Reading and Learning in the Content Classroom

Reading and Learning in the Content Classroom

Diagnostic and Instructional Strategies

Abridged Edition

THOMAS H. ESTES
University of Virginia

JOSEPH L. VAUGHAN, JR.
The University of Arizona

Allyn and Bacon, Inc.

Boston London Sydney Toronto

Third printing . . . October, 1979

Abridged edition of *Reading and Learning in the Content Classroom.*

© Copyright 1978 by Allyn and Bacon, Inc.
470 Atlantic Avenue, Boston.

Library of Congress Cataloging in Publication Data

Estes, Thomas H   1940-
    Reading and learning in the content classroom.

    Bibliography: p.
    Includes index.
    1. Reading (Elementary) I. Vaughan, Joseph L.,
1942-   joint author. II. Title.
LB1573.E84   1978   372.4   77-20038
ISBN 0-205-05986-4

Contents

Units of Study in Content Classes   233

Dedication

In the frantic daily routine of milk money, attendance checks, bus duty, hall patrol, and the inevitable "squawk box," in the midst of plans and scheduling, overviews and lessons and guides, materials we need or have for one period only, it is all too easy to forget that the real purpose of education centers on children—real, live kids. It is to our students, some young, some now older than we when we taught them, some with more teaching experience than we have age—to all of them we are indebted for what they taught us and it is to them we would dedicate this book.

What one knows is, in youth, of little moment; they know enough who know how to learn.

Henry Brooks Adams

Preface

The philosophy and format of this book are related to two ideas. First, we believe that teaching is not something someone does to someone else. Rather, it is the careful structuring of an environment in such a way as to maximize the possibility that students will learn. Ideally, this structuring results from cooperation between teachers and students. Second, we believe that learning to read is a life-long process and that the objective of formal education is to help students become learners as well as learned. The *process* of learning, or ability to continue to learn, may well be more important to students than any *product* of learning, or possession of knowledge. In the words of Carl Rogers, "The most socially useful learning in the modern world is the learning of the process of learning, a combining of openness to experience and incorporation into oneself the process of change." (From *Freedom to Learn*, p. 163.)

Reading and Learning in the Content Classroom should provide you with an opportunity to structure the learning environment of students in such a way that they: 1) learn both in light of their abilities and in spite of their problems with reading; and 2) simultaneously develop skills and understandings necessary to their functioning as literate persons in a literate society.

Today, more than ever, subject matter teachers need to understand the relationship between reading and content instruction. They continually face decisions about what to teach and how to teach it. Their job might well be defined as one of maximizing the possibility of learning for students. Very often the learning they seek to effect is tied to students' reading abilities.

However, most content area teachers receive no training in reading instruction and are thus unable to respond to the inability of numerous students to get something from their textbooks. Fortunately, many undergraduate and graduate schools are realizing this and making an effort to correct what they see as a deficiency. Increasing numbers of states are requiring reading courses for secondary certification in an effort to heighten awareness that reading can be—must be—taught concurrently with subject matter. The greatest progress is being made by those teachers and prospective teachers who recognize that reading in content areas means 1) teaching reading and learning skills along with content, and 2) making appropriate instructional provisions for those students who find the reading task interferring with the learning task.

To assist teachers and prospective teachers in becoming more aware of and sensitive to reading in content classrooms, we have designed this book with a dual focus. Our concern is for both *diagnostic* and *instructional* techniques in content area instruction. Content area teachers need the skills with which to diagnose reading and learning difficulties of their pupils. They also need understandings with which to prescribe learning environments and provide learning opportunities for pupils in response to diagnostic information. It is such diagnostic and prescriptive insights that we hope this book will enable you to acquire.

The understandings to which we lead you through this book, however, may extend far beyond that which we may offer directly. In fact, our hope is that each user of this book will come individually to better understandings of the same concepts through different combinations of activities and experiences. In that spirit, we open each unit with a specific statement of conceptual objectives—general understandings toward which the unit is directed. You may consider these objectives a sort of overview of each unit. Think to yourself as you begin each unit: What do I know about these ideas? What might I like to know? Where could I get more information about the ideas? And so forth. It is such questions we want to help you answer.

In education and psychology we often hear that one learns only in proportion to his or her own effort. With that in mind, we have included two additional items immediately after the conceptual objectives for each unit. They are "Selected Readings" and "Suggested Activities." Traditionally, these sections follow chapters or units of books. We want you to view the sections, or units as we call them, as an integral part of your study, a part which you might utilize to at least as great an extent as you do the text of the book per se. These readings and activities may be most important for preservice teachers as they are intended to stimulate the practice and familiarity with strategies and devices which is so important for "second-nature" application in a classroom.

What we are really trying to do with our suggestions for readings and activities is to help in your search for information and understanding of the concepts related to the topic of the unit. We have keyed the readings and activities to those concepts and have cross-referenced activities within the text. As you come to references to activities and readings in the margins of the text, consider their value to you. Certainly, no one will be able or need to recall all we reference, nor do we expect any reader to engage in every activity we suggest. It is certain, however, on the basis of work with our own students, that your learning from this book will be proportional to your active response to it. For this reason, we don't leave your response to chance alone.

As you study any unit, examine the parts and begin to make some decisions. Which concepts are most intriguing to you? Which of the headings are familiar to you, which have you previously thought you might want to explore? Which of the activities do you think would be most helpful to you in developing the skills you feel you need? How do the chapters treat the concepts? In other words, try to get the gist of each unit before you settle in to specific and individualized study. When you do settle in, make your study as purposeful as possible. Direct your effort to the search for understandings and information that you need to have rather than allowing it to be restricted to what we need to say. To the degree this becomes possible, authors and readers both will have accomplished an important purpose with this book.

T.H.E.

J.L.V.

Acknowledgements

Throughout earlier chapters, we have made continued reference to units of study as the leitmotif of instruction. We include the following examples as concrete examples of what we consider to be the heart of organized instruction. What you find here of interest may lie in the overall organization, the various activities, or the specific devices exemplified.

Whatever you do find of immediate use, we hope that these units demonstrate what imagination can create. We do suggest, however, that you not limit yourself to examining only the unit in your own content field; much is to be learned and transferred from all of these units, different as they are.

In the main, what you see here is what two teachers thought they needed and are now using. If some of it does not exactly match the theory or suggestions we have put forth, this has concerned us very little. What we have expected of each of these teachers, and what we expect of you, is to see a practical carrying out of practical suggestions. If these teachers' work helps you, we know you will want to join us in expressing appreciation

to   *for*

Helen M. Friedman   *Self-Development and Self-Awareness*
Pueblo High School
Tucson, Arizona

Margaret Donaldson   *Oceans of Fun*
Salem Elementary School
Chesterfield County Schools
Chesterfield, Virginia

UNIT 1

Reading in the Content Classroom

CONCEPTUAL OBJECTIVES

1. *Nothing is so unequal as the equal treatment of unequals.*

2. *What readers do when they read must determine how they are taught to read.*

3. *Reading materials can and should be assessed for difficulty and appropriateness.*

4. *The objectives of content area instruction include both the product and the process of study.*

Activity and Selected Readings Key

SUGGESTED ACTIVITIES

Cross references to the following entries are denoted by a single star in the margin, followed by reference to the entry number in this list.

	CONCEPTS			
	1	2	3	4
1. Investigate the range of reading abilities of pupils in your classes, using school records of achievements. (p. 8)	X			
2. After responding to the attitude scale (p. 9), discuss your responses and opinions with your colleagues. (p. 11)				X
3. How would you define reading? Write out your definition. (p. 11)		X		
4. Interview persons you know whose reading ability you respect. Ask them why and how they think they read well. (p. 14)		X		
5. Visit a professional library in your school system and survey different authorities' views of reading in content areas. (p. 11)		X		X
6. Systematically skim this text and identify the relationships among the various parts of the book. (p. 16)		X		
7. Superficially read the summary of what you consider to be "key" chapters in this book. Compare the basic ideas inherent in this book with your concept of "higher levels of reading." (p. 16)		X		
8. Determine the readability level of several different chapters in a text or selections in an anthology to see whether the difficulty is consistent throughout. (p. 28)			X	

CONCEPTS

	1	2	3	4
9. Examine a reading selection that you might use with your class; list the major concepts the author is discussing. Then, conduct a discussion with your students to see how much they seem to know of the concepts. (p. 34)			X	X
10. Using the information you obtained in activities 1 and 9, compare the results to the difficulty of the book as estimated by the Fry formula.	X		X	
11. Administer both a cloze passage and a maze to your students. Evaluate the relative appropriateness of the procedures. Compare both to results obtained from the Fry formula. (p. 33)			X	
12. Check with the librarian of your school to see what information is available on the difficulty of materials related to your subject area. For example, there are various guides to books for young people which might be helpful in selecting materials. (p. 35)	X		X	
13. Among members of your school staff organize a committee for evaluation and collection of supplementary materials to use in your courses. For example, in social studies, consider the wealth of "fictionalized" books and materials. (p. 35)	X	X		X
14. Examine the curriculum guide available for the course you teach. Try to determine whether the objectives of instruction described there are or might be set in conceptual terms (p. 41)				X
15. Make a list of the reading assignments you have given your students over the last six weeks or so. What kind(s) of reading was required and how satisfactory do you think it was for the students? (p. 39)	X		X	X
16. Consider the curriculum of the course you teach in terms of your own background and ability. Evaluate your perceived success with each topic or chapter to determine whether what you teach best is what you most like to teach. Ask whether the emphasis of your course is appropriate to your strengths and interests.				X

	1	2	3	4
17. Choose a random sample of twenty students from your classes. Investigate their background and interests through cumulative folders and personal knowledge to determine how appropriate what they are expected to learn in your course is to them. (p. 42)	X			X
18. The concept of "Foxfire" is more than a magazine. How could you use the "Foxfire principle" in your classroom?	X			X

SELECTED READINGS

Cross references to the following entries are denoted by double stars in the margin, followed by reference to the entry number in this list.

CONCEPTS

	1	2	3	4
1. Wiggington, *The Foxfire Book; Foxfire II;* and *Foxfire III.* Specifically, the introductions to each of these. Hitch your wagon to these stars!	X			X
2. Rogers, Carl. *Freedom to Learn.*	X			X
3. Mager, Robert. *Preparing Instructional Objectives.*				X
4. Adler and Van Doren. *How to Read a Book.*		X		X
5. Spache and Spache. *Reading in the Elementary School, 4th edition.* Specifically chapter 1, "Ways of Defining the Reading Process."		X		
6. Klare, George. "Assessing Readability."			X	

(Full bibliographic information for these items will be found at the end of the book under Bibliography.)

1

Reading and Learning

Nothing is so unequal as the equal treatment of unequals.

What readers do when they read must determine how they are taught to read.

SUMMARY

There are two principles underlying the relationship among students, teachers, and content. First, of all that might be taught, what *is* taught must be determined by what can be learned. Second, how to teach is defined by how students learn. To ignore either of these principles is to jeopardize the possibility of learning. *What* can be learned and *how* it can be learned are often related to the reading ability of learners. This ability must be at least approximately sufficient to the demands of content area reading; otherwise, either the ability or the demands must be modified. "Teaching reading in content areas" implies an attempt to do whichever is more efficient.

Effecting changes in students' reading abilities would necessitate an understanding of the developmental nature of reading. With this understanding, teachers may be able to "place" students and to respond to their developmental needs in reading by what they require of them and what they do to help them read.

Mortimer Adler and Charles Van Doren have elaborated a model of reading, describing it in terms of four stages: reading readiness; beginning reading; elementary reading; and reading maturity. Wherever the reader is on such a developmental "scale," the demands of his reading in content areas should be adjusted accordingly.

THE FOXFIRE PRINCIPLE

The Foxfire Book, enjoyed by thousands since its first appearance in 1972, is a testament to the frustrations of one English teacher and, even more important, to

5

the way in which he solved those frustrations. In his first six weeks of teaching, Eliot Wiggington had his lectern burned, his chalk stolen, and his chart of the Globe Theatre mutilated. In the next six years, he published three collections of articles from many editions of *Foxfire,* a magazine produced by his students and distrib uted through subscriptions in every state and many foreign countries. *Foxfire* was born because a teacher decided to design a curriculum around students rather than around a subject in school.

It is easy for most of us to empathize with Mr. Wiggington in his nearly disastrous, first-year experience. Unfortunately, most of us, like him, began our careers teaching as we were taught, with less regard for whom we would teach than for what we would teach. The training teachers receive in college which prepares them for teaching a content subject primarily concerns the subject and not the students. This is unfortunate because the real job of teaching happens to involve students, not subjects. For most teachers, the anomaly is soon resolved and a successful career proceeds. The principle behind that resolution is the first principle

**, 2 of instruction: *of all that might be taught, what is taught must be determined by what can be learned.* Thus, Eliot Wiggington made several decisions. First, he de cided that English could be defined as "communication—reaching out and touching people with words, sounds, and visual images" (*The Foxfire Book,* p. 13). Second, he decided that the lore and legend of Rabun Gap, Georgia, could form the basis of that communication. Thus, he decided that the immediacy of the content would facilitate mastery of the communicative art. In other words, English might be learned as communication if what was communicated was immediate and real to the learners. Accordingly, Mr. Wiggington's success was not so much a function of

**, 1 *Foxfire* (that was evidence of the success) but was a result of defining and teaching his subject matter in a way that it could be learned.

What was true in Rabun Gap—Nacoochee School, grades 9 and 10 English class in 1968—remains everywhere true today. The co-occurrence of what students *can* learn with what they *might* be taught in a course determines what *should* be taught. For example, what might be taught in a science class is virtually anything within the domain of natural phenomena. But what tenth grade science students can learn includes only a portion of that domain and thus defines that part of natural phenomena they should be taught. This basic principle of instruction holds true for any subject in school. It is ignored when we teach as if what might be learned were synonymous with what might be taught, as if what might be learned included all that might be taught.

Reading and learning in the content classroom depend on sound diagnostic and instructional strategies. The purposes of diagnosis (including diagnostic instruc tion) are: 1) to define what students can learn of a particular domain; and 2) to suggest appropriate instructional procedures to cause that learning to occur. Figure 1-1 depicts the intersection of two circles. One represents what students can learn, the other represents what might be taught, i.e., the domain of the subject within the course. The intersection of these two circles delimits what should be taught, and defining that intersection is the primary purpose of diagnosis and diagnostic instruction.

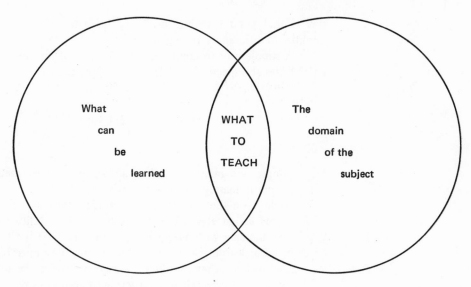

Figure 1-1   *What to teach.*

What to teach is only part of the story of diagnosis, as you might guess. It is, however, so important that much of what we have to say about diagnostic instruction will be directly or indirectly related to determining what to teach. Thus, the intersection of what can be learned and what might be taught is the major focus of our attention.

RANGES OF STUDENTS' ABILITIES

If determining what to teach is half the story of teaching in a content classroom, how to teach it is the other half. Eliot Wiggington knew this when he revamped the English curriculum in Rabun Gap. Having defined the curricular domain (communication) and what could be learned (to communicate content of genuine interest), the problem remained of how to involve all the students in the learning. "It hasn't always worked, but we try" is Wiggington's understatement. To involve everyone requires attention to the range of individual abilities and learning styles in the classroom, an educational goal made no easier by the fact that almost every curriculum guide adopts it.

Individual differences in reading ability can be found at all levels of a curriculum, and the nature of this diversity raises an interesting question. What is the relationship between grade level and range of individual differences in reading ability? To delineate the question somewhat more specifically, does the range of reading ability in a classroom decrease, remain constant, or increase with successive grade levels? The answer to this query becomes more evident if one realizes that what pupils learn is directly related to what they already know. The implication of this is that good teaching inevitably leads to increased rather than constant or diminished differences among individuals.

A simple way to approximate the range of differences among students' reading abilities at a specific grade level is to apply the following formula:

$$\text{RANGE} \approx \text{grade level} \pm \frac{\text{grade level} + 1}{2}$$

For example, the range of reading ability in a heterogeneous seventh grade classroom is approximately ($\approx$) 7 $\pm$ 8/2, which is 7 $\pm$ 4, or grades three to eleven. Thus, some students in the typical seventh grade class may be reading on a third grade level, others on an eleventh grade level; and the ability range among these same pupils will increase with successive grade levels! Clearly, if all these students are to be involved in learning in the same classroom, they must be given opportunities to learn as individuals; they should not always be taught as a group.

*, 1

Our second principle of instruction, therefore, is this: *how to teach is defined by how students learn.* Some students found it possible to write feature articles in *Foxfire;* for others copying and placing paragraphs in the layout was a challenge. BUT—all were involved, and all were learning since each was allowed in the setting of that English class to function first as an individual and second as a member of the class.

Can there be any other way for schools to succeed in their mission? Consider the social studies teacher in eleventh grade, for example. In many schools, eleventh grade social studies is United States history, and the domain of study includes the government, geography, history, and sociology of the United States. *What* students can learn of that can be determined by diagnostic instruction. *How* they can learn it is also critical. Some will be able to read in primary sources; others will find the text appropriate; and yet others will learn from simpler material like comics, picture books, magazines, and other media. It is likely each will learn from various sources, but *all* can be involved. That is the point and purpose of individualized instruction.

CONTENT AREA READING TEACHERS: THE NEED

Reading, like attendance and attention, is an assumed prerequisite for academic success. For many pupils, however, reading in content area textbooks is a very real problem. Not uncommonly, up to 50 percent of the students in an upper-grade class cannot read their textbooks. This is not to suggest that these students cannot read; on the contrary, most are quite literate. Literacy, however, does not guarantee success with all types of reading assignments. Because a student can read some material successfully does not ensure that he or she is proficient enough to learn effectively from a content area textbook.

There is a need for reading in content area classrooms. How that is to be effected and what it entails we will examine throughout this book. At this point, however, consider this question: Isn't teaching reading in content area classrooms a reasonable proposition? If taught how to learn and read better, might not students learn more now and in the future? Consider what an affirmative answer to these questions might mean to you. Better yet, reserve a definite answer at this time and give serious consideration to Activity 1-1.

This activity is designed to help you do the following: 1) Examine your opinions regarding a set of statements which are often heard as teachers argue the merits of teaching reading in content areas; and 2) expound on the ideas that you have regarding teaching reading in content areas.

ACTIVITY 1-1

WHAT DO YOU THINK?

Instructions   Place a check in the box that best represents your agreement with the corresponding statement.

	STRONGLY AGREE	AGREE	TEND TO AGREE	UNDECIDED	TEND TO DISAGREE	DISAGREE	STRONGLY DISAGREE
1. A content area teacher is obliged to help students improve their reading ability.							
2. Technical vocabulary should be introduced to students in content classes before they meet those terms in a reading passage.							
3. The primary responsibility of a content teacher is to impart subject matter knowledge.							
4. Few students can learn all they need to know about how to read in the first six years of school.							
5. The sole responsibility for teaching students how to study should lie with reading teachers.							

	STRONGLY AGREE	AGREE	TEND TO AGREE	UNDECIDED	TEND TO DISAGREE	DISAGREE	STRONGLY DISAGREE
6. Coursework in how to teach reading in content areas should be required for secondary teaching certification.							
7. Only English teachers should be responsible for teaching reading in secondary schools.							
8. A teacher who wants to improve students' interest in reading should show them that he or she likes to read.							
9. Content area teachers should teach content and leave reading instruction to reading teachers.							
10. A content area teacher should be responsible for helping students think on an interpretive level as well as on a literal level when they read.							
11. Content area teachers should feel a greater responsibility to the content they teach than to any reading instruction they may be able to provide.							
12. Content area teachers should help students learn to set purposes for reading.							
13. Every content area teacher should teach students how to read material in that teacher's content specialty.							
14. Reading instruction in secondary schools would be unnecessary if elementary schools were successful in their jobs.							
15. Content area teachers should be familiar with theoretical concepts of the reading process.							

*, 2   The problem of reading in content areas is not given a solution in the phrase "every teacher is a teacher of reading," which was bandied about several years ago as the nostrum to cure all reading ills. Actually, it is self-defeating to say every teacher is a teacher of reading, just as it is self-defeating to think that a successful English teacher like Eliot Wiggington teaches English. He teaches students. That is the essence of reading and learning in any classroom, and content area teachers cannot be divorced from such a mission.

*, 5   Operationally defining "reading in content areas" is but one part of defining the role of the content teacher in helping students become better learners and readers. The content teacher's role also hinges on his or her understanding the nature of reading itself. Reading ability, much like knowledge or understanding, is a phenomenon that develops over a lifetime.

Before we launch into a discussion of reading to learn, we suggest you take a few moments to synthesize your definition of reading so that you can compare your ideas to ours. So:

*, 3

Think, and then write out your definition of reading. (Don't cop out by running to the nearest dictionary. Compose *your* ideas here.)

Now let's see where we stand. Our guess about your definition is that you included ideas or terms related to meaning, understanding, and/or comprehension. That is, you probably conceive reading to be something that occurs when one obtains meaningful information from print, much as we hope you are doing now.

We agree. In our view, to assume reading means anything less than obtaining meaning from print (for example, that reading is correctly saying words) would be very unrealistic, especially in relation to reading in a content classroom. What your students need to do when they read is to understand; and their ability to pronounce all the words may be quite irrelevant to that understanding. If you are interested in pursuing the issue of various definitions of reading, George and Evelyn Spache do a good job of surveying the issue, and we refer you to the first chapter of their book, **, 5 *Reading in the Elementary School,* Fourth Edition.

DEVELOPMENT OF READING MATURITY

Let us now elaborate on a related topic, the developmental nature of reading to learn. Before being considered a mature reader, a person must progress through several well-identified stages of development. These stages include: 1) reading readiness; 2) beginning reading; and 3) elementary reading. (These are illustrated in Figure 1-2.) In order to perform effectively in a content classroom, it is all but imperative that a student develop his or her reading ability gradually through each of these stages.

Reading readiness is the stage that begins at birth and extends until a child can perceive words on a page as meaningful symbols. During this time, a child develops the necessary physical, intellectual, affective, social, and linguistic abilities which are the basis for learning to read. The physical traits most often associated with reading are visual and auditory acuity. Elements of intellectual development that are related to readiness include visual and auditory perception, the ability to reverse operations and think conversely, the ability to think in symbols, and the fledgling ability to focus on an entire operation rather than its isolated parts. In essence, the intellectual capabilities required for learning to read are equivalent to those characteristics of the upper range of Piaget's stage of cognitive development known as preoperational thought. Social factors necessary for learning to read include elements of social interaction such as the ability to work with others, to be attentive for short periods of time, and to follow simple directions. Linguistic abilities include the child's awareness of the basic elements of language, development of a speaking vocabulary, and the ability to manipulate the syntax of language to communicate orally in complete sentences.

In general, having developed these basic abilities, the child is ready to learn to read. Only one other major factor needs to be present—the interest in learning to read. This affective factor is vital, for unless a child develops an interest in learning to read, he or she probably will have difficulty in beginning reading.

Beginning reading, the second developmental stage, is difficult to restrict with boundaries because it overlaps with both readiness and elementary reading. This

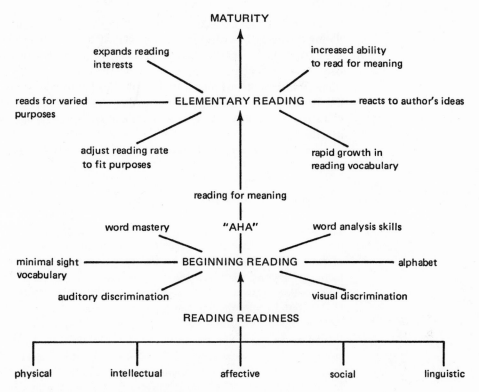

Figure 1-2 *The development of reading maturity.*

stage is characterized by an occurrence referred to by some as the "Ah-Ha" phenomenon, an instantaneous, perceptual "click" which occurs when the child recognizes that the squiggles on a page represent meaning which he or she can extract. It is an event as necessary for reading as vocal chords are for speaking. It is this event that is the critical turning point in the child's development as a reader. Older students who have not achieved this point are in deep trouble when asked to read for meaning, and they often require the help of a special reading teacher if they are to "turn the corner."

The elementary reading stage is also a vital one in determining the eventual success a person will have as a reader. This stage is most frequently associated with rapid growth in sight vocabulary and an increased ability to read for meaning. As each child builds a sight vocabulary, awareness of using reading to obtain meaning develops because the reader is less concerned with identifying words. The child begins to read for varied purposes, both in and out of school and begins to compare authors' viewpoints and to react to an author's ideas. Reading interests expand and the developmental reader learns to adjust reading speed to fit purposes for reading.

The gradual progress a student makes through the elementary reading stage is extremely critical to developing as a reader. The student must become fluent in the ability to assimilate information from print; he or she must be praised and supported, pushed and challenged, for if the student confronts failure or stagnation during this stage, frustration may result. If all goes well, as it usually does, the fledgling develops strong wings during this time and begins to soar. The end of the period comes when the reader can, however sophomorically, read practically anything to which interest may lead. Usually this happens so gradually, neither teachers *, 4 nor students mark the time or notice the change. However, like other benchmarks of maturity, the attainment of a functional and practical ability to read to learn is a quietly dramatic event.

Figure 1-2 depicts the succession of "steps" which lead to reading maturity.

THE ADLER AND VAN DOREN MODEL

The attainment of maturity in reading, possession of the ability to read to learn, does not mark the end of learning to read. More accurately, it marks the commencement of learning how to use reading to its fullest advantage as a tool in learning. Beyond maturity comes sophistication, and it is sophistication that the typical adolescent in grades seven through twelve is trying to find.

Content area reading—perhaps at any grade, but certainly at secondary levels —represents an awesome task for many students. Often, the reading strategies required by assignments in content area classrooms are simply beyond the level of sophistication possessed by otherwise normal, "grade level" readers. Thus, content teachers may inadvertently *require* of students the very skill the students need to learn. Unfortunately, perhaps, the material from which students learned to read differs from that which they are later required to read to learn. A few examples are: material from which students learn to read is fiction, but that which they are asked to read to learn is expository; vocabulary in the practice material is controlled for difficulty and familiarity, but words in content texts are specialized, the concepts often abstract and unfamiliar.

Effective reading in content areas requires mastery of learning strategies which the good reader applies automatically in an attempt to comprehend what he or she is reading. These strategies include setting purposes, adjusting rate to the demands of the task, and relating old and new information; these and other strategies will be discussed in the context of comprehension development. More generally, however, the mature reading demanded by content area study includes such abilities as surveying before reading, reading critically, and reading comparatively. A model which is built on these more general dimensions of reading is suggested by Mortimer Adler and Charles Van Doren in their book, *How to Read a Book*.

The Adler-Van Doren model is superimposed onto Figure 1-2 by the upper half of Figure 1-3. This model is the same as the one in Figure 1-2 up to "maturity" which is replaced by "elementary maturity." The three levels beyond elementary maturity are identified as 1) inspectional reading, 2) analytical reading, and 3) syntopical reading. Inspectional and analytical reading abilities are built on a solid foundation of basic reading ability and are developed concurrently during the high school years. In fact, the authors state that "a good liberal arts high school, if it does nothing else, ought to produce graduates who are competent analytical readers" (p. 29).

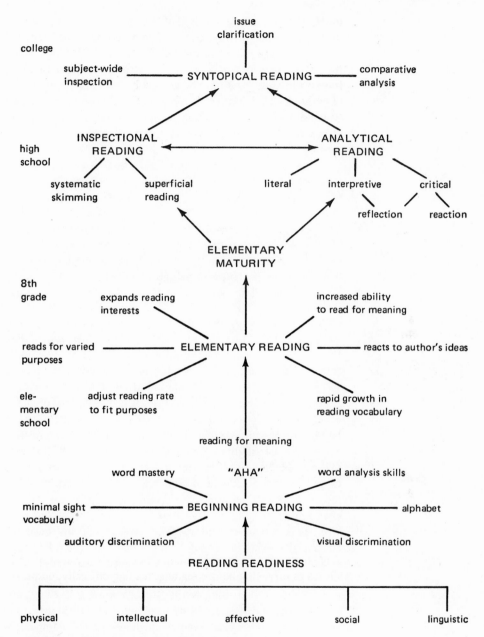

Figure 1-3   *The Adler-Van Doren Model completed.*

A reader who can effectively read to learn can manipulate reading speed according to the needs and purposes for reading. Many adults are, in a sense, handicapped readers because they tend to read everything at the same speed, and such inflexibility reflects a very inefficient reading habit. Inspectional reading is closely akin to the concept of flexibility in reading. One of the underlying themes of *How to Read a Book* is that "some books are to be tasted, others to be swallowed, and some few to be chewed and digested," as Francis Bacon put it.

The inspectional reading level is an essential ingredient in analytical and syntopical reading, but it is also a basic strategy familiar to readers who can effectively learn from their reading. The aim of inspectional reading is "to examine the surface of a book, to learn everything that the surface alone can teach you" (p. 19). Because such surface reading can vary according to purposes, the two constituent elements of inspectional reading are 1) systematic skimming and 2) superficial reading.

Systematic skimming is a valuable first step in diagnosing and examining a book or reading passage. It is similar to survey reading, which involves finding out what a book is about, and is sometimes referred to as "prereading." Through systematic skimming, a reader can decide whether a book will be worth the time. The reader can also establish a perspective on the book—a step which will facilitate more productive learning. The basic strategies involved in systematic skimming include thinking about the title, examining the table of contents, looking at pictures, maps, and graphs, and reading publishers' blurbs and chapter summaries.

*, 6

Superficial reading is very much like scanning. The principle underlying this strategy is that in "tackling a difficult book for the first time, read it through without ever stopping to look up or ponder the things you do not understand right away" (p. 36). Most readers tend to slow down when the going gets tough, but that is exactly what they should *not* do. While it may seem illogical, "slowing down is not an efficient way to read if you are having difficulty comprehending" (Smith, 1975, p. 251). Instead, one should attempt to get an overview of the material by reading faster. Thus, superficial reading is a basic tool of the really good reader.

*, 7

Analytical reading is the ability to read critically, and as such it requires highly developed cognitive skills such as drawing inferences, making judgments, and evaluating the validity of an author's ideas. It is an "intensely active" process that involves literal understanding *and* the ability to interpret what the author means. Once a reader understands and interprets an author's message, if learning is to be effective, the reader must also scrutinize the message to isolate the grain from the chaff. Such probing occurs through reflecting upon and reacting to what has been said. This reflection and reaction is a search for meaning. That is the pith of analytical reading, and analytical reading is what reading to learn is really all about. It will take the remainder of this book to treat analytical reading adequately. (In the meantime, you might also want to read *How to Read a Book,* Part II.)

**, 4

Syntopical reading is the "most complex and systematic type of reading of all" (p. 20), and it is predicated on the student's ability to read inspectionally and analytically. Syntopical reading might be called comparative reading, "but mere comparison of texts is not enough. . . ." (p. 20). A syntopical reader must, in fact, go well beyond obtaining meaningful information from print. An objective, comparative analysis of a topic must be constructed through subject-wide inspection and issue clarification.

What is expected of students in content classrooms can rarely be achieved through reading alone. Such learning requires a basic reading maturity, an ability to adjust reading speeds, and the thinking skills associated with scrutiny and analysis.

Few readers have such sophisticated skills when they enter secondary schools, but developing that sophistication is both an opportunity and a responsibility of the secondary school.

POST SCRIPT

To those of you who:

1. Often tell your students to pursue a topic out of class, and/or

2. are interested in the topics created in this chapter,

we refer you to the Activity Key at the beginning of the unit for further activities and suggested readings.

To those of you who:

1. read summaries first, or

2. can't find the summary of this chapter,

we refer you to the first page of this chapter, because we felt that the end of this chapter should really be the beginning.

2

Materials in a Content Classroom

Reading materials can and should be assessed for difficulty
and appropriateness.

SUMMARY

Many of the reading problems which interfere with learning in content classes can
be traced to the material rather than the students. Before throwing up their hands
in despair or charging headlong into a crash remediation program, content teachers
should examine carefully the material they have chosen for their classrooms and
determine whether the students can realistically be expected to learn effectively
from it.

While several devices are available to teachers for both predictive and measuring analysis of reading material, such devices can be considered no better than the
person who interprets their results. Any analysis of reading materials must include
an examination of their conceptual complexity, vocabulary difficulty, and skills
requirements. The various devices currently available provide little more than a
place to begin.

The purpose of analyzing reading materials is to determine how well the
students will be able to learn from them. If the students are to learn content
material effectively, they must be given tasks with which they can succeed, and one
of the prime requisites for this success is materials that are at least on their instructional reading level.

THE RIGHT STICK

When a little league manager begins batting instruction, he hauls out the canvas bag
and empties the contents in the vicinity of home plate. Out spill brown bats, white
bats, yellowish bats, and two-toned bats—short bats, long bats, skinny bats, and fat
bats. The players eagerly scramble among the bats as the manager helps them find

18

the "stick" that will be best for each of them. When a classroom teacher begins content instruction, the teacher hauls out a briefcase, opens it, and takes out the book for that course. It may be brown, red, green, yellow, or chartreuse—fat, skinny, short, long, easy, or hard. But, there is usually only *one* book. Of all this, one thing is certain. The little leaguers and the readers will not all succeed equally well with their respective tasks, but at least the baseball players will have the best chance of finding the right stick.

Failure to learn in a content classroom is often attributed to a reading deficiency inherent with the learner. Efforts are made to correct such deficiencies because the students could succeed if they could read better. Whenever such a tack is taken, someone is implicitly assuming that the reading material the students have been given is appropriate, but that they are inappropriate for it. That is, they have the right stick; the problem is that they can't use it. Unfortunately, such an assumption is often invalid, because many of the reading difficulties which exist in content classrooms could be eliminated if the material were chosen on the basis of criteria that reflected realistic expectations for students. Frequently, however, the materials are neither adopted on the basis of such criteria nor are they examined as the potential source of learning difficulties in a classroom. If success is to be the goal of education, teachers would benefit from remembering this formula: students + the right task = SUCCESS. The right task must include the right stick.

BASIC COMPONENTS

A reading selection can best be analyzed in terms of three basic factors. These are: 1) the concepts presented in the material, 2) the language used to convey those concepts, and 3) the skills needed by a reader to extract those concepts. If the purpose of analyzing a reading selection is to determine its suitability for a group of students, the analysis should be based on an understanding of the interrelatedness of these components.

The primary function of a reading selection is to convey information, usually in the form of ideas, facts, and inferences. The aggregate of these comprise what may be referred to as the concept load. Basically, the concept load reflects the complexity of the ideas which a reader is to grasp. Therefore, any analysis of a reading selection must include an examination of its conceptual complexity, especially in relation to the experiential background which will be required for readers to understand those concepts.

The ideas or concepts in a reading selection are conveyed by specific words, and the degree of sophistication of those words, taken collectively as language, represents the vocabulary load for that passage. Since words are the outward manifestations of concepts, or verbal labels for concepts, the vocabulary load of a reading selection can provide an index of its conceptual complexity. Unfortunately, the universality of such a premise must be suspect in the face of such sentences as "The Child is father of the Man." The sophistication of the concept in this sentence far exceeds the simplicity and familiarity of the terms used to express that concept. It is evident, therefore, that conceptual complexity is determined by factors other than vocabulary alone; however, that the reader's familiarity with the vocabulary affects his ability to understand the concepts cannot be denied. A reader's chances of learning are significantly decreased if the ideas are couched in terminology that isn't recognized. Thus, it should come as no surprise that vocabulary familiarity has long been regarded as a primary variable in determining the difficulty of reading selections.

The skills load represents the reading skills required to extract concepts from a given passage. For a beginning reader, this may be as basic as realizing that the printed symbols on a page represent words; for a mature reader, the necessary skills could include the ability to interpret symbolism successfully. In a sense, the skills load demanded by a reading selection is an index of the author's style. The intricacy of the stylistic conventions which an author employs determines what reading skills will be required to get meaning from a passage. If a reader is to learn from a given selection, he must be familiar with the author's mode of presenting the information, be it flashback, dialogue, comparison, contrast, simile, metaphor, or analogy. If an author's style requires skills that a reader does not have, the learner's potential for successful processing will certainly be limited. The ideas and the vocabulary in a passage may be well within a reader's grasp, but to get to the information so it can be learned, a reader must also be sufficiently familiar with the author's stylistic devices.

All three of the components inherent to the composition of a reading passage are usually considered by an author, especially when the author is preparing materials to be used in a classroom. Certain things are assumed about the readers' conceptual and linguistic abilities, and the author adjusts the ideas, choices of language, and stylistic conventions to accommodate these assumptions. Once the material is introduced into the classroom, the author's assumptions become inconsequential because of the reality represented by the students. If the students' abilities are in fact equivalent to the author's assumptions, the material can be used appropriately in that classroom. It is the teacher's responsibility to ensure this match and by so doing to enhance the probability of successful learning. If a teacher is to make decisions about the appropriateness of specific materials for students, he or she must first understand what relationships can exist between those materials and students.

READING LEVELS

Most readers of any age experience varying degrees of understanding every day when they read the daily newspaper. The comics and sports pages offer little or no difficulty; the front page can be perplexing; the editorials and comments are often enigmatic.

Success in reading is determined by such variables as prior knowledge of the topic, conceptual complexity, vocabulary familiarity, and author's style. In the jargon of the reading specialist, three levels of understanding have been delineated and identified as 1) the independent reading level, 2) the instructional reading level, and 3) the frustration level. Each of these levels predicts a varying degree of success which a person will have with a specific reading task.

The *independent reading level* is the level at which a reader can completely understand material without outside help. That is, the reader can virtually learn everything the author has to offer and can do so with ease. In such situations, the reader is familiar with the vocabulary, has the necessary skills to extract the ideas, and can understand the concepts being conveyed. Thus,

What the author assumed		What the reader has
vocabulary load	=	vocabulary
skills load	=	skills
concept load	=	conceptual awareness

Unfortunately, such an exact match between the author's assumptions and the reader's abilities rarely occurs, especially in a classroom situation. Perfect congruence, however, is not necessary for students to learn from a reading selection. When students' abilities in skills, vocabulary, or conceptual awareness fall slightly below an author's expectations, they may not learn with the thoroughness or ease associated with a perfect match, but they will be able to learn. In fact, this is what usually happens in academic situations; students struggle with assignments and learn what they can. If students can learn from material in a limited way, often a teacher can provide instruction which will help them read with greater ease and understanding. Thus, when

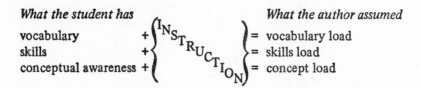

What the student has		What the author assumed
vocabulary	+ {INSTRUCTION}	= vocabulary load
skills	+ {INSTRUCTION}	= skills load
conceptual awareness	+ {INSTRUCTION}	= concept load

the material is said to be on the student's *instructional reading level*. In essence, instruction can bridge the gap between the student's abilities and those necessary to read with satisfactory understanding.

Sometimes material which is used in classrooms is so difficult for students that a reasonable amount of instructional assistance will not be sufficient to bridge the gap between the students' abilities and an author's assumptions. In such cases the learning potential is notably limited because of the frustration and anxiety which often accompany the students' efforts. This reaction frequently produces negative results because the student associates failure and frustration with reading. The *frustration level* therefore reflects material where

What the student has		What the author assumed
vocabulary	+ {INSTRUCTION}	≠ vocabulary load
skills	+ {INSTRUCTION}	≠ skills load
conceptual awareness	+ {INSTRUCTION}	≠ concept load

All readers perform with varying degrees of proficiency, depending on the demands of the particular task. Some general guidelines suggested by the aforementioned reading levels might be:

Reading Level	Appropriate Use
Independent	Homework; extended learning activities; basis for discussion of concepts
Instructional	Discussion in class with directed help through instruction; homework *after* appropriate "bridging of the gap" instruction
Frustration	NONE

A teacher's awareness of the relationship between students' abilities and the reading materials in the classroom should enable the teacher to realize maximum utility from those materials. Furthermore, it should suggest to a teacher the kinds of materials that will be necessary as a supplement to the basic text(s) of a course.

ANALYZING READING MATERIALS

The difficulty of reading material can be determined by either predictive analysis or measurement analysis. Predictive techniques are restricted to the material; measurement analysis requires interaction of readers with material. Either type of analysis can be accomplished with both formal and informal procedures, and the objective is almost always the same—to determine whether the designated readers can learn from the material.

Predictive analysis   The most common method of predictive analysis requires the use of readability formulas. Readability is a term which is applied to "the question of what makes the language in materials easy or difficult to read" (Bormuth, 1968, p. v). Readability formulas generally tap linguistic variables within a passage and these variables are used as indices of its complexity. Primary among these variables are 1) sentence length and 2) vocabulary difficulty.

Underlying the application of readability formulas is the premise that material consisting of short, simple sentences and familiar vocabulary is more easily understood by readers than material written with complex sentences that include difficult or unfamiliar words. Consider the following sentence:

Sally ran down the street.

The familiar vocabulary and the simple sentence structure suggest that few readers would have difficulty understanding that sentence. However, many young readers, and even some older ones, would not learn much from the sentence:

> The only aim now is to hurt the enemy, in any way possible and, with every available weapon, to destroy not only his will to resist but also to eliminate every ability to implement that will effectively.

Analyses of materials with readability formulas enable a teacher to make reasonably accurate predictions about the success students will have in learning from a particular book or passage. They can further serve as the basis for a more complete estimate of that selection's overall difficulty.

Historically, classroom teachers have not used readability formulas because most of the reputable ones have been very time consuming and complex to administer. These formulas, such as the Dale-Chall (1948) and Spache (1960), have been widely used in reading research and textbook preparation, however, and their complexity lies primarily in the process of determining vocabulary difficulty. Both formulas require that each word in a passage be compared to a graded list of familiar words. Thus an adequate administration of these formulas may require as much as an hour per book or passage. This demands time which few teachers are able to devote.

Recently, however, two new formulas have become available to teachers which are neither time consuming nor complicated. These are the Fry Readability Formula (1967) and McLaughlin's SMOG Readability Formula (1969). The time-consuming strategies of earlier devices have been eliminated and yet the results that these newer formulas yield are highly correlated with those obtained by using the Spache and Dale-Chall. Only the Fry and SMOG formulas will be examined in depth here. References to other formulas are provided in the review by Klare ****, 6** (1974) which is particularly good.

Fry Readability Fry's formula is actually a graph. Several simple calculations must be applied to a
Graph selection and the results then interpolated by plotting them on an accompanying graph. This analysis begins by determining the average sentence length of three 100-word samples and continues with an estimate of vocabualry familiarity by a count of the syllables in each sample. The specific steps suggested by Fry are:

1. Randomly select three 100-word passages from near the beginning, middle, and end of the selection or book. Don't count numbers. Do count proper nouns.

2. Count the total number of sentences in each hundred word passage (estimating to the nearest tenth of a sentence). Average these three numbers.

3. Count the total number of syllables in each 100-word sample. There is a syllable for each vowel sound. For example: cat (1), blackbird (2), continental (4). Don't be fooled by word size. For example:

polio has three syllables, *through* has one. Endings such as -y, -ed, -el, or -le usually make a syllable. For example: ready (2), bottle (2).

When counting syllables, Fry suggests that you put a mark above every syllable over one in each word and add 100 to your total count of marks. This simplifies the syllable count since one-syllable words would be included in the adding of 100, as would the first syllable in each word with one or more marks.

Average the total number of syllables for the three 100-word samples.

4. Plot on the accompanying graph the average number of sentences per 100 words and the average number of syllables per 100 words. The perpendicular lines mark off approximate grade level areas.

5. If a great deal of variability is found, more samples to determine an average should be used.

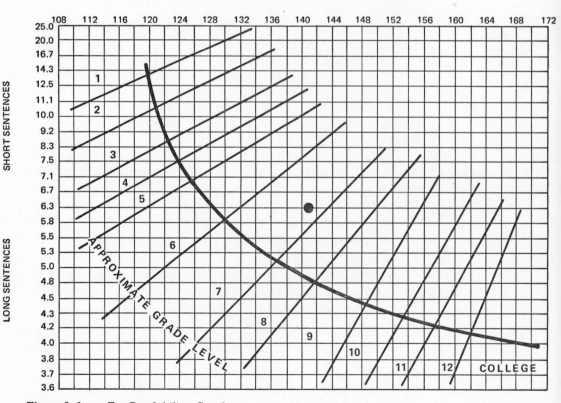

Figure 2-1   *Fry Readability Graph.*

McLaughlin's
SMOG
formula

This formula is probably the least complicated of all those available and its efficiency has made it widely attractive for many content teachers. It is based on the interrelationship of sentence length and vocabulary difficulty, though the inclusion of these two variables is not clearly evident at first glance. McLaughlin has approached these two variables from a slightly different direction than other designers of readability formulas. The SMOG formula requires determination of the number of polysyllabic words in three ten-sentence samples. The premise behind this is that if the sentences are short, then there is diminished possibility for many polysyllabic words to be included, and the difficulty of the passage can be determined by the number of polysyllabic words in it.

The specific steps included in McLaughlin's formula are:

1. Count ten consecutive sentences near the beginning, ten in the middle, and ten near the end of the selection.

2. In the thirty sentences (total), count every word of three or more syllables when they are read aloud. Recount polysyllabic words (of three or more syllables) if they are repeated.

3. Estimate the square root of the total number of polysyllabic words by taking the square root of the nearest perfect square.

4. If the total number of polysyllabic words falls exactly between two perfect squares, take the lowest of the two.

5. Add three (3) to the estimated square root to determine the reading level.

Consider the following example.

	Number of polysyllabic words
10 sentence sample # 1	6
10 sentence sample # 2	9
10 sentence sample # 3	7
Total	22

The nearest perfect square to 22 is 25 (5 × 5). Add 5 + 3 and the reading level by the SMOG formula is 8. The simplicity of this formula and its slight deviation from the procedures of other formulas more highly regarded through time and research has caused this formula to be somewhat suspect among some reading professionals However, it can serve some vital purposes for content teachers, and the real value of such formulas comes not in the specific grade level they reveal, but in the interpretation of their results.

ACTIVITY 2–1

Directions   Before proceeding to a discussion of an interpretation of readability formulas results, try this short activity. Assume that the following passage is one of the sample selections which you would use to try out the Fry and the SMOG formulas. Determine the results with both formulas and insert your results into the other data provided in the table following the selection.

It was a cold winter morning in 1925. Everywhere, the Arctic was covered with ice and snow. Beside a frozen sea, the little town of Nome, Alaska, lay hundreds of miles away from the nearest railroad.

Suddenly came a radio call for help—sickness in Nome. Twenty-five people lay sick with diphtheria! Four people were dead. The lives of all were in danger—the townspeople of Nome and the Eskimos of the region. Only shots of antitoxin would keep the diphtheria from spreading. The need was desperate.

In the south of Alaska, a doctor heard the call for help. At once he packed up a twenty-pound supply of the antitoxin and sent it by rail as far as the train could go. He telegraphed Doctor Welsh in Nome that the antitoxin was on its way.

	Fry	
	Sentences per 100 words	*Syllables per 100 words*
100-word sample # 1	?	?
100-word sample # 2	7.7	139
100-word sample # 3	8.9	135
Average	3 ⟌	3 ⟌
	SMOG	
		Number of polysyllabic words
10-sentence sample # 1		?
10-sentence sample # 2		8
10-sentence sample # 3		9
Total		

Table of results for readability activity.

Using the Fry procedures, the 100th word is "once" in the third paragraph. In this sample, there are 10.1 sentences and 146 syllables. (If you're close, don't worry about minor discrepancies.) Adding these results to those already provided, you can determine average counts of 8.9 and 140. Plotting these scores on the graph indicates that this is sixth grade material, but since the mark is not very close to the curved line for typical material, something may be awry.

Using the SMOG formula, twelve polysyllabic words can be found including "twenty-five." Twenty-five" is *a* word, even though hyphenated, and numbers are not words, *per se,* unless written out, and are not included in counts by either the SMOG or Fry. Thus, 1925, a numerical symbol for several words, is disregarded in each procedure.

The total number of polysyllabic words, then, as determined by the SMOG formula, is 29. The nearest perfect square is 5, thus the reading level is (5 + 3) or 8. Had the sample results of the SMOG administration been widely inconsistent, for example, 4, 10, and 16, further samples would need to be taken to provide greater accuracy.

Interpreting readability formulas

Since the results of the preceding activity indicate different grade levels for this material, a natural assumption may be to consider one or both formulas to be inaccurate. In fact, however, both are accurate. Herein lies the importance of accurate interpretation.

An examination of the validation procedures for each formula provides an explanation for the discrepancy. The Fry formula estimates the reading ability a reader will need to understand the material with 50 to 75 percent accuracy. On the other hand, the SMOG formula predicts the reading ability required for 90 to 100 percent comprehension. Thus, these two formulas are each providing valuable information, but information that cannot be applied appropriately without an understanding of the underlying criteria.

To relate this discussion to the reading levels presented earlier, the SMOG formula predicts an appropriate reading ability equivalent to reading on an independent level while the Fry graph suggests a level somewhere between the frustration and instructional reading levels.

Because of the variance which exists in the validation criteria of these two formulas, it would be inappropriate for a teacher to assume that the average sixth-grade reader would be able to understand this material, on his or her own, with 90 percent accuracy. Such assumptions have been made in the past with consequences that have been unfair to students. Thus, if teachers intend to use readability formulas, they must assume responsibility for interpreting their findings accurately.

Once a readability score is determined, a further examination of the results is required if a teacher wants to use the material appropriately. As has been implied, these formulas tap *only* linguistic variables. Concept and skills factors are only tangentially related to formula results. To assess reading materials thoroughly, readability formula results must be accompanied by informal examinations of the conceptual complexity within the material to determine whether the difficulty level indicated by a formula is also a reasonable representation of the concept load. If not, further adjustments must be made of the expectations that can reasonably be established for a reader's success. Likewise, if the author's style is such that it will pose difficulties undetermined by an analysis of the linguistic variables through a formula, this factor must be accounted for when determining the applicability of the material for particular readers.

While readability formulas can provide a basis for examining the difficulty of reading materials, they must not be considered infallible or definitive. Properly used, they can be very helpful aids in instructional planning, but when realistically examined, they provide only a rough estimate of the difficulty of a reading selection, and not much more. Thus, as teachers use readability formulas and other predictive techniques, they would be admonished to consider these cautions:

1. The predictive criteria for comprehension does vary among some of the formulas, and users should be aware of what they are determining when they use a particular device.

2. Readability formulas directly tap some linguistic variables, but not concept load; they provide only a basis from which to extend an analysis of the difficulty of reading material to a consideration of its conceptual difficulty.

3. The scores derived by such devices are only estimates and cannot be assumed definitive.

4. Readability formulas are not very helpful when used with poetry or other forms of material that do not conform to the basic characteristics of regular prose.

5. The true value of such devices can be derived only in tandem with knowledge of the reading skills of the students who will use the material.

It may seem that predictive analysis through readability formulas is subject to so many restraints that they are of little value. Consider, however, these realistic and valuable uses:

1. As the basis for analysis of the difficulty of a particular reading selection.

2. As a means of evaluating materials for adoption without having to rely blindly on a publisher's analysis.

3. As a comparison of books to be used within a course to determine which would be more appropriate for certain times or certain students.

4. As a comparison of stories, chapters, or sections within a required text.

*, 8
5. As empirical data to indicate whether adopted material is appropriate to the reading abilities of students with whom it is to be used.

Measurement analysis

As described earlier in this chapter, measurement analysis is based on an interaction between the reader and the material being examined. There are times when the readers are not available, and it is then that predictive procedures are most useful. However, when analyzing material for use in a classroom, the pertinent issue is how well specific students will be able to learn from it. Thus, an analysis based on an interaction between the readers and the material will prove more fruitful than one based on prediction. Several devices will be presented which can be used as the basis for a measurement analysis.

Cloze procedure

In 1953 Wilson Taylor introduced to reading specialists a technique of measuring how well students could read a particular text or reading selection. He called it the cloze procedure. It is based on the psychological percept of closure (hence, cloze) and the linguistic concept of redundancy within the English language. Since then, the cloze procedure has been intensively researched and applied in many ways. One of its most frequent uses has been as a method of determining the appropriateness of reading material for a particular group of students. The cloze procedure may be defined as a "method of systematically deleting words from a prose selection and then evaluating the success a reader has in accurately supplying the words deleted" (Robinson, 1971, p. 2).

Consider the following sentences. As you read, try to replace the words which have been omitted:

Their accounts may be _____, but many consumers write _____ anyway during periods of _____ and inflation. Their intention _____ is to try to _____ to the bank with _____ before a merchant turns _____ the check.

The degree to which you were successful in replacing the exact words deleted from the sentences can be considered an index of your ability to read the material from which it was taken. (The words deleted were *empty, checks, recession, often, get, money,* and *in.*)

The following steps are recommended in the construction of a cloze passage:

1. Select a reading passage that your students have not yet read. It should be approximately 300 words in length.

2. Type the first sentence intact. Starting with the fifth word in the second sentence, delete every fifth word until you have fifty deletions. Replace each deletion with an underlined blank fifteen spaces long.

3. Finish the sentence in which the fiftieth deletion occurs. Type one more sentence intact.

Once a cloze test has been constructed, it is a simple matter to administer it in a classroom. To guide you in this, follow these steps:

1. Provide directions which might read: "You are to fill in the blanks in the following selection with the word that has been left out. Try to supply the exact word the author used. Only one word has been deleted from each blank. You will have as much time as necessary to complete this exercise."

2. If the students are unfamiliar with the task, show them some examples prior to handing out the test.

3. The students are not to use any books or materials when completing the test.

4. Let students know that they should try to use context clues to determine what word fits each blank.

5. Allow them as much time as necessary to complete the test.

While a cloze test can be administered easily in a classroom, several cautions should be observed if the results are to be meaningful. Often the task itself interferes with obtaining valid scores. If the students have never taken a test like this, they may become very frustrated and not apply themselves in a way that is essential to obtaining valid scores. Thus, teachers should familiarize their students with the task prior to administering a passage from which meaningful results are to be determined. Initially, let them work on short passages and even let them work in pairs or teams. Try to make the task a challenging game and help them become involved in the process. Cloze passages are often used as instructional devices to improve the use of context clues, so introducing the task in an instructional setting may be the most productive method of familiarizing students with the procedures.

The scoring procedure can also cause unforeseen problems. While the scoring process will be discussed later, it is not unusual for students to get only 30, 40, or 50 percent correct, and few students are accustomed to being only 30 percent successful with a task. Thus, an anxiety factor can interfere with their production, and teachers need to be prepared to lend support and encouragement during the testing, especially for students with limited language awareness. Finally, the real purpose of a cloze test is to "test" an author's assumptions in relation to a particular group of readers. Many reluctant students respond to an opportunity to test an author, and such an approach often relieves them of feelings of anxiety.

Scoring a cloze test is the easiest part of the procedure, though interpretation of results requires experience. The most widely researched aspect of the cloze procedure has been in scoring and interpretation. Ruddell (1964), Bormuth (1966), and Miller and Coleman (1967) have shown that the most valid scoring system with cloze tests is to accept only the *exact replacement* as correct. That is, do not give credit for synonyms. (One should, however, count misspellings correct if it is clear that the intent was to provide the exact word deleted.) Once the total number of correct replacements is determined, compute the percentage score for each student.

The value of accepting only exact replacements is twofold. First, it does not require a subjective evaluation of the subtle connotations of synonyms, and thus retains objectivity. Second, it allows a set of stable criterion scores to be used in interpreting the results. Teachers and students often express scorn, disdain, and a few four-letter words for such seemingly arbitrary procedures. However, if synonyms were allowed to be correct, valid interpretations of the results would be all but impossible. It may help to mention that the rank order of scores rarely changes appreciably when synonyms are included as correct responses. However, as a person interprets the results he or she must consider the possibility that the responses may in fact be better than the words used by the author. When a person consistently includes more sophisticated or more expressive words than the author, the results for that individual may not be valid. Because of such possibilities, individuals' scores are often uninterpretable without a careful examination of the relationship among the various types of miscues they have inserted in the blanks. (This is facilitated by an understanding of the syntactic and semantic relationships suggested by Goodman and Burke (1974) in the *Reading Miscue Inventory*.)

Once percentage of exact replacement scores have been determined for each student, record them all and *compute the average for the class*. To our knowledge, no research has found cloze to be valid for an individual's score. Hence, it is the *group's average score that is compared to the criteria*. It may be advantageous to chart individual results in a format like the one that follows. This will allow comparison to criteria modified from the research of Bormuth (1968).

Cloze Test Results

Material _____

Class _____   *Date* _____

Above 60%	Between 40% and 60%	Below 40%

Table 2-1   *Interpreting Cloze Results.*

The difficulty of the material can then be determined by comparing the class average to the following set of criteria.

If the mean score is:	*The material is probably:*
60% or higher	Easy for this group and will be on their *independent* reading level.
between 40% and 60%	Suitable for this group and is within their *instructional* reading level.
below 40%	Difficult for this group and will be on their *frustration* level.

To summarize, the following guidelines may be helpful:

1. Count only exact replacements. Do not include synonyms.

2. Determine the percentage scores for each individual.

3. *Compute the class average and compare it to the criterion scores.*

4. Use the material appropriately or discard it as being unsuitable for that group of students.

Maze technique   Guthrie (1973, 1974) has modified the cloze procedure for use as a measure of comprehension, and his maze technique seems to be a suitable alternative, simpler to use than the cloze. Though this device lacks the substantial research support of the original cloze technique, its potential is evident.

The maze technique consists of:

1. A series of sentences extracted from a passage that the student has not previously read.

2. The text is altered by substituting three alternative words for every fifth or tenth word in the passage. (Presumably the same deletion techniques as those previously discussed for cloze would be appropriate here.) The three choices that are substituted are:

   a. the correct word,
   b. an incorrect word from the same word class, such as noun, verb, etc.
   c. an incorrect word from a different word class.

   Guthrie cautions that the order of these choices be altered at random. An example of this procedure would be:

   The boy walked down the   1. dog.
   2. causeway.
   3. cautiously.

3. The student reads the passage silently and selects the alternative he or she believes to be correct.

4. The percentage of correct choices is commensurate with comprehension of the material in the passage. Thus, if a reader correctly identifies fifteen of twenty choices, he or she can be said to be reading with 75 percent comprehension. Apparently, twenty items are sufficient for valid results.

The potential of the maze technique is evident, but two factors are immediately troublesome. First, the reliability and validity of this technique was based partly on an .82 correlation with the Gates-MacGinitie Comprehension Subtest. While this is a very reputable test, a similar procedure is used to determine the comprehension score on it as that used in the maze technique. One would expect the results to be highly correlated, even higher perhaps than the obtained coefficient of .82. Second, the validation study was conducted with six-, seven-, and eight-year-olds, and thus the ability to apply this technique in the upper grades remains to be determined.

Guthrie suggests that the optimum instructional range is between 60 percent and 75 percent as determined by the maze technique. If scores are obtained above 85 percent over several sample passages, the material is probably equivalent to the reader's independent reading level; if scores fall below 50 percent, the material is likely to be frustrating for the reader. This device requires further development and research, but content teachers might be able to use it in situations where the cloze procedure is inefficient or less desirable, perhaps as an introduction to cloze tasks.

*, 11

Informal measurement procedures

In this age of scientific investigation, the older, more subjective methods of determining the appropriateness of materials for a group of students seem to have been shoved in a closet. Whatever happened to the idea of giving students a book, asking them to read from it (silently), and then having them explain what they learned? Such an uncomplicated, unobjective method may seem to be out of tune with today's computerized, technological world. But the time-proven validity of assessments based on informal procedures and teachers' intuitions makes it unwise to abandon such methods. In fact, such assessments may at times be more valid and practical than any scientific, objective analysis such as those based on readability formulas and the cloze procedure.

If you would like guidance in measuring a reading selection informally, try this procedure:

1. Select a passage from the material that the students have not previously read. Choose a length that is complete in itself and will approximate the length that they might be expected to read as an assignment.

2. Ask the students to read it.

3. Administer a ten-question test based on:
   a. main idea
   b. factual information
   c. inferences
   d. vocabulary.

4. Go over the test with them. Discuss the answers and determine through intuition and their opinions how well they will be able to learn from this material.

Informal assessments of reading material can be extended beyond these suggestions and can become rather complex, depending upon the ability of the teacher to interpret the results of the testing. Rather than deal with some of the more advanced methods of classroom diagnosis here, it will be more appropriate to treat them at length in two later chapters: *Standardized Testing* and *Analyzing Reading Comprehension.* It should be noted, however, that the criteria for determining, as measured by an informal assessment, whether or not to use a book must remain the responsibility of the individual teacher. This relates to the various purposes for specific materials that a teacher might want or expect within the classroom. Thus, while 80 percent comprehension might be needed in one situation, 40 percent comprehension might be acceptable in another. Rather than suggest criteria that may not be appropriate in certain situations, it is preferable that teachers realize and accept the responsibility of modifying criteria based on individual purposes and expectations. To do otherwise would, in effect, violate the inherent attractiveness and utility of informal assessments.

*, 9

CRITERIA FOR EVALUATING MATERIALS

When examining materials for adoption or use with groups of students, teachers should be alert to other elements of the material which extend beyond the limitations of "the right stick" concept. Materials should be chosen for their maximum utility in helping children learn. The following suggestions might be considered.

1. Does the material include sufficient directions to the user so that it does not require students to have the very skills and understandings it purports to develop?

2. If a teacher's edition or manual accompanies the material, does it provide sufficient examples and suggestions for instruction?

3. Do the skills to which the material is directed relate to problems confronted in more realistic reading tasks?

4. Is the material appropriate to students' abilities, interests, and needs?

5. Does the material seem to lend itself to flexible, individual application in the classroom setting?

6. Will the content and format of the material promote interaction among pupils and between pupils and teachers?

7. Is the purpose of the material apparent to students, and will they be able to use it independently, given sufficient reading and study skills?

8. Is the appearance of the material attractive?

9. Does the material include a bibliography or additional resource material?

10. Is the material conducive to divergent, creative thinking, or is it convergent and dogmatic?

*, 12, 13

While this list is not all-inclusive, it may suggest other criteria which deserve examination to meet the needs of a specific classroom—YOURS! The overriding question, of course, has to be, "Does this material provide the students with the maximum opportunity to learn, and does it do it as well or better than anything else?" If the answer is "No," keep looking.

3

The Student, the Teacher, the Content Class

The objectives of content area instruction include both the product and the process of study.

SUMMARY

Objectives of instruction must be based on the interface which exists between students' needs, the teacher's goals, and curricular demands. A well-known critic, Marshall McLuhan, once said that children interrupt their education to attend school. This attitude can be changed if schools can derive their objectives—their reason for being—out of consideration for developmental needs of pupils, adjusting and adapting the goals of the teacher and the demand of the curriculum in light of such consideration.

 There are two types of instructional objectives in a content area classroom. There are conceptual objectives related to students' understanding of general ideas and principles. There are process objectives related to the development of various processes or skills of learning. Both of these types are important to content area study and instruction, and they are both most effectively developed when the teacher recognizes their interdependence

Out of these ideas, we are able to distill three principles of good instruction. First, content reading must be assigned and completed in a framework that allows the practice of reading strategies, or processes, and at the same time works toward conceptualizations appropriate to the needs of pupils. Second, students should be provided with materials that supplement their study, often in the form of study guides, which help them to understand what they are reading and to develop skills appropriate to such reading in other settings. Third, related to both of the preceding considerations, pupils need to know that their purpose in content study is to develop understandings of what they are studying and to acquire strategies of study that can make them better able to continue the development of their understandings in the future.

CURRICULAR FOUNDATIONS

Kohlberg and Mayer (1972) make the argument that the most important aim of education is the development of the child. In their view—and ours—schools exist to provide a structured opportunity for children to develop in terms of both what they are and what they know. The object of education is to foster intellectual and personal growth. This goal is best accomplished by allowing the learner the chance to interact with the learning environment while receiving help and guidance of the kind he or she needs. This is the basis for our first principle of instruction: What is taught must be determined by what can be learned.

There is a necessary interaction which must be considered among 1) student's needs, 2) a teacher's goals, and 3) curricular demands. In fact, an understanding of this interaction is essential if what is to be taught is to be determined judiciously. John Dewey (1902) was speaking of this when he wrote:

> The child is the starting point, the center, and the end. His development, his growth, is the ideal. It alone furnishes the standard. (p. 95) Abandon the notion of subject-matter as something fixed and ready-made in itself, outside the child's experience; cease thinking of the child's experience as also something hard and fast; see it as something fluent, embryonic, vital; and we realize that the child and the curriculum are simply two limits which define a single process. Just as two points define a straight line, so the present standpoint of the child and the facts and truths of studies define instruction. It is continuous reconstruction, moving from the child's present experience out into that represented by the organized bodies of truth that we call studies. (p. 95-97)

In light of these ideas, materials and activities that are used in content instruction must be 1) appropriate to the abilities and interests of pupils; 2) feasible for the teacher to arrange; and 3) honest to the curriculum or domain of study under scrutiny. We might, then, extend our first principle of instruction to suggest that what is taught must be determined by the appropriate interaction of students' needs, a teacher's goals, and curricular demands:

These three aspects of curricular foundations deserve careful consideration if the content teacher is to create an effective learning environment in his classroom.

STUDENTS' NEEDS

Given a topic for study and its related concepts which the teacher hopes pupils will come to understand better, the needs of pupils must be considered in light of three categories: 1) personal needs, 2) skill needs, and 3) learning needs. The following kinds of questions are essential to the planning of instructional objectives

1. *Personal Needs:* What are the possibilities for personal fulfillment in the students' study? Do the information and skills to be explored and taught offer any

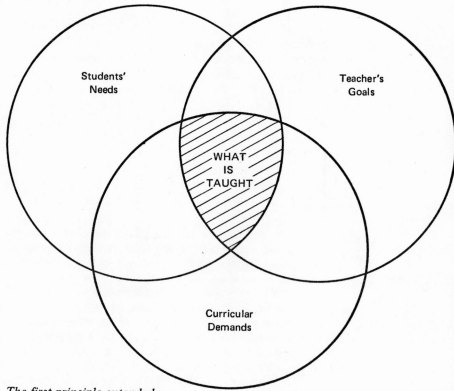

Figure 3-1   *The first principle extended.*

possibility of personal application *or* fulfillment for the students? For example, career interests might be sparked for some; information and skills that are useful in other courses might be explored. Any unit can offer varied opportunities for application of personal talents (drawing maps, making collages, designing displays, sharing experiences, etc.). The success which is insured by a concern for each student's personal needs may foster more general success and a feeling of personal satisfaction.

2. *Skill Needs:* The specific kinds of skills to be required should be delineated as precisely as possible in the planning of instruction. To what extent are the students adept with the skills required for successful learning? To what extent are you, the teacher, aware of their abilities? For those students who are deficient in requisite skills, what instruction should be provided? What alternative modes of study might be made available? Success in learning may well depend upon appropriate diagnosis and consideration of specific skill needs exhibited by students, followed by appropriate instruction.

3. *Learning Needs:* Of all that might be taught, what can the students learn that will benefit them? What provisions are made for multi-level material? What do the students already know about the subject? What are the basic concepts that

they must know? In this aspect, the content teacher must be the authority. Decisions about what to include, as well as what can be omitted, must be made on the basis of what students know and what they will be able to learn.

*, 15

TEACHER'S GOALS

The teacher's perspective of the breadth and depth of a course largely determines what is taught at a given time. Within any content area there is infinitely more that might be taught than can be taught. Choices must be made. Certain understandings are often necessary for subsequent study of other concepts. This is obviously true in a course such as mathematics, where so much skill work depends on previous understandings, but it is true in other studies also. Learning is itself a preparation for learning; thus, the teacher must orchestrate instruction to simultaneously account for past, present, and future learning. At any moment, a teacher must be able to answer certain critical questions, namely:

1. Why am I teaching this particular lesson or unit?

2. What are the resources which I might use to help students learn? (These could easily include the teacher's own personal experiences, supplementary reading of all kinds, guests to the classroom, field trips, the librarian and other resource persons, or films and video tapes.)

3. What is my purpose for each part of the overall plan and how much of that purpose and plan will require explanation to the students?

4. How much time will this study require? How much time will be available for diversion?

5. In what ways can I, the teacher, learn along with my students?

*, 16

Answers to such questions (can you add more?) are helpful in structuring any learning environment.

CURRICULAR DEMANDS

**, 3

Curricular demands means the content information that is traditionally accepted as what *must* be taught. It represents the third factor on which many instructional decisions must be based. Curricular demands appear in the tertiary position here by no accident; too often they have formed the only foundation for instruction and, yet, they may well be least important after pupils' needs and teacher's goals. We *can* de-emphasize them by minimizing their importance. However, school boards and courts by right can and do say what is to be taught in schools (and, for that matter, what is *not* to be taught).

In planning instructional objectives, therefore, teachers must give attention to curricular demands, all the while keeping students' needs and his or her own goals and resources in mind. A teacher must determine what curricular demands are appropriate for the students. In making such decisions, the teacher outlines the *curriculum,* which we define as "what *is* taught."

An effective way to integrate pupil needs, teacher goals, and curricular demands is to identify and plan each unit around specific concepts. These concepts should be stated and their development fostered at a level appropriate to the needs and abilities of the students. In this way, the teacher can at least partially insure that the abilities and needs of the students are in consonance with the learning demanded by the curriculum.

Effective instruction is the direct outgrowth of careful planning, and careful planning is based on these three curricular foundations. All that takes time, certainly. Nothing is more professionally rewarding, however, than well-planned, smoothly executed instruction, especially since the result is likely to be effective, productive learning.

INSTRUCTIONAL OBJECTIVES

When Robert Mager published his book, *Preparing Instructional Objectives* (1962), even he probably didn't guess the impact it would have. Educators at every level were literally swept off balance by behavioral objectives. Anything taught in school could be translated into behavioral terms and tested with micrometer-like precision. Curriculum guides were translated with haste; the bandwagon filled quickly. The result is that today many teachers can hardly think of what they teach without relying on behavioral terminology. Where the use of these objectives proves difficult, many begin to question their ability to teach: "Am I doing something wrong? Is what I want to teach wrong?" —Probably not. More likely, the trees have eclipsed the view of the forest, and the purpose of teaching is often obscured in the mire of objectives made for purposes of evaluation.

While some objectives lend themselves well to behavioral terms, others that are equally important do not. Though many objectives of education may result in changed behavior, observable behavior does not necessarily provide the most convenient way to view all objectives. Our work with content area teachers has shown us the need to emphasize two kinds of objectives; one that is conceptual, the other process-related.

Conceptual objectives are those objectives that are primarily related to ideas and understandings rather than to behaviors. They can be written in behavioral terms by identifying a behavior that may evidence the learning of them, but the focus of conceptual objectives is on an idea or concept. In other words, conceptual objectives are related to students' understanding of basic, general ideas, for example, "Habitat influences both life forms and life styles of organisms." The emphasis is on the idea or concept to be developed. Another example, one appropriate to social studies, might be, "Man constantly encounters conflict and seeks its resolution." In this case, the basic concept—conflict and its resolution—is identified as

*, 14 the major focus of study. Additional examples of conceptual objectives are identified at the beginning of each chapter within this book.

Process objectives, by comparison, can be related to the development of various processes or skills of learning, such as, "the ability to preread or inspect a selection for the purpose of establishing a set for information acquisition and determining an appropriate reading approach." Of particular importance in the context of reading in a content area classroom is that process objectives are concerned with *how* students learn. The process objectives, then, are those objectives that relate to students' abilities to acquire and develop understanding.

Integration of meaningful conceptual and process objectives is fundamental to reading and learning in a content classroom. The behavior required by mature reading can best be developed in a setting where there is meaningful content to be read. On the other hand, students are most likely to develop meaningful concepts when they are taught how to deal effectively with subject matter. The content teacher who designs instructional objectives with emphasis divided between learning process and learning content, whose instruction reflects the complementary relationship between processes and conceptualizations, will serve both sets of objectives.

INSTRUCTIONAL CONSIDERATIONS

How many games, battles, and arguments have been won on paper only to be lost in the heat of the engagement? Likewise, what purpose can be served by discussing instructional objectives without considering how to use them? To be more specific, content area teachers are faced daily with problems in teaching that are the direct result of an inequitable relationship between their students and the material chosen to help those students learn. This book is dedicated to those teachers and their problems.

The units and chapters to follow will delineate specific diagnostic and instructional strategies which can be used to solve or help minimize instructional problems. What we suggest, however, is based on the idea of teaching content and process in consonance. That is the fundamental premise of all that follows, and that premise becomes possible when instruction is characterized by three essential considerations.

First, content area reading can be systematized. That is, it can be approached from the perspective of a clearly-identified framework. This system or framework should be highlighted in any lesson structure used in a content area classroom. Furthermore, the system should be made obvious to students so that they can realize that the procedures they are being led through in their study will transfer to other settings. (In chapter 9 we will examine this concept in detail.) The object of such structured lessons is to ensure that in every encounter with reading in a particular content area, students will become better able to deal with similar content in future contacts.

Second, teachers should, where necessary, construct guide materials to accompany students' reading and study. These materials should guide students in their interaction with reading assignments at levels commensurate with their ability, purposes, and background of reference. (This will be the focus of chapter 11.) Both materials and students must be evaluated to determine when such guidance is necessary. (Unit 2 is designed to examine this problem.) Generally speaking, the worth of any guide material is related to the degree to which it fosters conceptualizations and develops increased abilities to read similar materials.

Third, students must be aware that their content area study involves both skills development and content understandings. They should become familiar with and habituated to information acquisition processes that will stand them in good stead in their independent study. For example, to borrow some terms from Adler and Van Doren, students need opportunities to develop abilities to read inspectionally, analytically, and syntopically. Concurrently, they need to be taught how to decide when one of these approaches is most appropriate. For this to happen, students must learn to ignore the temptation to read everything with precision. We say "temptation." Likely, most of us were taught to do exactly that! The result of such teaching is that most adults, even college graduates, are rather inefficient readers. Too often we've been told (and are telling students ourselves), "Read pages 35 to 47 by Friday." And so we read and they read, word by word, trying to recall every detail in hopes that some of what is remembered might appear on the inevitable and ubiquitous Friday test. For content reading instruction to work, for students to acquire facility in reading content area materials, they must become familiar with a variety of strategies rather than continuing to rely solely on one *, 17   approach to reading and learning

Identifying Reading Needs in a Content Classroom

The skilled teacher sees diagnosis as a first step in planning appropriate instruction and materials for his students.

Mary Austin

CONCEPTUAL OBJECTIVES

1. *Standardized reading tests can be useful to the classroom teacher when their results are interpreted within certain limitations.*

2. *Analyzing students' study skills is an important aspect of diagnosis for a content teacher interested in improving students' ability to learn.*

3. *Reading comprehension is the best window through which to observe reading ability.*

4. *Attitudes are a measurable outcome of learning.*

5. *Vocabulary and conceptual development are essentially related.*

A THESIS

In chapter 1 we expressed our conviction that diagnosis and instruction are inseparable. To isolate one from the other is like basing a good marriage on the absence of one of the partners. The value of amalgamating diagnosis with instruction lies in what we described as the first principle of instruction. The determinants of curricular content must include what can be learned as well as what might be taught. The first step of teaching, therefore, is to determine what students can learn.

Instruction in any classroom can only approach maximum effectiveness when it is designed to bridge the gap between what a student knows and what he or she needs to know. To us, this is the *raison d'etre* of instruction. Diagnosis is that aspect of instruction that enables a teacher to identify what the student knows. Without diagnosis, instruction is likely to be based on conjecture, and the extent of "the gap" tends to be veiled by uncertainty.

Figure II-1: *The true purpose of instruction is to bridge the gap between what the student knows and what he needs to know.*

If instruction is to bridge this gap, it must be based on a definite awareness of what the student knows, in terms of both content and abilities; it cannot be based on suppositions and conjecture.

Our purposes in this second unit—*Identifying reading needs in a content classroom*—are two: 1) to suggest various ways by which content teachers can identify what students know about reading and learning; and 2) to lay the groundwork for unifying diagnosis and instruction in a content classroom. We are isolating diagnosis in this unit as a convenience; our ultimate objective remains that of fostering unified diagnostic reading instruction in content classrooms. In examining diagnosis by itself, we are paving the way for a discussion of diagnostic reading instruction in its entirety, and that is the subject of Unit 3.

As you proceed through this unit, we hope you recognize that we treat reading diagnosis from the perspective of the content teacher, not the specialist. Furthermore, consider one overriding concern: *instruction is more likely to be effective when a teacher can discover what students are trying to do and when the teacher can then provide the students with appropriate activities to help them succeed.* Thus, while it may be valuable for you to become familiar with basic diagnostic strategies, it is more important that you become diagnostically aware.

Effective use of the concepts set forth in the preceding chapters may well depend upon how diagnostically aware you can become rather than on how many devices and strategies you may come to know. Familiarizing yourself with specific aspects of diagnosis may lead you into the trap of "Diagnosis . . . then what?" To be diagnostically aware means simply that one can approach the students with the intent of being responsive to their needs rather than feeling an overriding responsibility to a given body of knowledge or a predetermined curriculum. The teacher who understands the interrelationship between diagnosis and instruction is the one who will become diagnostically aware, hence the most responsive and the most effective.

*, 1

Activity and Selected Readings Key

SUGGESTED ACTIVITIES

Cross references to the following entries are denoted by a single star in the margin, followed by reference to the entry number in this list.

	CONCEPTS				
	1	2	3	4	5
1. Propose an antithesis to the preceding one. (See p. 41.) Which do current educational practices exemplify?	X				
2. Collect standardized test data on the reading ability of your students from their cumulative files and analyze them for any value you think they might have to you in your own teaching.	X				
3. Make a point of going by the guidance or testing office in your school or central offices to discuss the standardized testing program they employ. Find out what sources are available to teachers as aids to test data use and interpretation. (If not currently teaching, you might visit a school for this purpose.)	X				
4. Devise a study skills program for your class by the steps we suggest in chapter 8.		X			
5. List your objectives for a content reading inventory as we suggest on p. 69, chapter 6.			X		
6. Conduct analyses of students' responses to the sample IRI we provide on pp. 75–93.			X		
7. Using the suggestions provided in chapter 6, devise a group inventory of your students' comprehension of material required of them to read in your course. Analyze the results and continue to more careful diagnosis of students who would seem to need it. (See p. 94.)			X		

CONCEPTS

	1	2	3	4	5
8. Using data of the sort you collected in Activity **2** pick out the half-dozen or so students in each of your classes who are probably in deepest trouble in reading. Either on your own, or, preferably, in cooperation with a reading specialist, conduct an individual, in-depth assessment of these students.			X		
9. As preface to chapter 5, identify achievement tests and attitude scales of which you know. (See p. 58.)				X	
10. Analyze the study skill requirements of the course you teach, as suggested in chapter 8, p. 110.		X			
11. Following the guidelines suggested in chapter 5, design an attitude scale for your class. (See p. 62.)				X	
12. Select a passage from material you would use with your class. Identify the key concepts and the key concept words for that selection. Then describe how you would assess your students' knowledge of the concepts and the terms that reflect those concepts. (See p. 103.)			X		X

SELECTED READINGS

Cross references to the following entries are denoted by a double star in the margin, followed by reference to the entry number in this list.*

CONCEPTS

	1	2	3	4	5
1. Lyman, Howard B. *Test Scores and What They Mean.*	X				
2. Thomas, E. L., and Robinson, H. S. *Improving Reading in Every Classroom.*		X			
3. Shepherd, David. *Comprehensive High School Reading Methods.*		X			

Full bibliographic information for these items will be found at the end of the book under References.

CONCEPTS

	1	2	3	4	5
4. Valmont, William J. "Creating Questions for Informal Reading Inventories."			X		
5. Sanders, Norris M. *Classroom Questions: What Kinds?*			X		
6. Edwards, S. L. *Techniques of Attitude Scale Construction.*				X	
7. Hoffmann, Banesh *The Tyranny of Testing.*	X				

*Full bibliographic information for these items will be found at the end of the book under References.

4

Standardized Tests and Reading Diagnosis

Standardized reading tests can be useful to the classroom
teacher only when their results are interpreted within
certain limitations.

SUMMARY

Diagnosis is a matter of making qualitative judgments. Testing is a matter of quantification. While it is true that diagnosis and evaluation may overlap in purpose, it is
good to keep the differences between the two activities in mind and never to try to
substitute the administration of tests for the conduct of diagnosis.

Several basic references on testing are to be recommended. Some are stand-
bys like Buros' *Mental Measurements Yearbook* which provides scholarly reviews of
most tests in print. Other references, equally creditable, take a much less charitable
view of the whole business of testing, and with just cause, we think. The very idea
of standardized testing is suspect and is being questioned on several fronts. The
matter boils down to validity and use of tests. Do the tests we administer to
students serve us or them as evidence of achievement of either our goals or theirs?
One could even go so far as to say that not only do tests fail to test what we teach
but, worse still, schools have fallen into a trap of trying to teach what they test.

It is possible that standardized tests have a purpose to serve. They may
indicate the range of ability among groups of students. They may serve to indicate
which students should be looked at more closely to see what may be special
problems or special talent. In any case, we will borrow a phrase from an article by
David Harman (1975) that should well set the tone for what we want to say about
standardized testing. *Si duo idem faciunt, non est idem* or "If two people do the
same thing, it is not the same thing."

A MINI-REVIEW OF SOME PERTINENT LITERATURE

Standardized testing in this country is very big business today, and there are more tests of reading achievement available than of any other dimension of the curriculum. Their pervasiveness alone should cause an interest in standardized reading tests. Here is a brief review of several references which you might find it helpful to know.

The exemplar of reference sources for standardized tests is *The Mental Measurements Yearbook,* by O. K. Buros. It is not a yearbook in the strict sense; there have been eight editions published since 1938 when the first one appeared. Virtually all tests available are reviewed in M.M.Y., in one or more of the editions, with basic information and authoritative reviews included, usually both pro and con.

Buros also published *Tests in Print,* a simple listing of tests, and offers a collection entitled *Reading: Tests and Reviews* amassed from various editions of M.M.Y. These two additions to the line of service provided by Gryphon Press, the publisher, makes the service invaluable to the intelligent consumer of tests and related services. Chances are that any adequate professional library associated with a public school or college of education would have copies available.

The Educational Resources Information Center (ERIC) also has available good information on testing. The *Guide to Tests and Measuring Instruments for Reading,* for example, is straightforward and helpful. It is available from the ERIC clearinghouse on reading, NCTE (National Council of Teachers of English).

Educational Testing Service (ETS) serves as a base for the ERIC clearinghouse on testing. A treasurehouse of free or inexpensive material and information is available from either the company or the clearinghouse. The best way to get to resources in the clearinghouse is through the ERIC references, and again this source will be found in most sizeable professional libraries in education.

The references we have mentioned thus far are all more or less neutral in treatment of the topic of testing. Many other sources do not take nearly so neutral a stance. Niether do we, for reasons which we hope will become apparent. Much of the ammunition one would need to argue against the use of standardized tests, or to argue for more discretion and caution in interpretation as we will do, is available in a few sources.

The classic attack on standardized tests is *The Tyranny of Testing,* by Banesh Hoffmann (1964). In similar tone, and a little more up to date, is *Uses and Abuses of Standardized Tests,* by George Weber (1974). These two books are imperative for the serious critic. It is our opinion that school officials who haven't done so, should take a closer look at the warnings and recommendations in these books. In fact, the National Association of Elementary School Principals devoted two recent issues of *Principal* to attack the wrongs perpetrated by standardized tests. Volume 54, No. 4, March/April, 1975, deals with "the great I.Q. myth." Volume 54, No. 6, July/August, 1975, is devoted to "The scoring of children: standardized tests in America." The issues are available from NAESP or are likely in the professional collections of many school principals.

Even commercial television has had its say in recent years, and many educators watched with no small pleasure as CBS aired its "special" on I.Q. They called it a great myth, and their criticisms gave the industry no quarter. With so many people up in arms over the issue, can the problem be summarized fairly? What good can be said about testing? What guidelines can be offered the teacher who may want to make the best use of standardized tests? These are the concerns we hope to address in what follows of the present chapter.

THE WOLF IN SHEEP'S CLOTHING

Let us begin by saying that the most serious problem with standardized reading tests is that they are not what they seem. The basic idea of standardized tests is to compare groups of children or to compare individual performance to that of a group. Aside from whether that might have any value in and of itself, there is simply no way it can be called diagnosis. Standardized tests have virtually *no* diagnostic value, and to use their results as if they were diagnostic is to abuse them in the worst way. Decisions about individuals cannot be made on the basis of performance on a group measure. While diagnosis may involve standardized tests, it certainly need not, often does not. To ignore this basic understanding, a point cautioned in the manuals of many standardized tests themselves, is one of the easiest and most common ways to misuse them.

Let's look more closely at the basic idea, however, and try to strip away some of the façade of standardized tests as we view their complicated inner workings. There are seven reasons we might say that the basic idea, comparing individuals to groups or groups to groups on standardized test performance, is as insidious and dangerous as a wolf among the sheep.

1. There is nothing to suggest that the "average" performance of a group on a very particular task is necessarily a "standard" of performance for an individual which can be generalized to his or her performance overall. And yet that is precisely what we assume when we say "Johnny is reading on a fourth-grade level" because he scored grade 4.0 on a standardized test of reading ability.

2. People are different in more ways than they are similar; in fact, every person is unique in every ability, reading ability most certainly. It is cruelly ironic that in a country built on "rugged individualism" we should judge success in school by conformity, that we should reward convergence and punish divergence with standardized tests.

3. Objective tests, of reading or any other skill, are graded so that only the answer to an item, not the reasoning behind the answer, will figure into the data for the final score. Yet, as the eminent child psychologist Jean Piaget noted long ago, the reason for a "wrong" answer may often be better than the reason for a "right" answer. "Wrong" answers on a standardized test are always plausible and often attractive to the creative reader. (That's why students are

often told, "Your first guess is more likely to be right than your answer on second thought.) Clearly, the implication, and truth, is that thinking can get you into trouble on standardized tests!

4. Tests are set up in a subtle version of Joseph Heller's "catch-22" so that a predetermined and rather large portion (actually 15.86 percent) of students will score "low," the same portion will score "high," assuming the group tested is like the group against which comparisons are being made. Now why the students score low or score high or whether on a different sort of test of the "same" ability or understanding they would score differently, is quite irrelevant, at least in standardized test terms. As a matter of fact, the likelihood is rather good that the test scores of people who score either very high or very low would change if the same test were given again. How they might score on a different measure altogether is practically anybody's guess. Whatever the case, extreme scores are the least stable and are the very ones for which the danger in accepting them at face value is the greatest. Yet it is exactly these scores, the ones of students whose performances are outstandingly good or bad, that are the basis on which most "diagnostic" decisions are made!

5. The more "representative" the sample of pupils against whom comparisons are being made, the less likely it is that comparison of a "typical" student's performance will be fair to that student. On the other side of this coin, for the so-called ethnic youngster, even if a number of Chicanos or blacks or Eskimos or whomever are included in the "representative" sample, the number will be so small as to be insignificant to the individual. On the question of representativeness, you're damned if you do and damned if you don't.

6. There seems to be a certain respect for numbers in the thinking of most people, a respect that is unwarranted. While numbers *are* precise, the application of numbers to results of imprecise measures makes those measures no less imprecise. A score of 3.8 on a reading test sounds very scientific, but it may not be so at all. The concept is a tough one, but there is a very real qualitative difference between saying, for example, that a person is 103 months old and that that person reads on a grade level of 3.8. You can count the months since a person's birth, but you can in no comparable way "count" grade levels of achievement in reading.

7. We tend to assume that standardized test results must mean something. We publish reading scores in newspapers, comparing schools and school systems. We judge the quality of a program of free reading in a school on the basis of standardized reading test scores. We pass out scores to children and parents, make decisions to retain or promote individuals, all without realizing the basic assumptions we are making.

And what are these basic assumptions? They concern two ideas, each of which is as confusing as the other: reliability and validity. Whether one realizes it or not, every time a standardized test is used, someone very likely is assuming: 1) that the test is a reliable measure, and that this means something about its quality as a measurement tool; and 2) that the test is a valid measure, and that evidence for validity is available somewhere for anyone who would want to look at it. Both of these assumptions are false enough to give anyone who realizes it pause to wonder about the whole idea of standardized tests.

For a test to be reliable merely says that it agrees with itself, that for example, any half of the test items would agree with the other half. It's called "internal consistency," in fancy words. Yet no matter how consistent it might be, any test can at the same time be completely useless as a measurement tool.

For example, we could administer a reading test written in Latin to a group of third graders. The test would probably be very "reliable," since the students would score about as well (or poorly, it doesn't make any difference so long as it is consistent) on one item as on the next. You might say this is nonsense since no one would do such a thing anyway. Right you are. But let's administer the same reading test, written in English this time, to a group of third-grade Spanish-speaking children. Or to a group of inner city black youngsters. In the same vein as our Latin example, the results would be highly reliable, and yet this fact would say nothing about the quality of the test or its results for these children.

In its common sense, "reliable" means "dependable," and connotes a good quality—usually. Just as even the habitual criminal is reliable, in the technical sense the word means only "internally consistent," and to label a test as such is to say very little about its value. Of course, we would want a test to be reliable, but only in *hopes* that it might be valid. Knowing a test is reliable gives us no *assurance* at all of its validity.

And now to the *sine qua non:* VALIDITY. Does the test measure what it says it measures? Does the reading test measure reading ability, does it measure achievement in reading? Test makers try to say yes by pointing to either one or both of these facts about their test:

1. Experts think it does, or it looks like it does, if you accept that these skills, the ones we think our test items measure, are what define ability and achievement in reading.

2. The test measures as well as other reading tests since we know that scores on the two tests tend to be very similar.

In fact, that's very little reason to think a test is valid. The first claim depends on acceptance of what amounts to a very narrow and probably unrealistic definition of reading. The second claim is circular: Test 1 is like Test 2 which is (when you look at it) like Test 3 which is (when you look at it) like Test 1. —So all three tests are valid measures of reading?

We think not, actually. Reading comprehension is very complex. The criteria for its accomplishment are not to be captured in a number. In fact, reading comprehension defies quantification. To maintain otherwise is to trade teacher judgment in diagnosis for test reliability in measurement—a poor trade for those who make it.

Test performance is often very unlike real-life performance and only vaguely related to it. What students are asked to do on standardized tests of reading often doesn't even look like reading. It ignores the matter of interest, of reading strategy, of purpose for reading. Yet all these things are the critical factors that determine the success of the act of reading.

What tests do measure is performance on a test. The caution is clear: Make sure you know what performance on a reading test can and cannot be taken to mean before you use that performance to judge the ability of a reader.

SEVERAL FUNDAMENTALS

Can anything good be said about standardized tests of reading ability? Do they have any saving virtue to recommend them? We think so, though we hope we've made the point that they're no substitute for diagnosis. (The matter of reading diagnosis will be discussed in the next three chapters in terms of diagnosis of comprehension, vocabulary, and study skills.)

On the positive side of the question of standardized tests, we want to make these points now:

1. That test results are reported in various ways, some more useful than others.

2. That standardized test results can be used as rough indices, useful for estimating the range of a group's achievement, and that from such results it is possible to make group instructional decisions.

3. That standardized tests can help in picking those children for whom specific diagnosis is to be recommended.

The form of test results
Three common forms in which standardized reading test results are reported are 1) grade equivalents, 2) percentiles, and 3) stanines. Of these, grade equivalents and percentiles are the most common, and stanines are the most reasonable way in which to express test results.

It is easy to think that a grade score, say grade 4.6, is equivalent to the performance on the test by pupils at the sixth month (February) of the fourth year of school. It is as if in the standardization process, students of all possible grade levels (scores) were tested. But not so, despite what "equivalent" may mean to most people. To test makers, "equivalent" means "estimated." It is likely that in a test standardization program a test is tried out at only one time of year with children of different grades. Then, taking the scores from each grade, it is possible to divide differences between grades into intervals and to thereby "interpolate" or at least roughly estimate the scores that would have been obtained had there been any children of such grade taking the test. For example, on a test intended for grades seven, eight, and nine it is possible to score such "grade equivalents" as 5.2 or 8.6 or 11.0, and yet no one at any of these exact grade levels would have taken the test. In fact, there is little if any real reason to think that if, for example, an eleventh grader or a fifth grader or an 8.6 grader has taken the test, he or she would have gotten the number of items correct which the grade equivalent score would lead one to believe. And so the grade equivalent is a guessed grade; it may or may not reflect anything very true about a person's real performance.

The percentile score is also estimated, but it has nothing to do with grade level. What it does express is the relative standing of a score in a group of 100 scores, pretending for the moment that 100 scores were obtained on the test. The fact that 100 raw score points is usually *never* the number of scores obtained simply means we're back to guessing. We take all the scores we do have and put them in a list from highest to lowest. We then take the score halfway down the list as the 50 percentile. Then we simply estimate the raw score which should be at a given percentile rank *or* we calculate the percentile of a given raw score on the basis of how many (what percentage of) scores fall above or below it. Then we say that someone scores at the 70 percentile or the 90 percentile or whatever. But a *warning* is in order. The difference between 50 and 70 in percentile terms is the same as the difference between 70 and 90. Yet the difference between a score at the 50 percentile and one at the 70 percentile is much smaller than the difference between a score at 70 and one at the 90 percentile. Because most obtained scores fall near the mean and few fall at the extremes, a small raw score difference can make a big percentile score difference among scores on the middle range while the opposite is true for scores at extremes. There is no doubt that percentile scores are tricky; like most test scores, they may not mean what they seem to mean.

Stanines are the easiest to understand, the safest to use, and yet may be the most difficult scores to accept. We say "difficult to accept" because test users often want more precision in a score than the stanine affords. But that's exactly the point. The manner in which results are expressed by stanines is about as precise as most standardized tests can measure to begin with, which is why we call them "safest."

Many standardized tests report results in stanines or, where this is not done, converting from some other "standard" score is a fairly simple matter. The most rudimentary text on tests and measurements should explain the procedure.

The basic assumption of any standard score, stanines included, is that whatever is being measured is "normally distributed." This in turn, assumes that most of the scores obtained on the test will be fairly close to the average score. Scores not close to the average are relatively few in number, and there are as many very low scores as very high scores.

Now back to the stanine score itself. "Stanine" is a coined word, from STAndard NINE-point scale. Stanines have values from 1 to 9. In the conversion to stanines, scores are divided into nine groups, each group a certain distance from the average. Actually, the average score is included in stanine 5, the middle group. And since it is the middle group and since most scores occur near the middle, a rather high percent of scores fall in stanine 5. By the same token, few scores fall in either stanine 1 or 9.

Table 4-1 expresses the story in a way that should make clear the meaning of stanines. Each number in the middle column is a stanine score. Percentages of raw scores which are included in each stanine group are indicated in the first column. A guide to interpretation of performance indicated by a given stanine score is indicated in the third column of the table.

Percentage of Scores Represented	STANINE SCORE	Evaluation
4%	1	Poor
7%	2	
12%	3	Below Average
17%	4	
20%	5	Average
17%	6	
12%	7	Above Average
7%	8	
4%	9	Superior

Table 4-1   *Interpreting stanine scores.*

The use of test results

You probably have the feeling that if we're right in our assessment of the situation, standardized tests are limited in their use. While this is true, they do have some uses, and in some ways are very efficient.

For example, we mentioned in chapter 1 that in a "normal" classroom the range of reading ability is quite wide. Certainly one of the most common problems of the classroom teacher is to identify the divergent reading needs and abilities of students in the class. No class is really "normal" though, and the formula we gave in chapter 1 can only demonstrate the diversity which is theoretically possible in a heterogeneous class. By using standardized test data, however, a teacher can get a much better estimate of the range of reading ability in a class. This is usually a matter of collecting standardized reading test data from students' folders and identifying the number of students that fall into each of the stanine classifications.

After studying such information about the group to be taught, the teacher can make selections of appropriate reading materials. The use of group test results in conjunction with readability formulas can provide guidelines for planning an instructional program or unit. Decisions can be tentatively made about who probably can or cannot read the textbook in the course. A lot of frustration might be avoided if a teacher were to know before being tempted to require the reading of a text that it was probably too difficult for many students to tackle alone. Naturally, standardized test and readability formula results are only part of the picture, in some cases a minor part. But our position is that if standardized test results are available anyway, teachers and others in schools may as well make the best use of them, taking every pain not to misuse them.

Picking children for diagnosis

We have tried to make the point that testing is what one does to groups, diagnosis is what one does to individuals. But to carefully diagnose the complex learning needs of all students is probably unnecessary, if not impossible. One of the strongest points in favor of group standardized tests is that they may help to pinpoint those students whose needs may be exceptional enough to warrant a detailed diagnostic workup. Students whose scores are in stanines 1, 2, or 3, or 9, 8, or 7, may be in particular need of special attention. (Recall, these stanines include roughly the lower and upper 20 percent of students.) The standardized test in this use is like a net whose openings are large enough to let through the students whose needs are more common while picking out others whose needs may be exceptional. The net will "catch" this latter group because of either suspected exceptional weakness *or* exceptional talent. Certainly, it won't always be accurate, for many reasons, but as a rough screening device, the group standardized test does have usefulness. With its results, teachers, guidance personnel, and other ancillary staff can cooperatively deal with instructional problems, treating individuals as individuals, once their needs have been identified by careful diagnosis.

Remember when . . . ?

It wasn't so many years ago in education—and reading education was hit particularly hard by this—that performance contracting was the rage. Problems in education were promised a sure cure through applying the methods of industry to the needs of education. Companies that put out these programs of reading education were going to perform for the schools what schools had been unable to perform for themselves. And they would guarantee results on a money-back basis.

*, 3

There was one big hitch to it all, and it did them in. The tests that the education industry had been providing as measures of educational outcome for so many years now became that industry's nemesis. When one company was criticized for low reliability of one form of one of its tests, it answered that these tests were never intended to determine whether a company be paid for its performance in instructing children! (Elam, 1970). Ironically enough, the national sales manager of one of these companies once remarked, "We have excellent programs, but I'd hate to see them evaluated by our present evaluation instrumentation." (*Nation's Schools,* 1970) Might not any parent or teacher or school say precisely the same thing? Is the 150 million dollars a year we spend on standardized tests worth the price? (Dollar figure from Kohn, 1975.) In how many other ways do we "pay" for the use of standardized tests, and do we know what we're getting in the bargain?

5

Measuring Attitudes

Attitudes are a measurable outcome of learning.

SETTING THE STAGE

Before you read over the summary of the chapter, we want you to begin with an activity. This will prove a point we will make later.

*,9   ## ACTIVITY 5-1

1. Identify several achievement tests that are used in your subject area.
2. Identify a scale that might be used to measure students' attitudes toward the subject you teach.

[To do this, you might discuss the activity with fellow teachers and the guidance counsellor or check publishers' catalogs and references such as Buros, *Mental Measurements Yearbook.*]

SUMMARY

Attitudes of students toward school subjects are often misunderstood and usually ignored in assessment programs. However, there are scales available for measuring attitudes and there are techniques by which teachers can construct their own scales. Supplemented by informal but careful diagnosis, paper and pencil "tests" of attitudes could easily be a standard part of assessment of the objectives of instruction. Whether one would choose to measure attitudes, given the availability of techniques for doing so, probably comes down to a matter of priority.

The Estes Attitude Scales, one form for middle-school-age and up, another form for elementary school use, is a direct measure of attitudes toward English, math, reading, science, and social studies. Scale scores can best be interpreted in light of behavioral observations of students whose attitudes may be more extreme than those of their peers. Taken together, formal testing and informal assessment will likely yield the best information about attitudes.

THE IMPORTANCE OF ATTITUDE MEASUREMENT

Few teachers would quarrel with the notion that attitudes are critical determinants of learning. However, students' attitudes toward specific subjects or toward school in general are not usually included as a part of a school's regular testing program. Formal or teacher-made achievement tests are used almost exclusively to assess or plan teaching and learning. Why is this so? Why is attitude measurement so conspicuously absent from assessment programs? Need it be so?

While the selection is rather narrow, there are several good alternatives from which to choose in the measurement of attitudes. The reasons for absence of such measurement in most schools is anyone's guess, but two explanations seem most tenable to us. First, attitudes are not well understood by most people, other than to say they probably exist. The affective domain is not a major part of the professional study of teachers. Second, even among those who would wish to do so, few people really believe attitudes can be measured. While cognitive measures, the achievement and intelligence tests, are accepted with frightening indiscrimination, skepticism has been the common reaction to affective measures.

Despite their often misunderstood nature and the infrequent attention they receive, attitudes can and should be measured in planning for and evaluating students' educational experiences. To do so will require: 1) an understanding of attitude measures that are possible; 2) a familiarity with published scales that are available; and 3) some feeling for techniques of informal observation and assessment of attitudes.

KINDS OF ATTITUDE MEASURES

Basically, there are two ways of measuring attitudes, since attitude scales can be classified as either direct or indirect measures. Direct measures are distinguished by the fact it is clearly evident what the scale is measuring. Such measures have the advantage of relatively high reliability, though critics will point out that answers to direct measures can be easily faked, that students may try to lie for fear of admitting dislike for a socially or academically desirable behavior Research done on attitude measurement belies this criticism, however.

Indirect measures attempt in some way to disguise their true meaning. The supposed advantage to this is that students cannot easily "lie" to the scale. The main problem with indirect measures, though, is that one can never be sure that the attitude inferred from any behavior or judgment is justified. For example, when you see someone crying you may be tempted to conclude he is unhappy. You may, however, be wrong. If the person is happy, the attitude you infer (sadness) from the observed behavior (crying) is unjustified. In the same manner, many variables might be reflected in the scores of indirect scales, and the validity of purely inferential assessment is open to serious question.

Often, you may wish to measure pupils' attitudes toward something for which there is no available scale. For example, a department may want to know how pupils feel about a newly instituted elective program. A locally designed scale will have to be constructed for this. It is impossible that the commercial market could meet every conceivable need in educational diagnosis. Most tests given in schools will continue to be teacher-made, and so with attitude measures. The following two sections of this chapter concern the construction of attitude scales. Such information should also be helpful in selection of scales that are commercially or otherwise available for use. These will be given review in the next major section of the chapter.

CONSTRUCTION OF DIRECT MEASURES

Direct measures are those which 1) are rather obvious in intent and 2) require little if any inference in interpretation. Raw scores on such measures are directly interpretable; the higher the score, the better the attitude.

One of the most popular and perhaps the best direct method of measuring attitudes was designed by R. S. Likert (1932). Likert scales present the respondent with a series of statements related to a "psychological domain" (e.g. school, English class, curriculum design, or anything about which people might hold varying opinions). The task of the respondent is to indicate his or her agreement or disagreement with each statement. For example, in a scale to measure attitudes toward school, the following might appear:

5 will mean "I strongly agree"

4 will mean "I agree"

3 will mean "I cannot decide"

2 will mean "I disagree"

1 will mean "I strongly disagree"

	Strongly Agree	Agree	Cannot Decide	Disagree	Strongly Disagree
1. School is worthwhile.	5	4	3	2	1
2. Most courses in school are useless.	5	4	3	2	1

There are two points to be made concerning these items. First, notice that item 1 is positive, item 2 is negative. This means that the scored values of responses to the items are opposite in magnitude. For example, *strongly agree* to item 1 would be scored 5, whereas *strongly agree* to item 2 would be scored 1. (The numbers in the response boxes merely refer to response choices.) The general rule is this: from *strongly agree* to *strongly disagree*, score positive items 5, 4, 3, 2, 1; score negative items 1, 2, 3, 4, 5.

The second point about scoring is that an individual's score on a scale is the sum of response values across all items. For every item, an individual's response is scored 5, 4, 3, 2, or 1. These values are then summed across all items on the scale. The total represents a quantification of the person's attitude. For example, if a scale had 15 items, the possible scores for any individual would range from 15 to 75, or 15 × 1 to 15 × 5. Do you see why?

**, 6   The writing of items for any attitude scale is the most critical step. Criteria for items have been published by Edwards (1957) in an excellent little book called *Techniques of Attitude Scale Construction*. The following suggestions for writing items are adapted from Edwards' list. Examples are provided to illustrate the criteria. Each item refers to and should call to mind the school subject "Science."

1. Avoid statements referring to the past rather than the present.

    Poor: Science was an exciting subject in elementary school.
    Better: Science is an exciting subject.

2. Avoid factual statements.

    Poor: Science is a required subject in the eleventh grade.
    Better: Science should be a required subject in the eleventh grade.

3. Avoid statements capable of multiple interpretation.

    Poor: The job of the science teacher is to transmit information. (Is *to transmit information* good or bad?)
    Better: The study of science offers the opportunity for search and discovery.

4. Avoid statements irrelevant to the subject.

    Poor: School is worthwhile.
    Better: The study of science is worthwhile.

5. Avoid statements likely to be endorsed by almost anyone or no one.

    Poor: All of man's progress has stemmed from his scientific endeavor.
    Better: The most important aspects of man's progress stem from scientific endeavor.

6. Use simple, clear, direct language in the form of concise statements.

Poor: The study of science, while beneficial to the welfare of mankind, is nevertheless a double-edged sword, since it has the potential for accruing to man either his guaranteed immortality of his inevitable destruction.

Better: Scientific endeavor provides a better way of life.

7. Each statement should have only one complete thought. (See examples for 6.)

8. Avoid terms such as *all, always, none, never, only, just,* and *merely.*

Poor: All students should try to major in science in college.

Better: Majoring in science in college would be worthwhile.

9. Avoid use of words perhaps incomprehensible to students.

Poor: Indefatigability is high during the study of science.

Better: Studying science is less tiring than studying other subjects.

10. Avoid use of double negatives.

Poor: It is not true that not enough science is offered in high school.

Better: More science should be offered in high school.

The use of these criteria is essential. By adhering to them, the content validity of the attitude scale is achieved. To the degree that items conform to the criteria, the scale is likely to provide a true measure of attitudes.

*, 11

PUBLISHED SCALES

Until recently, there were very few scales available for measuring attitudes toward school subjects. Those that were available were typically constructed for use in research or evaluation projects where the validity of the scale was not a primary concern. In 1967, Shaw and Wright, in their book, *Scales for the Measurement of Attitudes,* pointed out that most scales of attitude toward school courses were to measure attitudes of college students. They chose to exclude many existing scales from their compilation because of generally poor quality. In their terms, the "functional characteristics" of many scales were unsatisfactory.

In the ten years since the Shaw and Wright book appeared, the picture has changed somewhat. Alexander and Filler (1976) list eighteen attitude assessment instruments in their booklet, *Attitudes and Reading.* Only four of these bear pre-1967 dates. Most have appeared since 1970. Note that these are only scales to measure attitudes toward reading, which says nothing of scales that may have appeared as measures of attitudes toward other school subjects.

It was in response to the conditions deplored by Shaw and Wright that Johnstone (1973) sought to validate the Estes Attitude Scales. The success of her study led to the subsequent publication of the scales (Estes, Johnstone, and Richards, 1975). Five subscales of this instrument allow measurement of attitudes toward English, reading, math, science, and social studies among middle school and older pupils. An elementary form (Estes, *et al.,* 1976) measures attitudes of children in grades two through six.

The main value of these scales is that they allow teachers to 1) pinpoint students' present positive or negative attitudes expressed in interpretable terms; 2) make curricular and instructional modifications in response to those attitudes; and 3) observe changes in attitudes over time, when the scales are administered on a pre/post basis.

INFORMAL OBSERVATION AND ASSESSMENT

Formal, paper-and-pencil tests of attitudes are but a part of measurement in the affective domain. Certainly they allow quantification of attitude, but careful and sensitive observation is the best method of "qualifying" pupils' attitudes. Numbers on tests are impersonal. They say nothing of why a person's attitude is what it is, let alone how the attitude is expressed in behavior. Informal assessment, on the other hand, gains in personalization what it gives up in precision. The implicit suggestion for all measurement is clear, especially for affective measurement: for screening and testing of groups, use formal scales; for diagnosis and counseling of individuals, add informal observation.

An attitude is both a feeling and a disposition toward a class of tangible or intangible objects to which the attitude is related. Behaviorally, this often translates to verbal statements and approach-avoidance actions, especially where alternative behaviors are available. For example, a good attitude toward reading will lead a person to read instead of watch television when the goal is entertainment. Obviously, there are exceptions where good television wins out over mediocre reading. But the general choice of reading over television can be attributed to a person's relative feeling for reading and television as entertainment. Therefore, observation of behavior should be indicative of attitude.

When a student has been identified by a screening test as having a poor attitude, or where the teacher thinks that attitude may be a problem, there are certain questions that can be asked. Answers to these, derived from informal observation, will bear qualitative implications for the student's attitudes. Thus, answers to carefully framed diagnostic questions can suggest modifications in a child's school experience.

1. What does the student's cumulative record indicate about past experience with similar courses?

It is as true that experiences determine attitudes as that attitudes determine behaviors. If a child seems to have an unfavorable attitude toward school or a particular subject, you might ask whether previous experiences with school or certain courses have been negative. It is possible that even the student does not realize the source of his or her feelings or what to do about it. A frank and open discussion about the causes of a poor attitude can be helpful.

2. Does the student express anxiety and fear about a subject?

People will often verbalize their attitudes when given an opportunity. Where a student has developed an unrealistic fear of a subject, he or she may say so in different ways. Graduate students, for example, often are afraid of measurement and statistics courses, or so they say. But more often than not, what they are really afraid of is having to memorize things that they do not understand. What they need is to be counselled into a section of the course that is likely to be taught on an intuitive level rather than an algorithmic level. For high school students, the story is similar.

3. Is the work the student does in a course careful or careless?

To continue the example of the graduate student and statistics, tests and measurements professors often complain that their students "can't add a column of figures, let alone multiply a negative and a positive and get a negative product!" But is it really that the students can't perform simple operations or is it that their predisposition toward mathematics, stemming from whatever source, leads to carelessness? When an attitude of fear mitigates against learning, the student needs counselling about the fear more than teaching directed to a weakness that doesn't really exist. The story is the same, repeated endlessly for countless "failures" in school. Diagnosis of attitude can have far-reaching effects on a student's academic life if followed by attempts at attitude modification. (This topic will be treated in chapter 13.)

4. By class participation, or lack of it, what is the student saying about his or her attitude toward the course?

Certainly not everyone who is quiet in class has a poor attitude and not everyone who participates in discussions has a good attitude. But by the way they do or do not participate in class activity and discussion, students may reveal their feelings toward a course. If the teacher is sensitive to this, he or she can often know when steps to remediate a poor attitude are in order. The antagonistic participant and the passive aggressive withdrawal are perhaps demonstrating similar attitudinal problems that demand attention.

5. What are the student's expressed personal and/or professional goals and how are these related to the course?

Students with good attitudes toward a course often aspire to occupations and endeavors that relate to the subject. Conversely, a student who sees no relationship between his or her goals and the requirements and content of a course will likely have a poor attitude toward the course. An informal survey of student interest and aspiration, given early in a course, can serve as part of an informal attitude assessment. Careful analysis of results may reveal the need for exploration of the relevance and relationship of students' interests and course content.

This brief list of informal questions is representative of the kinds of behaviors and statements that often indicate attitudes. Answers to such questions can be helpful in making decisions about causes and remedies of poor attitudes. There are, however, few if any simple solutions to attitudinal problems. Attitudes form over years and change slowly. To complicate matters further, the question of attitudes and behaviors is a question of chickens and eggs. While it may be logical to say that attitudes determine behaviors, it is as easy to say that behaviors can modify attitudes. This may, in fact, sometimes work to a teacher's advantage. For example, a social studies teacher might have a group of students who are very negative toward reading the text, discussing it in class, listening to the teacher, and taking tests every Friday. So, the teacher tries a completely different approach and sets up an activity-centered syllabus that includes many options for modes of learning the same thing. If not all, certainly many students give it a try and begin to behave as if they did like social studies—in fact, they come to do so because they are doing things in their study that they like and this affects their whole outlook on the subject. (Remember *Foxfire?*)

6

Analyzing Reading Comprehension

Reading comprehension is the best window through which
to observe reading ability.

SUMMARY

From an informal analysis of a student's reading comprehension, we can generate
hypotheses about that student's reading ability. As we do this, we can consider how
well a student reads on three levels: 1) literal, 2) inferential, and 3) applicative.

In designing a program for informally diagnosing reading comprehension, a
teacher should consider several factors. First, the abilities that one wants to assess
must be identified and the type of selection process must be chosen. Second, the
questions which are to be asked on the comprehension check should be designed
in relation to the purposes for administering the test. Third, the administration of
an informal reading inventory in a content classroom can serve several purposes.
Fourth, interpreting the results of an informal analysis requires more than simply
scoring a test objectively; it requires insights and perceptions which are developed
through practice.

WHAT'S IT ALL ABOUT?

Reading is a controversial matter surrounded by much heat and little light. Our
earlier guess was, however, that as you defined reading you included a dimension
related to comprehension. To try to do otherwise would be like trying to define the
game of football without mention of the attempt to advance the ball. Whatever else
it is or is not, football is a game of moving the ball. It is indefinable without that
idea. Reading is also essentially indefinable without the element of comprehension.
Comprehension is the object and the essence of reading; it is what reading is all
about.

Theoretically, it is possible that a football game could be played in which neither team was able to move the ball. Such a game, however, could only be called football because both teams were attempting to advance the ball, and that is the object of the game. So it is with reading. It is possible to say, "I have read this, but I can't comprehend it." But the person who says this can be said to have read only because he or she was attempting to comprehend. The fact that the person did not comprehend suggests that his or her attempt to read was unsuccessful. The success of the attempt to comprehend determines the quality of the reading act. Whatever else it is or is not about, reading is about comprehension.

LEVELS OF COMPREHENSION

Comprehension is the object and the product of reading. As such, comprehension is the best window we have for observing reading ability. That window may be frosted, and we may see through it darkly, but it is the best we have at the moment.

Through the diagnosis of reading comprehension, one can generate inferences about the quality of a student's reading ability. On the basis of these inferences, hypotheses can be formed about the expectations one might reasonably establish for a student's reading. Inferences may also be drawn for instructional activities appropriate for the student. Comprehension, then, is the key to effective reading diagnosis.

Perhaps the easiest way to understand comprehension is to realize that a reader can 1) read the lines, 2) read between the lines, and 3) read beyond the lines. Reading the lines is equivalent to *literal comprehension,* that is, comprehending what the author says. To read between the lines is to interpret what the author means and is *inferential comprehension.* The third level is reading beyond the lines by applying what is read and is called *applicative comprehension.* Analytical and syntopical reading require that a student function on both the second and third levels of comprehension. Thus, an analysis of a student's ability to comprehend on each of these three levels is an important aspect of diagnosis.

Literal comprehension is what most students obtain when they read material that is within their instructional reading level. It is what can be verified by referring directly to what an author has stated; there is no guesswork involved. Consider, for example, the following sentence, typical of an eighth-grade, history textbook:

> When Abraham Lincoln, the sixteenth President of the United States, took office, he faced the most difficult challenge in our history—to preserve the Union in the face of determined secessionists.

Assuming that the statements in this sentence are true, a student's literal comprehension will be determined by the ability to understand what the author said. If a student reads this as "Lincoln's challenge was to preserve the Union," he or she has comprehended literally what the author said. Literal comprehension is sometimes called factual recall because it refers to the facts that the reader remembers.

Inferential comprehension is based on one's interpretation of the facts that are presented. In a very real sense, inferences are the result of an "educated guess" because they cannot be proved by what is specifically stated. For example, in the passage about Lincoln, the author does not state why Lincoln's challenge was the most difficult in our nation's history. A student must infer from the evidence and make an informed guess about what the author meant. Thus, inferential comprehension is the ability to take what the author says and logically derive what is meant. Main ideas of passages are often left to inferential comprehension because they are not stated outright; students often need to be able to read on the inferential level if they are to identify the important concepts in a passage.

The applicative level is important because it is primarily through application that reading becomes meaningful and practical. The ultimate purpose of reading is to be able to apply what is learned through reading. Many students cannot transfer what they read to their own lives and situations, and reading for them is often perceived as a pointless and useless task. Reading a driver's manual and similar material may have obvious application to them, but a science textbook or a passage from *Walden* . . . ? Mature, critical readers actively seek application as they read, so their ability to comprehend and to analyze what they read far surpasses that of the reader who rarely transcends the literal level. The key to effective analytical reading is asking questions, and the student who constantly seeks application in his or her reading is the one who most easily learns to read critically. In addition, when a student comprehends on the applicative level, he or she is far more likely to remember the material because it has greater meaning for that student than for one who cannot apply what he or she reads.

INFORMAL DIAGNOSIS

When reading specialists diagnose reading comprehension, they rely on their knowledge and skills of observation more than anything else. The strategy they most commonly use is an informal reading inventory. It consists of providing a student with several reading selections, observing the student as he or she reads, and checking the student's comprehension when the reading is finished. Since the selections are of increasing difficulty, the diagnostician has an opportunity to determine what the student can do when reading easy material, challenging material, and difficult material. Because the testing situation is informal, the examiner can pursue a student's responses to determine exactly what has been learned and, in some cases, can even probe to ascertain how or why the student has learned.

The basic principles underlying the informal reading inventory (IRI) can be applied by classroom teachers in constructing and administering a content area informal reading inventory.

A systematically designed program to assess students' comprehension of content materials can be as simple or as elaborate as one wants. It should be designed to accommodate the needs of the teacher, and it can be as basic as giving a single passage to an entire class or as extensive as administering a series of passages to individual students. It might be best to consider something in between the two extremes. Whatever the case, careful attention should be given to preparing the testing material and to interpreting the results if the diagnosis is to be accurate and meaningful.

CONSTRUCTING A TESTING DEVICE

Whatever one hopes to determine from an informal diagnosis of reading comprehension, the value of the findings often depends upon how well the testing device has been constructed. At best, a testing situation can only provide *clues* about what a student knows or does. The accuracy of a reading diagnosis is determined, in part, by the degree to which the test reflects a realistic reading situation. In constructing a content informal reading test, a teacher must consider 1) what abilities he or she seeks to diagnose, 2) the selection of the passages that will measure those abilities, and 3) the design of the questions to be such that they do measure the identified abilities.

A content IRI must be constructed in relation to well-defined objectives. Identifying exactly what you want to discern is the first step in constructing such a device. For example, do you want your content IRI to:

1. assess abilities with material only from your specific content field?

2. assess abilities across a range of difficulty (i.e., multi-level materials)?

3. assess abilities with varied types of material (i.e., narrative, descriptive, expository, word problems, etc.)?

4. assess ability to identify main ideas?

5. assess ability to "read between the lines"?

6. assess ability to use context clues to identify new words?

7. assess ability to apply what is in the selections?

These and other questions must be answered before a test or inventory can be constructed if you are to be reasonably confident that the results you obtain are accurate.

*, 5

Consider the objectives for a content IRI in your classroom. What objectives would you identify on which to base the construction of your inventory or test? Are there areas that need to be considered that we have not suggested in our list of questions? What are they? A word of caution: because you identify your objectives does not guarantee that the inventory, when constructed, will provide accurate results. You must constantly monitor yourself during the construction process to determine how accurately the test reflects your objectives. If you lose sight of your objectives, it is likely that your inventory will diminish in its ability to yield accurate and meaningful information.

Having established the objectives for your inventory, carefully choose the passages you will include. Above all, the selections must be representative of the material students will be asked to read in your classroom. In selecting the passages, consider 1) the varied levels of difficulty for your course, 2) the predominant types of passages students will read, and 3) the length of the passage needed to obtain accurate results.

It is hoped a content teacher will be able to provide multi-level materials in his or her classroom. The diversity of reading ability in a content class has been discussed in chapter 1, and the need for multi-level materials is evident if one is to avoid frustrating reading assignments. If multi-level materials are to be used in instruction, a content IRI should be constructed from material at each of the available levels. This provides the teacher with an opportunity to analyze students' abilities at several levels of difficulty and makes it easier to determine which students would learn best from assignments in which materials. In addition, when a student's ability is sampled across several levels of difficulty, the task of planning instructional activities becomes easier because reasonable expectations are more likely to be established and the teacher's prognosis can be made with increased confidence.

If, on the other hand, circumstances require that a single textbook be used predominantly, the passages chosen for the IRI should be selected to reflect the variability of reading levels within that text. While one can ascertain an overall readability level for a textbook, rarely is that level consistently maintained throughout the book. Most textbooks include a wide range of readability levels, and the assigned readability level is only an average within that range. Thus, it would be prudent to include several selections from a single adopted textbook to assess students' abilities with material on the varied levels within that text.

Closely related to the diversity of reading levels are the varied types of passages students typically encounter in content area reading assignments. With the exception of that required in their English class, students read material which is almost exclusively nonfiction. The experience that many students have had with nonfiction material is limited and their problems in reading content material is often related to this lack of experience. Assessing ability to learn from descriptive and expository selections is an important purpose of a content IRI. In selecting passages for a content IRI, then, one should include those types of material that dominate a specific field. For example, at a minimum, a math IRI should include expository passages and word problems; an English IRI, narrative passages and perhaps even a poem; a history or science IRI, descriptive and expository passages. The selections in a content IRI must reflect the type of material that students will typically be asked to read.

A third factor to consider in the selection of passages for a content IRI is their length. On the surface this may seem trivial, but one of the major problems with many reading tests is that they create atypical reading situations by using selections far shorter than what is normally read. This results in a distorted image of a reader's ability. We believe that a selection of 200 to 250 words is minimal. The number of words, however, is not of prime importance. The objective of the content IRI is to determine how well a student will read a typical selection. We suggest a passage of this length because that will probably be necessary to assure that the selection is inclusive and has continuity.

The passage chosen should have a logical beginning and conclusion, the body of the passage clearly reflecting the development of a topic. Accurate comprehension of passages excerpted from the middle of a larger body of material is often dependent upon what has preceded that excerpt and what follows it. Thus, the length of a passage in a content IRI must be determined by the degree to which it is continuous and inclusive.

FORMULATING COMPREHENSION QUESTIONS

Good diagnosis depends upon the quality of the questions designed to assess comprehension; in the absence of good comprehension questions, the diagnosis of reading comprehension is almost surely inaccurate. Good questions can be formulated if three aspects of their design are considered. The neglect of any one of these is likely to result in an invalid assessment and a meaningless diagnosis.

IRI questions must measure the areas identified by your objectives. Typically, several aspects of comprehension are checked: 1) comprehension of main ideas, 2) factual recall, 3) inferential comprehension, 4) ability to apply and relate what is learned, and 5) ability to use context clues to understand unfamiliar vocabulary. You need not check all of these areas, but it is essential to know what areas of comprehension are being assessed. To check predominantly factual recall and then conclude that a student can or cannot comprehend the material can be both inaccurate and misleading. To conclude that the student can or cannot comprehend the material on a literal level may be accurate, but no information would have been gathered about other aspects of comprehension.

**, 4, 5 Exactly which aspects of comprehension to assess is each teacher's decision. We suggest that a teacher should check comprehension of main ideas, facts, and inferences. When these aspects of comprehension are assessed, the responses will provide information that can be used for an overall analysis of a student's comprehension. Each of the major aspects can be analyzed separately, and the interaction effect among them can be assessed. That is, if a student has difficulty with inferences, his problem may be an inability to recall the facts which are needed to make the proper inferences. An attempt to determine this should be made.

Questions that are not "passage dependent" may not be measuring what a student comprehends from that passage. This is not to suggest that one should avoid questions that assess a student's ability to relate what is learned from a passage to situations outside the selection. When you do so, however, be sure that the question incorporates *both* what is in the selection and what may be outside the passage's boundaries. For example, consider again the statement about Lincoln:

> When Abraham Lincoln, the sixteenth President of the United States, took office, he faced the most difficult challenge in our history—to preserve the Union in the face of determined secessionists.

An inappropriate question based on this statement might be: "Why might the challenge that Lincoln faced be more difficult than Washington's problems with his cabinet?" A student could answer this question from knowledge of Washington's problems and a general awareness of secession; he or she need not know the specifics of Lincoln's challenge. A slightly more "passage dependent" question might be: "Compare the magnitude of Lincoln's challenge to the problems Washington faced with his cabinet." But this "question," too, is probably inappropriate. Here the student must be aware of the details of the early problems of both presidents. If he or she cannot answer such a question, one must then ascertain whether this is because of 1) not knowing what Lincoln's challenge was, 2) not knowing how great that challenge was, or 3) not knowing about Washington's problem. Then and only then could an accurate diagnosis be made. If the diagnosis of comprehension is to be accurate, it must be directly related to the selection being read.

Another consideration in the formation of comprehension questions is that questions should not provide information about the answer. Frequently, too many clues about the right answer are included in the question itself. For example, consider the question "What problems did Lincoln face with the secessionists?" Immediately, the student is clued to secessionists, and if what secessionists were is known, a reasonable answer can be provided without reading the passage. A better question might be "What was the essence of Lincoln's challenge?" The answer can now provide a better clue to what the student learned from the reading.

In forming comprehension questions, it is important to bear in mind what you expect the students to learn from their reading. The questions should be similar to those you might ask on a test such as a weekly quiz or grading period examination, assuming now that those assessments accurately reflect your instructional goals and expectations. If the questions are easier or more difficult than what is typically asked, they may not help much in determining instructional strategies.

Finally, the questions you use in a content IRI should be designed to elicit short, essay-type answers. Sometimes, the answer may be only one word, such as a person's name, but you should avoid objective, multiple-choice questions. These questions tend to reveal too much information to the student and the answer may then be a guess based on the options made available. If there is to be a guess made, you want the student to guess on the basis of what he or she understands, not because you have provided a "right answer" and several distractors.

In summary, we might characterize good IRI questions as content related and open-ended. The classic open-ended question is "Retell what you have read," which may or may not be appropriate for a specific group administered content IRI. Certainly, the questions that are asked should require by various degrees retelling and evaluation of what has been read.

ADMINISTERING A CONTENT IRI

The way in which one administers a content IRI is an important aspect of informal reading diagnosis in a content classroom. This strategy may be used with an entire class or with individuals, but in either case, the emphasis must be on informality. By informal, we do not mean to imply overly relaxed, slouching students taking a test as they chat with their friends. Informal testing is to be contrasted with formal testing when the latter requires rigid, inflexible test administration. Flexibility is the byword of informal testing. A diagnostician is afforded a free hand in informal testing to pursue and probe students' responses in an effort to gain insights into their reading ability that are not immediately apparent from their responses. If a teacher takes advantage of the informality of a content IRI, the chances of obtaining valuable diagnostic information will be greatly enhanced.

When administering a content IRI, a teacher should consider several possible alternatives. The method that is eventually selected should, however, be in accord with the purposes and objectives established for using such a strategy in the first place. Among the available options, an individualized administration will provide the greatest opportunity for an in-depth analysis, but sheer numbers may make such an approach impractical for any but a small number of students. Another possibility is to administer a group inventory to an entire class simultaneously. This procedure certainly has the advantage of efficiency. Another option is to administer the inventory in small groups, where some of the opportunity to pursue answers remains open. A teacher should consider all possibilities, as the best option may not be any one approach, given the various limitations of time, space, and need. Perhaps the most feasible and appropriate strategy lies in some combination of these alternatives.

The approach we recommend is to begin with a survey inventory administered to an entire class. A survey inventory may consist of one or several passages, depending on how much screening information is being sought. If you prefer to use a single passage, it should be as typical as possible of the material you will use most often in your course. If several passages are employed, they should represent the range of available materials that will be used for instruction.

If you decide to use this group screening inventory approach, consider the following cautions. First, if you are interested in testing students' ability to recall what they have read, you should not allow them access to the passages as they answer the questions. If students can refer to a passage, you will be testing recognition, not recall, and those are two very different, though related, aspects of comprehension. Second, a major disadvantage of this screening approach is that students will have to write out their answers. This introduces a variable that may easily affect your results. If students write out their responses and their answers indicate that they had difficulty understanding what they read, one can never be sure whether the difficulty was in understanding the reading or in writing out the responses. For this second reason, if for no other, we suggest that you not limit your informal diagnosis of reading comprehension to a large group inventory.

The real value of this large group approach is to provide initial information which can be used to suggest additional diagnostic procedures. Since this is the primary value of this approach, you may prefer to use available standardized test data for screening purposes. (This is, we remind you, the most appropriate and valuable use of standardized reading tests.) Naturally, an informal screening inventory will yield results more directly related to your specific purposes than will a standardized test, and too, the inventory will be based more on material immediately pertinent to your course.

A second step in the approach we recommend involves the administration of several passages to small groups of students. These groups should be designed homogeneously on the basis of results obtained from the large group screening. Ideally, the size of these groups would be no more than four students, thus minimizing the interaction among the students as they respond to the comprehension questions.

When administering a small group inventory, ask the students to read each passage silently as they would an assignment in class. As they read, observe the students to identify any signs of strengths or weaknesses. For example, good readers may ask if they can write on the passage and may underline certain portions as they would when reading a homework assignment. A weak reader may indicate signs of difficulty or frustration by finger pointing, vocalizing, or being easily distracted. These observations during silent reading may be as important as the information obtained from the comprehension check.

When all the students have finished reading each passage, ask the comprehension questions orally. You will not be able to ask all students each question, but if you have a variety of questions, you should be able to determine to what degree each student was able to understand what was read. Having several students together can also be advantageous if you ask others to agree or disagree with a student's answer. You can then probe to find out why or how students arrived at their answers. If conducted properly, a small group inventory may provide you with as much diagnostic information as you will either need or want for most of your students.

After administering small group informal reading inventories, it is likely that you will want to obtain more information about a few of your students. This can be accomplished with individualized IRIs. When administering an IRI individually, you should pursue the same basic strategies used in the small group inventory. It should, however, differ in that you will have an opportunity to pursue and probe responses in greater depth. The student will assist in the diagnosis by explaining why he or she may be having difficulties. Also, in an individualized setting, you have the opportunity to provide instruction and to determine how well the student responds to your guidance and direction. Perhaps the student is totally disinterested in the subject and has no intention of trying to learn what is being read; if that is the case, you may be able to discover this problem and generate some interest in the material—at least enough to get the student to try to learn. On the other hand, you may want to have a chance to examine a good reader individually to determine exactly how far you can challenge him or her. Too, you may discover that a good reader can comprehend well on a literal level but has difficulty abstracting thoughts beyond the factual to more inferential or applicative levels of comprehension. One can discover much from an individualized testing that cannot surface in even a small group setting, and the limitations of such a diagnosis are determined only by the amount of perceptiveness and imagination that a teacher can provide.

INTERPRETING A CONTENT IRI

A good reading specialist interprets an informal reading inventory with the intensity of a bionic eye. Analyzing the facts and the implications in the Sherlock Holmes tradition, the diagnostician has but one purpose in mind—prognosis and recommendations; without these applications, diagnosis is of little import. Primarily, the intention is twofold: 1) to identify a student's instructional reading level (the level at which the student will benefit most from instruction); and 2) to determine the specific strengths and weaknesses of a student's reading ability.

When interpreting the results of a content IRI, one can begin by examining the percentage scores obtained by each student on the selections. These scores can *indicate* proficiency with similar material and can provide a rough, initial guideline for diagnosis. The following percentages are offered as estimates of several degrees of reading competence:

If a comprehension score is	that material is likely to be on the student's
90–100,	independent reading level.
70–90,	instructional reading level.
below 50,	frustration reading level.

If the score falls in the gray area between 50 and 70, it suggests that a student may find the material too difficult or that he or she may learn from it effectively when the reading is supplemented with appropriate instruction. When a score falls in this range, however, further analysis is required to suggest an appropriate competence level.

A word of caution is essential at this point. These scores can be misleading at times. Hence, we advise that the percentage scores be used only as initial indices or as evidence to corroborate findings based on more thorough analyses and understandings of a student's specific responses. For example, if a student skips, misreads, or misunderstands a major idea as the selection is read, it is conceivable that the student's total percentage score can be affected as much as forty points, depending upon how many comprehension questions are based on or are related to that idea. Therefore, accurate diagnosis can only be generated from an in-depth analysis of responses; it rarely emanates from a cursory examination of total percentage scores.

The in-depth analysis to which we refer is usually a result of an item-by-item examination of the responses to questions from each selection and from among various selections of varying degrees of difficulty. You should seek to identify trends in various areas of comprehension such as factual, interpretive, and applied. By determining specific strengths and weaknesses, you can relate the specifics to the whole picture and more readily understand what a student's real capabilities are.

ACTIVITY 2–2

*, 6   In this activity we have provided a passage typical of a ninth-grade history textbook. It has a tenth-grade readability level (Fry graph). Following the selection are

ten questions. To help you apply the principle of interpreting IRI findings, we suggest that you read this selection and answer the questions after it. This should help familiarize you with the selection and enhance your understanding of our discussion of the several examples which will follow.

Phil Sheridan in the Shenandoah Valley

Directions: Read this silently to find out why the Shenandoah Valley was valuable to both the North and the South in the Civil War.

During the Civil War, it was known simply as the Valley: an open corridor slanting off to the southwest of Virginia from the gap at Harper's Ferry. It was a broad land, lying between blue mountains with the bright mirror of a looped river going among golden fields and dark woodlands, and with pleasant towns linked along a broad undulating turnpike and rich farms rolling away to the rising hills.

Queerly enough, although it had been a vital factor in the war, in a way the war had hardly touched it. Stonewall Jackson had made it a theater of high strategy in 1862, and there had been hard fighting along the historic turnpike and near quaint villages like Front Royal and Port Republic, and most of the fence rails on farms near the main highway had long since vanished to build the campfires of soldiers in blue and gray. Yet, even in the summer of 1864, the land bore few scars. East of the Blue Ridge and the Bull Run Mountains the country along the Orange and Alexandria Railroad had been marched over and fought over and ravaged mercilessly, and it was a desolate waste picked clean of everything an army might want or a farmer could use. But the Valley had escaped most of this, and when Phil Sheridan got there it was much as it had always been—rich, sunny, peaceful, a land of good farms and big barns, yellow grain growing beside green pastures, lazy herds of sheep and cattle feeding on the slopes.

An accident of geography made the Valley worth more to the South than to the North, strategically. Running from southwest to northeast, the Valley was the Confederacy's great covered way leading up to the Yankee fortress, with the high parapet of the Blue Ridge offering concealment and protection. A Confederate army coming down the Valley was marching directly toward the Northern citadel, but a Yankee army moving up the Valley was going nowhere in particular because it was constantly getting farther away from Richmond and Richmond's defenders. Nor did a Confederate force operating in the Valley have serious problems of supply. The Valley itself was the base, and it could be drawn upon for abundant food and forage from Staunton all the way to Winchester and beyond.

When the 1864 campaign began, Grant tried to solve the problem of the Valley, and the solution then would have been fairly simple. All that he needed was to establish a Federal army in the upper Valley—at Staunton, say, or Waynesboro, anywhere well upstream. That would close the gate, and the Confederate's granary and covered way would be useless. But nothing had worked out as he planned. First Sigel went up the Valley, to be routed at New Market. Then Hunter took the same road only to lose everything by wild misguided flight off into West Virginia. So now the problem was tougher, and the solution that would have worked in the spring was no good at all in midsummer.

Grant studied the matter, fixing his eyes on the fields and barns and roads of the Valley, and he had a deadly unemotional gaze which saw flame and a smoking sword for devout folk whose way led beside green pastures and still waters. The war could not be won until the Confederacy had been deprived of the use of this garden spot between the mountains. If the garden were made desert, so that neither the Southern Confederacy nor even the fowls of the air could use it, the problem would be well on the way toward being solved.

Grant put it in orders. In a message to Halleck, sent before Sheridan was named to the command, Grant was specific about what he wanted: an army of hungry soldiers to follow retreating Rebels up the Valley and "eat out Virginia clear and clean as far as they go, so that crows flying over it for the balance of the season will have to carry their provender with them." He spelled this out in instructions for the Union commander: "He should make all the Valley south of the Baltimore and Ohio railroad a desert as high up as possible. I do not mean that houses should be burned, but all provisions and stock should be removed, and the people notified to get out."

The war had grown old, and it was following its own logic, the insane logic of war. The only aim now was to hurt the enemy, in any way possible and with any weapon: to destroy not only his will to resist but his ability to make that will effective.

Comprehension check: Do not refer to the selection while answering these questions. Write out your answers:

1. In the summer of 1864, Grant gave Halleck some specific orders about the valley. What was the essence of those orders?

2. Why didn't Grant just forget about the valley?

3. As used in this passage, what does *granary* mean?

4. Why was the valley strategically more valuable to the South than to the North?

5. After Halleck received Grant's orders about the valley, who was put in charge of the troops that were to carry out those orders?

6. Why did Grant specify "an army of hungry soldiers?"

7. How had Grant tried to solve the problem of the valley in the spring of 1864?

8. Why hadn't that plan worked?

9. What was the name of this valley that attracted so much attention in 1864?

10. What did the author mean when he referred to "the insane logic of war?"

The format of an answer sheet for this comprehension check would be just like the one you just completed if it were given in a written testing situation. If, however, it were designed for an oral testing situation, the format would resemble the one below. Note that the type of question is indicated in the margin by code for quick reference by the tester; namely,

MI represents a main idea question,

F represents a factual, hence literal, question,

I represents an inferential question, and

V represents a vocabulary question.

The answers which are provided in parentheses after each question are placed there for the tester's reference, but they are intended only as suggested responses, especially in the case of inferential and main idea questions.

In an oral testing situation, the tester must record the student's responses verbatim. (A tape recorder can be useful here.) Thus, when you prepare a comprehension page for an oral testing situation, you must leave ample room to record what the student says. If you administer such a test in a small group situation, you should indicate by some code which students answer which questions. Perhaps more than one student responds to a question, and you will need to record that information for reference when you analyze the data.

CONTENT INFORMAL READING INVENTORY:
U. S. History

Comprehension check:

(Sheridan in the Shenandoah Valley, Fry Graph = 10th Grade)

(F)   1. In the summer of 1864, Grant gave Halleck some specific orders about the valley. What were those orders? *(to take complete control and to make it desolate)*

(MI)   2. Why didn't Grant just forget about the valley? *(it provided supplies and a concealed avenue for attacks on the North; for other offensive maneuvers to be effective, the valley had to be destroyed)*

(V)   3. As used in this passage, what does *granary* mean? *(an area producing enough food to sustain an army)*

(F)   4. Why was the valley strategically more valuable to the South than to the North? *(it went toward Washington and away from Richmond)*

(I)   5. After Halleck received Grant's orders about the valley, who was put in command of the troops that were to carry out those orders? *(Sheridan)*

(I) 6. Why did Grant specify "an army of hungry soldiers?" *(high incentive to accomplish the purpose of destruction)*

(F) 7. How had Grant tried to solve the problem of the valley
(F) in the spring of 1864? *(establishing a Federal army in the upper valley to cut off supplies to the enemy and eliminate the concealed passageway)*

(F) 8. Why hadn't this plan worked? *(Sigel routed at New Market and Hunter forced to flee into West Virginia.)*

(F) 9. What was the name of this valley that attracted so much attention in 1864? *(Shenandoah Valley, in Virginia)*

(V, I) 10. What did the author mean when he referred to "the insane logic of war?" *(the logic of war meant that Grant had to destroy and hurt the enemy any way possible but it was insane because it caused so much hurt)*

As an introduction to informal comprehension analysis, we suggest that you compare your answers with those suggested following each question. Score each answer accordingly, allowing a maximum of ten points for each answer. (Partial credit may be given.)

When you have finished, answer this question:

How does your score compare with your overall feeling about how well you think you understood the selection?

Now, consider your responses and your score in relation to the criteria established for each question and what each question was intended to determine.

The most important question asked was item 2—the main idea question. Students who could answer that question would probably be able to read adequately material that this selection represents—that is, the text from which it was excerpted. This item cannot, however, be considered exclusively, and if you noticed, closely associated with item 2 is the factual first question which sets up the succeeding main idea question. These two questions, when taken together, will reveal a great deal about a student's overall comprehension of the selection. We placed these two questions in this position to provide us with an immediate indicator of a student's general awareness of what he or she had read. If the student could not answer these questions, we can anticipate problems with later questions, as they are designed to extend diagnostic insights.

The three remaining factual questions are all intended to provide varying degrees of information about a student's recall. Item 4, for example, deals with a major fact about the importance of the valley, and a student's response to this question will provide further insight into the depth of his or her understanding. If a student misses items 1 and 2, we would also expect the student to miss 4; if, on the other hand, he or she misses 1 and 2 but answers 4 correctly, we have additional data to try to figure out exactly what was learned from the passage. Thus, the interrelationships of a student's responses become a very important aspect of informal diagnosis.

Items 7 and 8 are less important details in terms of an overall understanding of the passage, but they can provide valuable information about the kinds of things a student learns as he or she reads. Item 9 is a minor, almost inconsequential, detail, but one which a student who thrives on isolated bits of information might get right, although he or she may have missed all of the other questions. The relevance of these three factual questions in terms of an analysis will become clearer as we undertake to examine several examples of students' responses.

The two vocabulary questions, items 3 and 10, are not arbitrarily chosen to test a student's ability to deal with unknown words in context. Instead, a student who can properly answer these items is likely to possess a depth of understanding well beyond the literal level and is probably indicating a comprehension at the upper ranges of the inferential level. Both items deal with connotations that require thought and nuances in conceptual awareness which may be beyond all but the very perceptive student. Good students will be apt to identify themselves by their ability to answer these questions.

The more typical inferential questions, items 5 and 6, really provide information about interpretive thinking more like that expected of average students. Item 5 is a very low level inferential question, while item 6 requires more of an intermediate level of inferential thought. Students' responses to these questions will reveal information that will allow an in-depth analysis that could not occur without them. In essence, with the inclusion of the two vocabulary questions as indicators of upper level inferential awareness, items 5 and 6 provide insights into a different dimension of inferential comprehension.

Responses to these ten questions can yield valuable information about students' reading comprehension. The total score, however, may not reveal very much as the succeeding examples will illustrate. The best chance of obtaining maximally useful information depends upon the selection of appropriate passages, the creation of incisive questions that will produce meaningful information, and an analysis which examines each item in relation to what information is being sought. With these ideas, criteria, and guidelines in mind, now examine several specific examples of students' responses and see how well you can interpret the results.

Liz[1]
_____

Name of Student

Write out your answers to these questions:

1. In the summer of 1864, Grant gave Halleck some specific orders about the valley. What was the essence of those orders?

[1] All names in the examples that follow are fictitious, but the answers are from real students at Marana High School, Marana, Arizona.

To burn the valley so no one would want to use it. Then they'd move in so they could get to the Confederates.

2. Why didn't Grant just forget about the valley?

Because he needed to gain control over the South.

3. As used in this passage, what does *granary* mean?

4. Why was the valley strategically more valuable to the South than to the North?

South

5. After Halleck received Grant's orders about the valley, who was put in charge of the troops that were to carry out those orders?

6. Why did Grant specify "an army of hungry soldiers?"

Because a hungry soldier would have need for more than one who was not. And a hungry soldier would think of things other men might not.

7. How had Grant tried to solve the problem of the valley in the spring of 1864?

He tried to set up a fort upstream to close off the valley.

8. Why hadn't that plan worked?

The person in charge of the troops that was to take over the valley ran away.

9. What was the name of this valley that attracted so much attention in 1864?

Shenandoha

10. What did the author mean when he referred to "the insane logic of war?"

He meant that how could there be anything logical about something as illogical as war.

ANALYSIS OF CASE

As we describe our analysis of Liz's responses, try your hand at each step before considering our interpretation. Your first attempt at informal comprehension analysis may be a bit wobbly, but give it a try.

Step 1   Begin by examining questions 1 and 2 on Liz's answer sheet. Read her answers, score them, and determine what they indicate about her comprehension. You may then wish to compare your analysis to ours, which follows in italics:

Liz's answers to both questions 1 and 2 are satisfactory. The response "needed it to gain control over the South" is somewhat vague but it indicates at

*least a general understanding, especially when considered in relation to her answer
to item 1. (We would give full credit of 20 points for these answers.)*

Step 2   Now examine question 4 since it is a major fact related to the ideas checked in
questions 1 and 2. Again, make notes of your analysis before considering ours.

    *Here Liz has not done well, but she indicates something important about her
comprehension. She has responded on a very literal level—"South"—as if the question were "To which side was the valley more strategically valuable?" Her answer
indicates that she may have problems with "why" questions, and probably with
inferential questions as well. That then is something to look for as you proceed.*
(We would give no credit for Liz's response to this question.)

Step 3   To continue examining her literal comprehension, move to items 7 and 8, then note
item 9. (Remember, try your own hand at it before looking to our interpretation.)

    *Here Liz reinforces what she has shown us in her answers to items 1, 2, and
4. She seems to have a general idea of what happened. First, in item 7, she remembered the idea of establishing an army in the upper valley to close it off. Note that
she said "fort," a term she associates with "establishing an army." While this may
well reveal a misconception, it nonetheless does indicate a fairly good understanding
of an important detail in the selection. (We would give full credit to Liz for this
answer.) In item 8, Liz shows again a general understanding of the idea, but not
much more. "The person in charge . . . ran away" does not accurately describe
what happened. (Here, we would probably want to give half credit for her answer.)
Liz answered item 9 correctly; perhaps the name of the valley stands out because of
the title, perhaps because of the river or a song she recalls. In any case, item 9 reveals little to us for analysis purposes, except that she remembers specific details.
(We would give full credit for the answer.)*

Step 4   Now examine Liz's answers to the inferential questions, specifically questions 5 and
6. As you work out your analysis, remember the hypothesis we projected in step 2.
There we saw reason to think she might find inferences difficult.

    *Liz's responses to these items are interesting. She doesn't remember Sheri-
dan; why, we don't know. Apparently, the title of the selection did not impress her
or perhaps she is confused by something in the question. Item 6 gives us an indication of what Liz can do, so we now have some indication of her true ability. She
does not directly state the inferred answer, but she certainly hints at it—enough so
that we know that she can read "between the lines" to some extent. (Thinking
back, could it be that the answer to item 5 was too obscure to allow Liz to pick up
the answer?) (Full credit for item 6, if we read between her lines!)*

Step 5   Next, you need to see how well Liz did with questions 3 and 10. Before you do,
though, on the basis of what whe know up to this point about her performance,

how do you think she will have done? Take a guess, then check it out as you analyze her answers.

Was your anticipation verified? Here's what we guessed we'd see. We judged, for two reasons, that she would completely miss item 3. First, she tends to deal with general ideas, not specifics, and "granary" is very specific. Second, she has never mentioned the concept of supplies—food, grain, and the like—and it seemed unlikely that she would answer item 3 correctly. Checking her paper verifies our guess, though we must suspend our judgment on the reasons for which she left the answer blank.

Item 10 deals with a general idea, so we guessed Liz might be able to provide a reasonable answer. That was our hypothesis, and WOW! what a guess! What more synthesized and appropriate answer from a fourteen-year-old? The final paragraph of the reading selection is subtle and powerful, and it has obviously struck Liz. (Ten points for Liz, more if we had it.)

Step 6   Now sum the objective score. On the basis of the item analysis, determine whether Liz can read this material independently, instructionally, or cannot read it with success.

In objective scoring, Liz gets a 65. But what does that tell us? What could any objective score really mean? A diagnosis of Liz's comprehension forces us to examine the general quality of her answers to our questions. That's quite a different matter from adding numbers, which can often be dangerously misleading. A score of 65 is marginal, but is Liz's reading so? She seems to grasp major concepts and general ideas, she draws logical inferences. Her weaknesses lie in recall of specific details ("granary," "Sheridan," and the like). But the material on this IRI is well within her instructional level, *objective sums notwithstanding.*

Before moving on to a second case, we feel compelled to iterate the value of examining a student's responses collectively. When considered all together, rather than in isolated segments, the responses usually represent the most accurate picture of the student's comprehension one can obtain. If we had asked Liz what this passage was about, her response might have been, "It's about Grant's burning the valley so no one could want to use it; then he'd move in to get to the Confederates. He needed it to gain control over the South. He told some hungry soldiers to do it because a hungry soldier would have need for more than one who was not and he would think of things to do which other men might not. Grant tried to do this by setting up a fort upstream to close off the valley but the person in charge of the troops that were to overtake the Shenandoah Valley ran away. None of it was logical, but how could there be anything logical about something as illogical as war?"

Look closely. We compiled this overall answer by simply tying Liz's specific answers together. Taken as a unified response, her answers certainly indicate a rather good understanding of the passage—and that's what we were trying to find out. The emphasis of this type of analysis must, then, be on what the student comprehends, not on any cumulative, objective score. The score itself is really of little value except when it might support a general conclusion suggested by a unified analysis.

Try the next example on your own and then compare your analysis witl ours.

Follow the basic steps outlined for Liz's case:

1. Check the main idea and related factual question (items 1, 2). These should provide a major clue for you.

2. Examine the factual question, item 4, as it is closely associated with items 1 and 2.

3. Analyze the other three detail questions for factual recall (items 7, 8, and 9).

4. Examine the responses to the lower level inferential items (numbers 5, 6).

5. Analyze the responses to the upper level inferential items (numbers 3, 10).

6. Evaluate the responses in total and synthesize your conclusions about the student's comprehension.

Ron
_____
Name of Student

Write out your answers to these questions:

1. In the summer of 1864, Grant gave Halleck some specific orders about the valley. What was the essence of those orders?

    To turn the garden into a desert

2. Why didn't Grant just forget about the valley?

    Because it was a natrul road to the Yankee citadel

3. As used in this passage, what does *granary* mean?

4. Why was the valley strategically more valuable to the South than to the North?

Because it ran southwest to north east.

5. After Halleck received Grant's orders about the valley, who was put in charge of the troops that were to carry out those orders?

6. Why did Grant specify "an army of hungry soldiers?"

so soldiers would eat most everything.

7. How had Grant tried to solve the problem of the valley in the spring of 1864?

tryed to set up a camp at the end of the valley

8. Why hadn't that plan worked?

his men had been attacked. and run off

9. What was the name of this valley that attracted so much attention in 1864?

just, valley

10. What did the author mean when he referred to "the insane logic of war?"

when you take sides in a war you try to help your side win even thogh you have to do some of the most logical things in a war, any other time they would consider it insane.

ANALYSIS OF CASE 2

Let's begin this analysis by examining our conclusions. You compare your conclusions to ours. Then we'll look at the specifics that led to the conclusions.

Ron is probably on a high instructional level with this material; perhaps he is independent with it. He has understood the main ideas of the passage in terms that are directly related to the passage. His ability to handle the inferential questions is basically sound even though he did not seem to pick up the concept of the valley being a source of food and supplies to the Confederate armies. His weakness lies in the area of specific details, but not in the same way Liz had trouble. Ron recalled some details that were important to his understanding the main ideas of the passage and they are reflected in his answers. Liz could not do that as well as Ron; her understandings were more general. If the instructional purpose of this passage is to have the students understand concepts rather than recall isolated pieces of information, then Ron has demonstrated his ability to do that.

If you are to learn much from comparing our overall diagnosis of Ron's responses, we need to go through the analysis step by step. Even if you came to the same conclusions we did, you may have arrived at them for different reasons. If you disagreed with our conclusions, then the following analysis may help you to see where we differ in our thinking.

The first thing we noticed was that Ron understood the main idea of the orders and why they were given; this can be determined by his responses to items 1 and 2. His answer to question 4 may appear superficial and insufficient unless it is examined in relation to the first two questions. We decided, therefore, to examine the interrelatedness of the answers Ron gave to items 1, 2, and 4. "Because it ran southwest to northeast" doesn't really reveal too much by itself, but when combined with "a natural road to the Yankee's citadel" the basic concept of the details and the main idea are clearly evident in his reasoning. Why didn't he repeat the idea of a possible invasion route in his response to item 4? Perhaps he saw little need to repeat himself from item 2. That is only a guess, but his answer satisfied us. Granted, there is a certain depth missing in his answers to questions 1, 2, and 4. He failed to mention the concept of supplies and the idea that Grant had to keep pressure on Lee at all points. All things considered, we felt that Ron's answers to these three questions, considered together, would warrant about two-thirds credit, or 20 points.

In the detail questions—items 7, 8, and 9—Ron does demonstrate a general understanding of what happened although he has not retained specific names of people and places. Consider the nature of these questions, though. Can we expect readers to recall such detail? Would we want them to? We think not. In fact, though Ron's attention and memory for detail is imperfect, it is quite sufficient for his purpose of general understanding and comprehension. Much better that than the other way around, we'd say! (So, we would give full credit for 7 and 8, none for 9.)

Among Ron's four remaining responses, we can see a confirmation of everything that the analysis has indicated so far. He missed the specific, low-level inferential item, but he did perceive why hungry soldiers might be more effective in carrying out the orders. The "granary" question we'd expect him to miss because, like Liz, he has not mentioned the concept of supplies and he does not seem to rely on specifics for his understanding. His detailed explanation in response to item 10 reinforces everything we have been led to expect by his previous answers. When scoring these items, we'd give no credit for items 3 and 5 and full credit for items 6 and 10.

To summarize Ron's case, his objective score is 60, but his comprehension is clearly greater than 60 percent. This analysis reiterates the inherent fallacy of objective scoring and the need for comparative, in-depth analysis of students' responses. Whether Ron can learn from this passage with independent level comprehension is dubious, only because he missed the idea of the valley as a supply source, and not for any specific details he may have failed to remember. To our way of thinking, Ron has demonstrated a very sound, mature approach to a reading task; hence, any instructional assistance he may need would be minimal.

It is hoped that Liz and Ron's cases both demonstrate the variability that can exist in students' answers and the fallacy of relying on strictly objective scoring. In an analysis of a student's comprehension, little is definitive; one must constantly seek clues to what each student has perceived and to each reader's success with the act of reading. The variability that exists among students is, to us, the exciting part of diagnosis and of teaching.

Now for another case. This one you may find a bit different from the others, but see how you would analyze Karen's comprehension, then compare your analysis with ours.

Karen
_____
Name of Student

Write out your answers to these questions:

1. In the summer of 1864, Grant gave Halleck some specific orders about the valley. What was the essence of those orders?

To take over the valley

2. Why didn't Grant just forget about the valley?

> *It was good land.*

3. As used in this passage, what does *granary* mean?

> *his army*

4. Why was the valley strategically more valuable to the South than to the North?

5. After Halleck received Grant's orders about the valley, who was put in charge of the troops that were to carry out those orders?

> *a hungry army*

6. Why did Grant specify "an army of hungry soldiers?"

> *To eat out Virginia clear and clean as far as they go.*

7. How had Grant tried to solve the problem of the valley in the *spring* of 1864?

8. Why hadn't that plan worked?

9. What was the name of this valley that attracted so much attention in 1864?

10. What did the author mean when he referred to "the insane logic of war?"

The weird way the war thought and worked.

ANALYSIS OF CASE 3

The first reaction one probably has when analyzing Karen's responses is that she is clearly frustrated by this selection. After all, her objective score is approximately 25! In every instance the answers she gave indicate minimal understanding, and she failed to respond to 4 items. But if we are to accept such conclusions, we must first reject several alternative possibilities. For example, is the problem here that she cannot express her ideas well enough in writing to handle the response part of the task? That is, can she do the reading but finds herself unable to compose written responses to questions on it? Obviously, this would require first-hand knowledge of Karen and her language abilities. We mention this, however, because it is a plausible explanation that cannot be dismissed lightly. On the basis of her teacher's observations, however, we can eliminate this possibility because the fact is that Karen can write reasonably well when given a task with which she is comfortable. A second alternative which must be explored is that Karen simply doesn't want to be bothered with this task. Interestingly, there is evidence that can be used to make a reasonable guess as to the probability of this alternative. Notice her answer to item 5, "a hungry army." This response seems to come from the wording of question 6! That Karen would go to the trouble to even attempt to manipulate the available information to fit another question is evidence that she has not taken the task lightly. In addition, her teacher knows that she is not the type of student who would simply throw down a few answers just to make it appear as if she had at least tried. She is a very conscientious student. Thus, the second alternative can be discounted along with the first.

There is one remaining point to be made about analyzing reading comprehension from this example. The fact that a student *does not* perform should not be taken as evidence that the student *cannot* perform. The IRI, as you may have guessed, is designed to give information about what students can comprehend. When a reader *fails* to comprehend, we may wonder why, but the answer to the primary question posed by the IRI must await further exploration.

Now, how are you doing? We want to present you with one final example of a student's responses to this comprehension check for two reasons. First, we think you can probably use a little more practice. Second, there are a few more things about informal comprehension analysis that we'd like to point out to you and they can be discussed in relation to the next example. Try your hand with Mary's case and then compare your analysis with ours.

Mary
_____
Name of Student

Write out your answers to these questions:

1. In the summer of 1864, Grant gave Halleck some specific orders about the valley. What was the essence of those orders?

   To take over the valley

2. Why didn't Grant just forget about the valley?

   Because the land, was rich, sunny

3. As used in this passage, what does *granary* mean?

4. Why was the valley strategically more valuable to the South than to the North?

North because the valley was a passage way to the Yankees fort.

5. After Halleck received Grant's orders about the valley, who was put in charge of the troops that were to carry out those orders?

Jackson

6. Why did Grant specify "an army of hungry soldiers?"

7. How had Grant tried to solve the problem of the valley in the spring of 1864?

8. Why hadn't that plan worked?

Because one troop was going to the New Market. The other lost almost everything.

9. What was the name of this valley that attracted so much attention in 1864?

Shendoah

10. What did the author mean when he referred to the "insane logic of war?"

ANALYSIS OF CASE 4

An analysis of Mary's answers stimulates more questions than it provides answers about her comprehension. A cursory analysis strongly suggests frustration, but a further examination causes one to wonder. That is, we think she is probably frustrated, but we can't be sure. Her answers to questions 1, 2, and 4, the main ideas and associated supporting detail, suggest a paradox of sorts. She remembers certain details related to the main idea but her response to the main idea question indicates confusion. Apparently, she thinks Grant wanted the land because it was good land. Her answers to items 1 and 4 tell us more about her comprehension. "To take over the valley" is an acceptable response and so is most of her answer to item 4, but why did she begin her response to number 4 with the word "North?" Does she think that the Yankees and the North are terms for different sides in the war? She has understood why the valley was strategically more valuable, but has she confused the two sides? Whatever the case, note that she may have provided us with a clue to her comprehension by getting several details correct, even if in a somewhat confused sort of way.

As we examine the three other detail questions, 7, 8, and 9, we are even more puzzled. "New Market" and "Shendoah" stand out, but the sense of her response to item 8 seems confused. The thing that creates confusion is the inclusion of "the" before New Market. What is her concept of this place, New Market? Is it a place to buy food? Or is this just a linguistic slip? We don't know, but we sure would like to know. Also, how does she remember the gist of the spring offensive if she doesn't remember what it entailed? Again, her answers suggest more questions than they provide solutions, and the more we see, the further we seem to be from being able to analyze what she has comprehended.

What, then, does she reveal in her responses to the higher level questions? Aha! Finally, we can say something with some confidence. Mary has missed all four questions—3, 5, 6, and 10. That we know, but that's really *all* we know! Can Mary handle inferential questions? How can we judge? She cannot read "between the lines" with this selection, or doesn't seem able to do so, but *why* can't she? We haven't many clues, but perhaps she is simply not interested in war stories. Our only recourse is to give Mary another passage at a different level of difficulty in an attempt to find something she *can* comprehend. Only then will we be able to judge the quality of her comprehension.

WHERE TO FROM HERE?

*, 7   Now that you've had the introduction and some practice, if your wobblies are beginning to go away, then we have accomplished as much as we hoped. After all, analyzing reading comprehension is rather complicated and one becomes good at it only through practice. Where to from here? We suggest that you create some passages for your own content area, collect some data, and analyze them. Then compare your diagnosis with a colleague and slowly, but most assuredly, you'll begin to feel confidence in this testing method.

7

Vocabulary Diagnosis

Vocabulary and conceptual development are essentially
related.

SUMMARY

Vocabulary diagnosis is diagnosis of the meanings which students hold for words
related to the concepts they are developing out of their experiences. The overriding
purpose of vocabulary diagnosis is to determine simultaneously students' conceptual development and their vocabulary facility. Different instructional approaches
will be implied by such diagnosis, depending on whether misunderstandings arise
out of a failure to conceptualize or a failure to acquire the vocabulary necessary to
express adequate conceptual awareness. Our position is that "vocabulary" problems
may often be the manifestation of a more serious problem, a lack of proper conceptualization. Furthermore, it is impossible to separate conceptualization and
experience from the vocabulary that ties the two together in the mind of the
learner or the language the learner speaks.

Several techniques of vocabulary diagnosis are possible, each a different twist
on the prevailing idea of conceptual analysis as we define it. Word association
activities for groups, a modified Maze procedure, an adaptation of cloze—all are
aimed at finding out what sort of balance exists in the student between what is
understood and what words the student can use to express that understanding. We
are not particularly concerned with word analysis skills that traditionally fly under
the banner of vocabulary—phonics, structural analysis, context, use of the dictionary. We are, rather, concerned with word meaning and its relation to conceptual
development, which we view as the proper concern of the content (reading) teacher
and, frankly, the more appropriate concern of any teacher involved with reading as
an activity directed at comprehension.

CONCEPTS, EXPERIENCES, AND VOCABULARY

In chapter 13, *Developing Meaningful Vocabularies,* we will discuss the inseparability of concepts, experiences, and vocabulary. Our major point in this chapter is that vocabulary analysis should be equivalent to an analysis of the stage of understanding that a student has achieved for the concept(s) to which the vocabulary is related. Obversely, while it may be the fact that students don't know words that keeps them from understanding what they read, it may as easily be that they don't have a firm grasp on the ideas that the words may represent. It is likely that their experience (learning) has been insufficient for the development of the concepts the words represent.

Einstein said that concepts develop in two ways, both of which are necessary to understanding. The first is by logical analysis, the procedure by which we see how concepts and judgments depend on each other. The second is by connection of our logic to experience.[1] In both cases, vocabulary is used. But only when that vocabulary becomes the bond between conceptualization and experiences will either the conceptualization, the experience, or the vocabulary have any meaning.

That master of the English language, Sir Winston Churchill, in an excerpt from his autobiography, *My Early Life,* conveys in a negative way the essence of our disposition toward vocabulary:

> I was taken into a Form Room and told to sit at a desk. All the other boys were out of doors, and I was alone with the Form Master. He produced a thin greeny-brown, covered book filled with words in different types of print.
>
> 'You have never done any Latin before, have you?' he said.
>
> 'No, sir.'
>
> 'This is a Latin grammar.' He opened it at a well-thumbed page. 'You must learn this,' he said, pointing to a number of words in a frame of lines. 'I will come back in half an hour and see what you know.'
>
> Behold me then on a gloomy evening, with an aching heart, seated in front of the First Declension.

Mensa	a table
Mensa	o table
Mensam	a table
Mensae	of a table
Mensae	to or for a table
Mensa	by, with or from a table

[1] Albert Einstein, from "The Problem of Space, Ether, and the Field in Physics" in *The World As I See It.*

What on earth did it mean? Where was the sense in it? It seemed absolute rigmarole to me. However, there was one thing I could always do: I could learn by heart. And I thereupon proceeded, as far as my private sorrows would allow, to memorize the acrostic-looking task which had been set me.

In due course the Master returned.

'Have you learnt it?' he asked.

'I think I can say it,' I replied; and I gabbled it off.

He seemed so satisfied with this that I was emboldened to ask a question.

'What does it mean, sir?'

'It means what it says. Mensa, a table. Mensa is a noun of the First Declension. There are five declensions. You have learnt the first singular of the First Declension.'

'But,' I repeated, 'what does it mean?'

'Mensa means a table,' he answered.

'Then why does mensa also mean o table,' I enquired, 'and what does o table mean?'

'Mensa, o table, is the vocative case,' he replied.

'But why o table?' I persisted in genuine curiosity.

'O table,—you would use that in addressing a table, in invoking a table.' And then seeing he was not carrying me with him, 'You would use it in speaking to a table.'

'But I never do,' I blurted out in honest amazement.

'If you are impertinent, you will be punished, and punished, let me tell you, very severely,' was his conclusive rejoinder.

Such was my first introduction to the classics from which, I have been told, many of our cleverest men have derived so much solace and profit . . .[2]

As young Winston was so emboldened to suggest, a knowledge of vocabulary without an understanding of its meaning (the concepts and experiences it expresses) is useless.

This implies a firm conclusion regarding vocabulary diagnosis: *to assess students' understanding and use of vocabulary is tantamount to assessing the sophistication of their conceptualizations.* This conclusion is justified because one's

---

[2] Reprinted by permission of Charles Scribner's Sons from *My Early Life: A Roving Commission* by Winston Churchill, © Copyright 1930, Charles Scribner's Sons. Also reprinted by permission of the Hamlyn Publishing Group Limited.

understanding of concepts is reflected in and demonstrated by the vocabulary one uses to express those concepts.

It is true, however, that at times a student may fail to understand something because of unfamiliarity with the vocabulary in which it is expressed. One's understanding depends on the appropriateness of the vocabulary with which an idea is expressed. That is, if a reader is to comprehend, the vocabulary of what is being read must be appropriately suited to the level, or stage, of conceptual development. If someone fails to understand what he or she reads, given at least minimal quality and style in what the person is reading, one of three things may be the case: 1) The concepts expressed may be so far removed from the reader's experience that little meaning is possible for what is said, even though individual words may seem familiar; 2) The vocabulary with which the ideas are expressed may presume a familiarity not yet acquired by the reader, even though the concepts might be understood if put in less sophisticated wording; or 3) Neither the concepts nor the vocabulary have places in the reader's cognitive store and thus it is all "rigmarole," to borrow Sir Winston's term.

To illustrate this point, we ask you to join us in a little exercise. Begin by reading this paragraph.

> It is particularly true in reading that the larger the context, the greater is the redundancy. And the more redundancy there is, the less visual information the skilled reader requires. In passages of continuous text, provided that the content is not too difficult, every other letter can be eliminated from most words, or about one word in five omitted altogether, without making the passage too difficult for a reader to comprehend—provided that he has learned the rules related to letter and word occurrence and co-occurrence.[3]

How well were you able to understand what the author is discussing? If you had difficulty, perhaps you feel that you lack the conceptual background to understand the meaning of the passage. Before deciding definitely, however, read this paragraph.

> In many reading selections, ideas are repeated several times, especially when the selection is of moderate length or longer. As the ideas are repeated, a reader has more chances to pick up the ideas and thus his chances of understanding the selection are increased. A reader can rely on this repetition instead of having to identify every letter or word in the selection. To prove this point, in many passages it is possible to eliminate every other letter from most words or eliminate every fifth word and yet not significantly impair a reader's comprehension. That is to say, the good reader is familiar with the rules of letter sequences within words and the rules of word sequences within sentences, and he

[3] From *Understanding Reading,* by Frank Smith, New York: Holt, Rinehart, Winston, 1971, p. 23.

can anticipate the letters and words which should come next. His comprehension is not dependent upon letter perfect or word perfect reading.

Now, compare your understanding of this paragraph to the previous one. If there were differences, can you determine what caused them?

When we have done this with teachers in person, we have seen one of three things happen: 1) they find both paragraphs difficult to understand; 2) they find that both paragraphs are clear; or 3) they find the second paragraph to be clearer than the first. We suspect that you found one of these to be true in your own case. What, though, are the implications of what occurred?

Typically, the teachers with whom we have conducted this exercise find that they understand the second paragraph far more easily than the first. Interestingly enough, the teachers who find the first paragraph considerably more difficult conclude that it is due to the complexity of the ideas. The intriguing thing here is that the ideas, i.e., the concepts, in both of the paragraphs are identical. In other words, the complexity of the first paragraph is inherent in the words chosen to present the concepts rather than in the concepts themselves, and any differences between the two paragraphs are merely rhetorical. Thus, if you found difficulty with the first paragraph but not with the second, then the factor that interfered with your understanding was the vocabulary in which the ideas were expressed rather than with a failure to understand the concepts or ideas.

When we diagnose students' vocabulary knowledge, we must also determine whether they understand the concepts associated with words. The purpose of vocabulary diagnosis is to determine what has to be taught so that students can learn. Recall, the first principle of instruction is that what to teach must be determined by what can be learned. If students understand concepts, the task is to help them learn new labels for their ideas, to bring their vocabulary up to par with their understanding of the concepts. If, on the other hand, students have superficial, inaccurate, or no understanding of a concept, they have little use for the vocabulary by which such understanding might be expressed. For these students, instruction must begin with a focus on concepts. While this latter case may be more difficult pedagogically, it is the more typical case. Vocabulary instruction comes down to providing experiences through which concepts and understandings may develop.

Let's return then to a consideration of the two paragraphs in our exercise, keeping in mind that the purpose of vocabulary diagnosis is to determine what students know of both vocabulary and the concepts it represents. If you found the first paragraph more difficult than the second, your difficulty with that material was with the vocabulary, not the concepts. Our instruction would then be designed to build on the concepts you knew by helping you associate new words with old concepts. If, however, you found both paragraphs difficult to understand, the implication is that you had problems with both the concepts and the vocabulary. In that case, instruction would probably need to provide opportunity for conceptual development. If you were among the lucky few who had no trouble with either paragraph, you probably understood both the vocabulary and the concepts, and for you instruction in either would be unnecessary.

TOLERANCE-TOLERATE: A CASE IN POINT

Students' conceptual awarenesses may not be what we assume them to be. For example, the following experience was shared with us by an English teacher who spent six weeks teaching a unit in which one of the key concepts was: "Social and emotional maturity is often exhibited through tolerance of others' ideas and beliefs." On the unit test, this teacher's students consistently indicated that tolerance meant "to tolerate." The teacher's dismay was understandable: her students hadn't understood the positive connotation of tolerance at all; how could they have understood the concept that characterized maturity as "exhibiting tolerance"?

Let's look closely at this common problem. The students had a preconceived idea of the concept associated with *tolerance.* Had the teacher realized that their idea was inappropriate in the context she was creating, she could have easily rectified the misconception at the beginning of the unit. Instead, problems arose for her students because she failed to analyze their conceptual perceptions. She made the unfortunate mistake of assuming that her meaning for a key word was similar to the meaning the students had for the word.

It is essential to begin vocabulary diagnosis by identifying 1) the most important concepts that are to be taught and 2) the terms that best convey those concepts.

By approaching vocabulary diagnosis from this perspective, instruction can be designed to meet both the students' conceptual needs and their vocabulary needs, in that order. To the credit of our English teacher friend, she did identify major conceptual objectives and the key words which students needed to know if they were to understand and discuss those concepts. However, she didn't go the next step to determine what the students' perceptions of those terms and concepts were. While it may sometimes appear that students understand terms and concepts, effective instruction is often dependent upon taking specific steps to verify initial assumptions. The by-word of vocabulary diagnosis, then, must be conceptual analysis. Whatever method of vocabulary diagnosis might be chosen, one of its essential features must be an analysis of students' developmental stages of conceptualization.

DIAGNOSTIC STRATEGIES

The word analysis skills approach

Typically recommended vocabulary diagnosis strategies are more appropriate to a diagnosis of word analysis skills than to vocabulary *per se.* Word analysis skills include phonics; syllabication; use of prefixes, stems, and suffixes; and the ability to use context clues. Such skills are of little concern to us here. Instead, we will address the ways to determine what terms students know and what meanings they associate with those terms. Very few content teachers can or should be concerned with traditional word analysis skills, except as those skills might pertain directly to the meaning of the content which the teacher is trying to help students understand. We believe it would be as foolish to recommend that content teachers teach phonics as that they be teachers of reading. The sense in which content teachers are teachers of reading, we would maintain, is limited to the sense in which they attempt to stimulate and guide students toward understanding content, through reading or other means. This is to us the most realistic and practical spirit in which to approach vocabulary diagnosis in content area classrooms.

Conceptual analysis Of the several techniques or approaches we will suggest, this is the one that best represents the essence of vocabulary analysis. The idea is to find out 1) what meaning students have for specific concepts, and 2) in what terms they might express the concepts.

As part of the introduction to a unit of work in science, we recently asked several groups of students questions such as this:

> What does it mean to you when I say 'A knowledge of the way in which the earth changes helps make a better world'? Do you understand the statement? Tell me what it means to you.

(Notice that the statement is typical of concepts that might be developed in a social studies or science unit on ecology. Following our question, a dialogue roughly equivalent to the ensuing occurred. S is student, T is teacher.)

S_1: The world doesn't change.

S_2: Things are today pretty much like they were when Christ was here.

T: Nothing is different?

S_1: Well, except that we now have telephones and airplanes. But those are inventions. They don't mean the *earth* is different.

T: No, they don't. But what about other things, like pollution?

S_1: Men have always polluted. That's not different.

S_2: Except that now you get fined $30 if you do it!

T: But does the pollution affect the way the earth is, do you think?

S_1: No. Not really. Just the way it looks or smells.

These were elementary students, grades 3, 4, and 5, children of rather normal intelligence and achievement. We found that there were many things they did understand, of course. We tried the procedure on a wide variety of conceptual statements. Often, the students' wording was an improvement on ours. We failed to guess how well they understood. Sometimes they had the idea, but required a little more explanation. But at other times, true misconceptions came out. Diagnostically, we were learning 1) what the students knew about the concepts, and 2) what vocabulary they used to express *their* meanings of the various concepts.

At the beginning of a unit, one of the best "pretests" possible is to ask of students "What is your understanding of the following concepts which we are going to study? In a few words, tell what each means to you." The answers students give to this sort of diagnostic question will tell much about what they understand and in what terms they understand it. The technique is invaluable, diagnostically, at any level of education, from primary school to graduate school. And, we might add, it is as effective a test as it is a pretest.

Word association games

A variation on the conceptual analysis technique is to engage the students in word association activities. These may be led by the teacher or played between teams of pupils under the teacher's supervision. The activities may call for student responses to stimulus words given by the teacher ("Tell me all the words which come to mind when I say _____.") or may be of the word-guess type. To get another team member to say a word in a given time, a person may say as many other associated words as he or she can think of, but not the word itself. Diagnostically, what pupils say will often represent the breadth and depth of their understanding.

The preparation of a word association task for vocabulary diagnostic purposes requires an identification of key terms related to concepts in a unit or reading selection. The diagnostic questions are, as you might guess: 1) what meanings do the students have for these words; and 2) what do they reveal about their level of understanding of the concepts to which the words are related? The advantage of the word association technique, used in whatever format, is that it tends to be "unobtrusive," in testing terms. That is, it is less easily perceived as a threat, as sometimes tests can be. We'll undoubtedly repeat, in a variety of ways, that the object of diagnosis is not to test but to structure an opportunity for students to demonstrate as naturally as possible what they do know and can do. That reveals what to teach and how to teach it.

Contextual synonyms

This procedure is a modification of the maze technique which we mentioned in chapter 2. Recall that maze asks the reader to choose from among alternatives that are provided for deletions. One choice is the correct (deleted) word, another is a word of the same part of speech, another a word of a different part of speech. The contextual synonyms technique asks the students as they read to *suggest* (rather than choose from) alternatives which they think would suit the context about as well as underlined key words.

This activity would have given our English teacher friend (tolerance-tolerate) some valuable information. Her students would have suggested "tolerate" as a substitute for "tolerance." She would have been looking for "understanding" or "broad-mindedness," perhaps "sympathy"; she would have gotten (she found out too late) words like "put up with" or "endure," perhaps "suffer." Information about the misconceptions students may hold, and reveal through their vocabulary misunderstandings, is invaluable diagnostic information.

Modified cloze

The cloze technique can be modified in a variety of ways to increase its diagnostic and instructional value. One obvious modification is to analyze the "synonyms" that students use as replacements for deletions. If the selection is one of particularly relevant conceptual load, the replacements that readers make will reveal much about their understandings of the concepts being taught. At times, the cloze replacements may indicate a conceptual attainment of *higher* sophistication than that assumed by the author. Given an opportunity to discuss their replacement words in a whole class or small group setting, students will usually make very clear their familiarity with vocabulary and concepts. The question becomes not what word was chosen but why it was chosen. *Which* word was chosen is a test question; *why* it was chosen is a diagnostic question.

Another modification of cloze which is often desirable is this: Make deletions systematically, to include key conceptual terms. Then, rather than have students guess at the replacements, have them pick from a list of words those that belong in specific blanks. Include in the list the deleted words, common synonyms, and potentially "misconceived" synonyms, words likely to be chosen if the reader misunderstands the concepts behind the words.

People who know and love the cloze technique may object that our modifications make the test invalid and leave the percentage exact replacement scores confused. This is a valid point but it is not our object here to test the appropriateness of material, in a readability sense of appropriate. What we are trying to get at is what the student knows. The key to diagnosis is a common sense understanding of what the student is doing, not an empirically derived percentage score that says nothing of why it is being done or what it means. The results could well mean avoiding the frustration of "Mensa . . . o table" when meaning takes first place among all vocabulary skills.

*, 12

8

Assessing Study Skills

Analyzing students' study skills is an important aspect of
diagnosis for a content teacher interested in improving students' ability to learn.

SUMMARY

Good and poor students alike can often become more efficient learners if they are
made aware of some basic, easy-to-learn strategies such as use of time, taking notes,
and taking tests. The most logical place in the curriculum to diagnose and teach
study skills is in the content classroom, for it is there that students find the greatest
need and most appropriate application of such skills.

Several different methods of diagnosing study skills exist, both formal and
informal. While there may be occasional need for the formal strategies, the informal
assessments are usually more informative. Teachers who are interested in improving
their students' ability to learn can devise their own program of study skills diagnosis
based on the various techniques discussed in this chapter.

A DISTINCTION

The ability to study efficiently is a distinctive characteristic of most good students.
Conversely, many poor students are unproductive because they lack good study
skills. A requisite for success in a content classroom may well be the ability to
distinguish between "studying" and "reading once-over-lightly." Good students
make that distinction easily; poor students rarely do, but often they *can* do so if
given the needed guidance and instruction to make them aware of the difference.

An improvement of students' productive learning in a content classroom is
often directly related to a concomitant increase in their awareness of effective

study skills. Of course, awareness is only the beginning, but without awareness, study skills development and application is haphazard at best. The ability to identify students' study skills and to discuss strengths and weaknesses with them may be among the most important diagnostic and instructional strategies for content teachers.

DELINEATING TYPES OF SKILLS

Reading and study skills are often discussed as though they were one and the same; we want to maintain their separateness as they are two different aspects of learning which are, at times, related. To identify and correct weaknesses in study skills will enhance a student's ability to learn effectively; that is not, however, to be considered equivalent to improving reading ability. Skills are specific, overt, demonstrable capabilities that are required to perform a specific task. Smith (1973) has amply discussed the fact that reading proficiency does not develop through learning a series of isolated skills. The distinction between reading and study skills is of utmost importance. The primary difference is that as one becomes a more proficient, experienced reader, one will also become a better learner, but the reverse is not necessarily true. While an improvement in reading may cause an improvement in one's ability to learn, improved study skills will produce a better student, but not necessarily a better reader. If we have belabored this point, it is because we do not sanction instruction in study skills as a means to improving reading ability.

Study skills may be classified into four categories: 1) work-study habits, 2) locational skills, 3) organizational skills, and 4) specialized skills. Our discussion of the different skills within each category will be necessarily general since we have tried to focus our discussion on areas of concern to all content teachers. If you want to pursue the concept of study skills in greater depth in your own specialized content field, we refer you to Thomas and Robinson (1977) or Shepherd (1973).

**, 2, 3

WORK-STUDY HABITS

Many students have little or no concept of basic work-study habits which can help them be more efficient learners. They often study at haphazard times, whenever "the mood strikes them," and in places that actually detract from rather than facilitate learning. Good work-study habits can foster students' awareness that dependable learning is based on the intent to remember. Simple exposure to information does not guarantee learning, nor does the passive repetition of an experience. When students learn to organize their study time and to establish a familiar place for study, they can become more proficient learners.

Efficient study can result from students' self-analysis of their use of time. A daily schedule, however, is a personal thing and should vary with each individual. Once established, it can indicate to a student how much studying is being done and it can give a better indication of how well the student is doing in a class. If a student is frustrated by his or her inability to learn, a motivation factor might be the realization of how much time and effort is being wasted. Few students are bored by learning; instead, they are frustrated and "turned off" by nonlearning. If a student can be encouraged to establish a reasonable daily routine where chunks of time for study can be set aside, it is likely that he or she will become more involved in study and perhaps motivated to learn more.

Finding the best place to study is another aspect of good study habits that can result in marked improvement in learning. Some students have no place where they feel comfortable studying. Usually, the best place is a special place, perhaps in a corner of a bedroom set aside for studying, or in a library carrel. Each person must find his or her own place; it must, however, be a productive place! Often students study where they are too uncomfortable (or too comfortable) and they find difficulty keeping their minds on their work. It is possible that where a person studies may be more of a distractor than a facilitator of studying. *Where* may be as crucial as *how* one studies.

LOCATIONAL AND REFERENCE SKILLS

Locational skills include knowing how to find information in various references sources. Many students are as bewildered by a library as they would be if transported by spaceship or time machine to a remote place. They don't know what is there that can help them. *Readers Guide, Masterplots, Oxford Companions,* or even atlases, almanacs, and encyclopedias of various sorts are often totally unfamiliar and unusable to students. More often than not, students are intimidated by libraries and their rules. Likewise, many students do not know how to use the table of contents, index, chapter summaries, or glossaries in their texts. Deficiencies in these skills are not due to low intelligence or other ability-related deficiencies; most students lack the experience that would lead to facility with these skills. They need instruction and guidance. Often, and this may be especially true of junior and senior high school teachers, the assumption is made that students do know how to use various reference materials; such assumptions are unwarranted in the majority of instances. Analyzing students' locational skill needs then is an important part of assessing their study skills. Deficiencies can often be rectified, and a whole new world opened for students.

ORGANIZATIONAL SKILLS

One of the more common weaknesses among junior and senior high school students is the inability to organize the material they are supposed to be learning. Yet, efficient learning often depends upon how well a student can organize the information that he or she is trying to learn. Good students tend to be able to organize their thoughts and their learning far better than poor or average students and this ability gives them a distinct advantage. Of all the study skills that a teacher needs to diagnose and provide help with, this is probably the most crucial.

That students are often not allowed to underline or write in the margins of their textbooks is a fact of which we are all too well aware. Nevertheless, underlining is a skill that students should be taught and encouraged to use to highlight the most important things encountered in their reading. Students need to become selective in what they underline, so that they highlight the key words and the key ideas that can be tied together as a summary of what the author is trying to emphasize.

Outlining is probably one of the most complex skills in learning because it requires analysis and synthesis of a very fine sort. Outlining requires that a student recognize the main ideas treated in a passage as well as the supporting details, examples, and reasons that are related to those main ideas. Consider, however, that it is possible—even likely—that a student's inability to outline the material being studied is not an indication of failure to understand the system of outlining, but an indication of failure to understand the material being considered. The perceptive teacher will recognize that the problem may not be a lack of organizational skills but a mismatch between student and material. To remedy this, the teacher's next step would be to switch to supplementary materials more appropriate for the student in trouble or to provide help in breaking the code of the particular pattern of organization the author is using, whichever may be the problem.

Notetaking is another organizational skill at which few students are accomplished. As most often used, it takes one of two different forms, lecture notetaking and reading notetaking. Most students do neither well. In lecture notetaking, students are required to listen, analyze, interpret, and synthesize while writing. In some cases, the lecture they are hearing is not well organized, and this makes notetaking even more difficult. That they only have one chance to hear something creates additional problems because they are afraid they will miss something; when they do miss a point, they tend to give up and not get down whatever else is said. Reading notetaking is closely akin to underlining and outlining, as it too is a difficult skill with which students often need assistance. While taking notes during reading, a student must analyze, interpret, and synthesize. It basically involves identifying key points made by an author and converting these key ideas to the reader's own words. Such a skill often requires rather sophisticated reading and thinking abilities if the end product—the notes themselves—is to be valuable. This is a difficult, if not impossible, feat if the material is not appropriate for the student. Unfortunately, students usually find their notes to be a word-by-word duplication of the textbook, so they perceive notetaking as wasted effort. Since it is a rather complex skill even when done well, students should practice reading notetaking and receive guidance from their teachers.

SPECIALIZED SKILLS

Specialized study skills include those needed for very specific purposes such as taking tests. In many cases, students know enough information about the material in a class to warrant their receiving a high grade, but they are unable to convey their knowledge to the teacher when test time comes around. The ability to express what is known is a major determiner of a student's grade in a class. Unfortunately, some students become confused by reading too much into a matching exercise; others fail to realize that one false element in a true-false item can make the entire item false. In addition, students at times do not understand what is being asked on an essay test. All of these situations create testing confusion and the confusion often results in students' failure. Thus, there are many strategies in taking tests that students need to know.

Other specialized skills include following directions and using graphic aids. Following directions is a specialized skill which is developed with practice; yet many students do not follow directions well at all. Such students need to be made aware of this weakness, and they need help avoiding distractions that cause them to ignore or be confused by directions. Using maps, graphs, and other graphic aids are other skills that usually can be developed through experience and practice.

Such simple things as these specialized skills can increase students' confidence in themselves and can stimulate their learning. A teacher who exposes students to specialized skills in a classroom can perceive how well the students are able to handle them and can help those who are having difficulty.

FORMAL ASSESSMENTS

A formal assessment of study skills may be obtained from a subtest of a standardized achievement test or from a standardized study skills inventory. As with other types of standardized testing devices, however, a teacher must exercise caution when interpreting the results of such devices. A formal assessment of study skills can be of value if it is used to indicate which students may have weaknesses in study skills. But to use these devices for purposes other than rough indicators would be assuming that they are more accurate than they are.

Many standardized achievement tests, especially those designed for junior and senior high school students, include a subtest intended to assess study skills. Such subtests are usually designed around a multiple-choice format and examine only tangential skills such as library awareness, using a map or graph, using an index, and ability to alphabetize. That they often do not sample the more important skills such as outlining, notetaking, use of time, or test taking is a significant deficiency in these tests.

A standardized study skills inventory, such as the Preston-Botel *Study Habits Checklist* (SRA, 1967) has several advantages over the subtest of a standardized achievement battery. First, most of these inventories cover major areas of importance such as use of time, notetaking, outlining, and taking examinations. Specific questions in these and other areas provide a greater degree of depth than an achievement battery subtest. A second advantage lies in students' responses. Rather than directly testing a specific skill, students are asked to analyze and describe their own study habits in reference to a very specific question. For example, students may be asked, "In taking examinations, do you read the directions and the questions with care?" (Preston and Botel, 1967). The response will be either "Almost always,"

"More than half the time," "About half the time," "Less than half the time," or "Almost never."

These inventories provide students with an opportunity to reflect carefully on their own study habits. This self-analysis is an important first step since areas of weakness may become immediately apparent. Such appraisals are of value to both students and teachers because they can serve as the springboard for fruitful diagnosis through private conferences.

If formal assessment devices of the standardized variety are to be used, we suggest the inventory over the achievement battery subtest. Each can be used as a screening device to indicate which students seem to have weaknesses in study skills that would impede academic success, but the inventory usually examines important areas rather than tangential ones. Each offers a teacher the chance to compare the students with established norms, but because of the nature of the questions posed, the inventory offers greater possibilities for intensive diagnosis based on an item analysis. The inherent dangers and limitations of any type of standardized device exist with both, but if a screening device of a survey nature is what is wanted, the advantages of the inventory are apparent.

INFORMAL ASSESSMENTS

An informal analysis of students' study skills may be the easiest aspect of diagnosis for a content teacher interested in helping students improve their learning abilities; it may also be the most important. Students who do not know how to learn are handicapped from the outset, and teachers cannot fairly assume that students, good and poor alike, automatically develop the necessary skills for effective study. Informal assessments are probably the most reliable and beneficial methods of evaluating students' study skills, and when appropriately utilized they can help perceptive teachers avert many problems before they arise.

One informal approach to study skills diagnosis is through daily observations of students as they perform the various tasks needed in the classroom. If lecture notetaking is important, a teacher can unobtrusively observe students as they attempt to take notes. Mental observations can be made of those who seem to be writing down the more important ideas which are expressed during the lecture. In fact, a written record may often be of value since a premium is not placed on remembering observations. Other skills that will enhance learning can also be observed in the course of daily routines such as test taking, outlining, and specialized skills such as knowing how to use a map or how to work a problem in math or science classes. A major advantage of this approach is that it requires performance and is based on realistic performance criteria.

A second means of informally assessing certain study skills is to create tests or exercises that are designed to assess specific skills. A tape might be made to check students' ability to take notes in a listening situation; a reading passage can be designed to assess underlining, reading notetaking, and outlining skills. A practice test can be devised that asks students to answer questions and then describe how they proceeded to take the test. To aid in study skills assessment, a checklist can be created to keep a record of strengths and weaknesses in those areas that seem to be most important in a given class.

DEVISING YOUR OWN PROGRAM

The most efficient method of assessing study skills is probably a combination of all the strategies we have discussed in this chapter. With this in mind, let us suggest a series of steps, with some examples, which can guide you toward devising a study skills assessment program that will be most appropriate for your classroom.

*, 10 First, analyze the courses you teach and the way you teach. What study skills are needed for success in these courses? Do students need to take careful reading notes because of your emphasis on the text and other outside readings? How important are lecture notes? Do students need to be able to outline material because the material itself is disjointed and needs to be tied together for clarity? Do they need to use maps and graphs, or research or locational skills? Is the terminology going to be very new and different so that they will need to refer often to a glossary? The identification of the specific study skills that are important in a course must be identified so that assessments can be related to the specific skills needed. As the year progresses, ask your students to help you revise the list; you may be surprised at some of their observations.

Second, once the list is compiled, construct a checklist. It may look something like Figure 8-1. We have based this checklist on specific skills identified as being important.

The preparation of such a checklist will enable you to keep a record of individual students. Other formats can easily be devised that may be more suitable for you, but without such a checklist, you will be forced to rely a great deal on memory. If the idea of keeping track of each student seems too overwhelming, you might consider letting the students do their own record keeping with individual checklists for each student separately. If you do, periodically hand out the checklist and let them make revisions as they think are appropriate. Perhaps a combination of your own observations kept on a separate sheet and the students' self-analysis will be appealing.

Third, prepare an inventory form to which students can respond with the emphasis placed on the skills you have identified as being important in your class. Published inventories such as those alluded to in the discussion of formal assessments can be used, but they frequently cover areas that are not of immediate interest to you and omit areas that might be vital in your class. If you do construct an inventory, it might look something like the one we have designed here.

STUDY SKILLS CHECKLIST

_____
teacher

_____
course/period

_____
date

3 = can do well
2 = needs improvement
1 = very weak

SKILLS

Figure 8-1   *Study skills checklist.*

NAME	KEY	Texts: table of contents	index	glossary	Underlining: highlights important ideas	underlines key words	underlines supportive information	Notetaking–Reading: based on underlining	will make sense several weeks later	cross references with page numbers	Notetaking–Lecture: brief, but clear	includes main ideas	includes supportive details	Outlining: headings reflect main ideas	subheadings include supportive data	headings reflect parallel relationships	Uses Maps: can use legends	can interpret historical data	Essay Test-Taking: reads directions and all questions before beginning	thinks before writing	organizes answer	proofreads
Bell, J.	1																					
	2																					
	3																					
Brown, S.	1																					
	2																					
	3																					
Carver, T.	1																					
	2																					
	3																					
Cotton, W.	1																					
	2																					
	3																					
Horton, G.	1																					
	2																					
	3																					
Ives, J.	1																					
	2																					
	3																					
etc.																						

STUDY SKILLS INVENTORY

_____
Student

                                                    _____
                                                    course/period

_____
date

Directions: Study skills will be important to your success in this course and this inventory is designed to find out what your strengths and weaknesses may be in these areas. Think carefully about each of the following statements and then _answer as honestly as you can._ This is NOT a test!!

Circle 1, 2, 3, or 4 next to each statement to indicate whether the statement would be true for you usually, sometimes, seldom, or never.

	USUALLY	SOMETIMES	SELDOM	NEVER
Use of Time				
1. I spend about forty-five minutes each day studying for each of my courses.	1	2	3	4
2. When I study, I can stick with it until I am finished.	1	2	3	4
3. I study where I will not be interrupted.	1	2	3	4
Using a Textbook				
4. I use the table of contents to help me understand how topics are related.	1	2	3	4
5. I use the index in my studying.	1	2	3	4
6. I use the glossary to find meanings of unfamiliar words.				
Underlining				
7. I underline all important ideas as I read.	1	2	3	4
8. I underline only key words and phrases, not whole sentences.	1	2	3	4
9. I underline details and examples.	1	2	3	4
10. I underline almost everything.	1	2	3	4
Notetaking				
11. When I study, I take notes from my reading.	1	2	3	4
12. When I take notes from my reading, they are clear enough to make sense several weeks later.	1	2	3	4

	USUALLY	SOMETIMES	SELDOM	NEVER
13. When I take notes from my reading, I put down the page numbers where I got the information.	1	2	3	4
14. When a teacher is lecturing in class, I take clear notes of what is said.	1	2	3	4
15. In my lecture notes, I make sure to write down the main ideas.	1	2	3	4
16. In my lecture notes, I include details and examples that help me clarify ideas.	1	2	3	4
Outlining				
17. I outline the major things I learn when I study.	1	2	3	4
18. In my outlines, I include main ideas in the primary headings.	1	2	3	4
19. In my outlines, I include details as subheadings that clarify the main ideas.	1	2	3	4
Using Maps				
20. I can use the keys and legends when reading maps.	1	2	3	4
21. I can interpret what the maps suggest about historical trends.	1	2	3	4
Taking Essay Tests				
22. When taking essay tests, I read the directions and all the questions before beginning to answer any of the questions.	1	2	3	4
23. When taking essay tests, I think about what I want to write before beginning.	1	2	3	4
24. When taking essay tests, I organize my answer so my ideas will be clear to the instructor.	1	2	3	4
25. I proofread my answers when I am finished and before I turn in my paper.	1	2	3	4
Taking Objective Tests				
26. When answering a multiple choice question, I try to eliminate first the obviously incorrect choices.	1	2	3	4
27. I trust my first guess when unsure of an answer.	1	2	3	4
28. I proofread to make sure no question is left un-answered, even if the answer is a wild guess.	1	2	3	4
29. I read through all of the choices given before marking an answer, even if the first or second one seems correct.	1	2	3	4
30. I look for clues in other questions that can help in answering questions of which I am unsure.	1	2	3	4

Fourth, design some evaluation exercises that are based on the most crucial skills you have identified as being important in your course. Have the students do the exercises and then evaluate them for signs of strengths and weaknesses.

Fifth, observe your students in daily classroom activities. Such informal observations can be used to reconfirm any tentative conclusions you might have drawn as a result of "testing exercises" or from an inventory or self-analysis by means of a checklist. As you use the observations in diagnosis, you should look for trends and not assume too much from an isolated situation. Students' performances are not usually consistent since many external variables affect them at any given time.

Sixth, compare your findings with those of the students. Discuss with them the areas you consider important and design ways that will help them eliminate any existing problems.

In summary, then, these are the six steps:

1. Identify the study skills that students will need for success in your course,

2. Construct a diagnostic checklist to record your evaluations of students' proficiency with the specific skills of importance,

3. Prepare a self-analysis inventory based on the study skills you consider important,

4. Construct evaluative exercises to assess the most vital study skills,

5. Informally observe students' ability to use their study skills as they perform tasks during daily classroom activities.

6. Compare your findings with your students.

In addition to these six, two more might be added:

7. Help students improve their study skills by providing direct guidance and instruction,

8. Periodically discuss students' progress on an individual basis. Make suggestions that will help them improve further. Above all, provide encouragement!

TEACHING STUDY SKILLS

Instruction in the various study skills we have described should be integrated into content reading lessons where the need arises. Students learn skills most efficiently in a meaningful context. The inclusion of specific skills in this way, however, requires perceptive, diagnostic teaching. To fragment and isolate skills instruction will rarely accomplish the desired objective. Skills instruction which originates from an observed need will help students see value and purpose in the skill.

Consider study skills as a means to an end, rather than as a separate entity worthy of active pursuit for its own sake. Application is the byword and, more often than not, effective instruction will emerge from students' need to acquire, assimilate, or synthesize knowledge. As you proceed through the next unit, seek ways to incorporate meaningful skills instruction into your activities. Be on the lookout for occasions when your students might need your help and guidance in studying. However, be wary that as you begin to consider and appraise their needs that you plan to meet those needs in a meaningful context.

UNIT  3

Diagnostic Instruction

CONCEPTUAL OBJECTIVES

1. *Organization is the key to effective teaching and learning.*

2. *What the reader knows is more important to comprehension than what the author says.*

3. *In their search for information, students may find opportunities to practice a variety of reading strategies.*

4. *The opportunity to reflect and react to what one has read solidifies learning.*

5. *Knowledge of vocabulary reflects a stage of understanding.*

6. *Attitudes toward school are changed by experiences in school.*

7. *Learning activities provide the conduit through which learners may make contact with educational objectives.*

A SYNTHESIS

Diagnostic instruction is instruction designed to adapt the curriculum to meet the needs of the student. Unfortunately, students in secondary school classrooms are often passive and unenthusiastic. For most teachers, this inertia is perplexing, especially when the same students are often seen engaged in witty, dynamic, animated conversations outside classroom doors. It is as if going to class is a price they pay for precious moments of socializing with their friends.

In the final chapter of *Psycholinguistics and Reading* (1974), Frank Smith discusses "Twelve Easy Ways to Make Learning to Read Difficult and One Difficult Way to Make it Easy." His one difficult way is the substance of diagnostic reading instruction in a content classroom: "Respond to what the child is trying to do." In other words, *identify what the students are trying to learn and then provide them with activities that will help them succeed.* The object of diagnostic instruction is to facilitate learning.

Students learn by continually attempting to make sense of their world. Their inertia would suggest that they perceive much of what takes place in their classes as making little sense in their world. Thus, they make little or no effort to learn it. Learning is an active process; passivity is counterproductive to learning. When students perceive neither purpose nor sense in what they find in their classes, they make no effort—and without effort, they do not learn.

Putting these comments in other words, the following quote from Arthur Combs in *Helping Relationships* (1971) seems particularly apt:

> Learning is the discovery of meaning. The problem of learning . . . always involves two aspects: one is acquisition of new information or experience; the other has to do with the individual's personal discovery of the meaning of information for him. . . . The discovery of meaning, however, can only take place in people and cannot occur without the involvement of persons. (p. 91)

In *The Naked Children* (1971), Fader describes a student, Wentworth, who never participates in class activities and who might best be described as the model of classroom inertia. His teacher explained that Wentworth could not read and that was why he never took part in class activities. Further, she explained, his malady could not be rectified in spite of all efforts to do so. When Fader pursued this problem, he found that, in fact, Wentworth could read. As Fader describes it,

> *Wentworth told me.* "Sure I can read," he said. "I been able to read ever since I can remember. But I ain't never gonna let *them* know, on accoun' of iff'n I do I'm gonna have to read all that crap they got." (p. 17)

This vignette dramatizes the problem of inertia all too well.

Combating the Wentworth syndrome   The diverse nature of students' backgrounds, interests, and needs is no more evident than in secondary content area classrooms. Similarly, the need for responsive, diagnostic instruction is nowhere more essential than in these classes. Through this type of instruction, a teacher can help students find sense and purpose in their study and can effectively combat the "Wentworth syndrome."

Diagnostic instruction is instruction organized by the teacher around the needs and interests of pupils with the goal of adapting the curriculum to allow pupils to find personal meaning in what they are doing. By accounting for the students' needs, teacher's goals, and curricular demands (discussed in chapter 3), and by creating a meaningful blend of these three instructional factors, a teacher can produce an activity-oriented classroom where students can learn in accordance with their own goals.

Students need to become involved, personally and collectively, in their learning. They need to discuss and debate the concepts being emphasized. They need to manipulate elements of the concepts and to make judgments about these concepts. They need to explore and examine issues in creative and meaningful ways, through open-ended questions where no "right" or "wrong" answers reign. They also need guidance in how to extract the personal content that will be meaningful and important to them.

Students in content classrooms need encouragement to ask questions—questions that will be self-stimulating, questions that will help them overcome inertia and guide them toward becoming active readers and learners. Students need the freedom to stick their necks out, to make intellectual progress. They need to ask questions, such as:

1. Why am I reading this? How can I best learn from it?

2. What do I want to know about this?

3. How can this information be valuable to me?

Such questions will help students pose more questions—probing questions of good quality that will help them make sense of their world.

What is more dynamic in an academic setting than to see and feel genuine learning taking place? When students become actively involved in learning, receive the proper amount of instructional guidance, and can have their creative drives nourished rather than stymied, they become as animated in the classrooms as they are in the halls. Such learning usually is characterized by the ability to answer three questions:

1. What am I doing? (This one's usually easy!)

2. Why am I doing it? (This one's essential!)

3. What am I going to be doing next? (This helps make sense in a larger perspective!)

Students must be able to answer these questions if they are to relate classroom activities to their world rather than to perceive them as arbitrary nonsense imposed by school. When students can answer these questions, diagnostic instruction is functioning at its best.

SELECTED READINGS

Cross references to the following entries are denoted by a double star in the margin, followed by reference to the entry number in this list.

	CONCEPTS						
	1	2	3	4	5	6	7
1. Sanders, Norris. *Classroom Questions: What Kinds?*	X						
2. Smith, Frank. "Twelve easy ways to make learning to read difficult."			X				
3. Herber, H. L. *Teaching Reading in Content Areas.*			X				

(Full bibliographic information for these items will be found at the end of the book under References.)

Activity and Selected Readings Key

SUGGESTED ACTIVITIES

Cross references to the following entries are denoted by a single star in the margin, followed by reference to entry numbers in this list.

	CONCEPTS						
	1	2	3	4	5	6	7
1. Keep a log of learning activities in your classroom for one week. Classify the activities by major categories in Figure 9-2, p. 127. Redraw Figure 9-2 to picture the way you teach. (If you are not now teaching, you can think back to the way you were taught and do essentially the same thing.)	X						
2. Make a preliminary examination of one of the units of study included at the end of this book. (p. 134)	X						
3. Try the structured overview process we describe on pp. 143–149, at first with a small group, then with a whole class. Compare your dialogue with the one we offered as an example.		X					
4. Try to use the ReQuest procedure with a group of students, modifying it as you see appropriate to your needs.			X			X	
5. Work through the example study guide on p. 157. Ask others to do the same thing and compare responses.			X				
6. Construct, use, and evaluate a three-level study guide, following the steps we suggest on p. 161.			X				

	CONCEPTS						
	1	2	3	4	5	6	7
7. Construct, use, and evaluate a patterns guide, following the steps we suggest on p. 163.			X				
8. Work through the concept guide for *A Patch of Blue* if you saw the movie or read the book. (see p. 171)			X				
9. Work through the concept guide for *The Outsiders* if you have read the novel.			X				
10. Construct, use, and evaluate a concept guide, following the steps we suggest on p. 174.			X				
11. Construct, use, and evaluate a combination guide, following examples that appear in units of work included at the end of this book. (see p. 174)			X				
12. Make an unobtrusive survey by listening to conversations among adults and/or students. What percentage of the conversation would you estimate is related to something one or more persons in the group has read about? How often does the word "read" occur? (see p. 178)				X			
13. Try your hand at a cinquain. Try the idea with your students or as a party game sometime. (see p. 183)				X			
14. Work the vocabulary exercises and puzzles scattered throughout chapter 13. Then, try your hand at constructing ones similar to those we provide as examples.					X		
15. List your favorite subject(s) and teacher(s) in school. Do they match?						X	
16. List the two best and two worst experiences of your life. Whom or what did they involve? (see p. 202)						X	
17. Rank various learning activities that we list on pp. 210–211, in the way we suggest on p. 210.							X

9

Organizing Diagnostic Instruction

Organization is the key to effective teaching and learning.

SUMMARY

Diagnostic instruction in a content classroom simultaneously facilitates students' gain in knowledge and acquisition of the strategies with which to acquire more knowledge. In using such instruction, a content teacher must orchestrate the basic elements that affect learning into a harmonious educational symphony. Those teachers who are most successful in achieving their objectives are often distinguished by their ability to create a stimulating learning environment in their classrooms. Usually, the teachers who create these environments rely on their ability to organize the separate elements that influence that environment. It is organization that is often the key to effective teaching and learning.

Operationally, diagnostic instruction can center on units of study that are based on concepts important to an understanding of a specific domain of inquiry. Materials and activities relevant to those concepts may be used by students in various combinations as their interests and abilities dictate. Through the use of individual assignments, kept in the form of weekly log sheets, the teacher and students can work together to create and respond to an environment that is maximally conducive to learning. The classroom can, through diagnostic instruction and organization, become an exciting place to be and to learn.

ORGANIZATIONAL FRAMEWORK

Diagnostic instruction incorporates all the elements of instructional demands relative to the students, the teacher, and the curriculum. It provides for the process of learning without slighting the content to be learned. When you discern these factors as merged within an organizational framework, the task of creating a stimulating learning environment is greatly simplified.

For a summary of the organizational framework that can mobilize learning through diagnostic instruction, examine Figure 9-1.

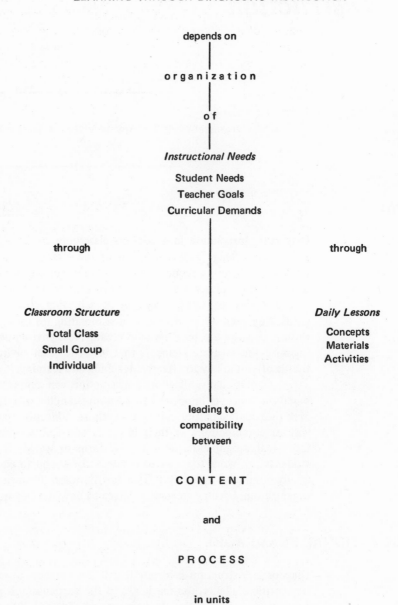

LEARNING THROUGH DIAGNOSTIC INSTRUCTION

depends on

organization

of

Instructional Needs

Student Needs
Teacher Goals
Curricular Demands

through   through

Classroom Structure   *Daily Lessons*

Total Class   Concepts
Small Group   Materials
Individual   Activities

leading to
compatibility
between

CONTENT

and

PROCESS

in units

Figure 9-1   *Organizational framework for process instruction in content classrooms.*

As depicted in this figure, the goal of diagnostic instruction in a content classroom is the successful learning of both content and process. Such learning is accomplished when the teacher structures the classroom and designs daily lessons on the basis of instructional needs. When identifying these needs, the teacher must take care to account for the implicit interaction among students' needs, the teacher's goals, and curricular demands. Once all these needs are identified and made compatible, the classroom must be organized to allow learning to occur through a structure of total class, small group, and individual activities. In addition, the conduct of daily lessons should be clearly designed in terms of the concepts to be emphasized, materials to be used, and appropriate activities that will precede, support, or reinforce the learning. The focal point of the overview in Figure 9-1 is instructional needs; it incorporates the concept of both behavioral and conceptual objectives as discussed in chapter 3. As you consider the other parts of this organizational framework, bear in mind that its parts are dependently related and that the whole may well be greater than the sum of its parts.

THE CRITICAL VARIABLE

The most appealing characteristic of many commercially prepared teaching materials is their organization. This is substantiated by the tendency of many teachers to rely on the organization of their material as they plan the sequence of their instruction. This tendency is especially evident when the material is accompanied by a teacher's manual delineating the scope and sequence (what is to be covered in what order) of the content.

Responding to this predeliction, publishers have sought to make their wares more appealing by providing minute organizational and instructional details for teachers, sometimes including dictations of exactly what the teacher is to say to the pupils and when to say it. At times, it seems that the publishers' objective is to tout materials as "teacher-proof." The implication is that what the educational community needs is material so well organized by "experts" that the function of the teacher is relegated to that of an overpaid clerk or expensive automaton.

No material is so good that poor teaching will not render it useless. Conversely, no material is so bad that a good teacher cannot find some use for it if someone mandates it into the classroom. In fact, materials are rather "avaluable," to coin a term. Hence, it has been said that to teach reading, all one needs is a stick and some wet sand. In other words, in and of themselves, materials have no inherent instructional value. Materials become valuable only when they are properly placed into the hands of students who can use them. Analogously, little leaguers don't hit home runs because of any inherent quality in their bats but because the bat they use is well suited to what they bring to the plate. To be effective, materials must be well suited to the learner, their use organized around the learner's developmental needs and abilities.

The major fallacy in organizing instruction around a set of previously sequenced materials is that no "expert" can possibly anticipate the contingencies that characterize any classroom—no expert except the teacher is in the classroom. The critical variable that distinguishes good from poor classroom instruction is a teacher who is able to systematize instruction around the individual needs of learners.

Organization, then, is the key to effective teaching and learning. This means, in practice, preparing for instruction by clearly determining what is to be taught to whom and why. In addition, it means creating an instructional environment that is conducive to learning. Given this line of reasoning, it is possible to discuss diagnostic instruction in three interrelated parts: 1) organization of the classroom; 2) organization of specific lessons; and 3) organization of instructional units.

CLASSROOM ORGANIZATION

The education to which most of us have been exposed is that of large group instruction. This is almost certainly true beyond the primary grades, although the practice is now changing. It is true that the reading we may have done and the "projects" we completed may have been accomplished individually (meaning with little help), but in colleges certainly, in high schools probably, and in junior high schools likely, the *modus operandi* is typically whole class instruction.

It has been said that this is because teachers tend to teach the way they have been taught; perhaps so. Perhaps also, however, few teachers have been convinced that it could be otherwise. "How can I break the class into groups? For that matter, why should I? They all have to learn the same things anyway and I would multiply my job and divide their learning time." Such a comment reflects a common misunderstanding of alternatives to large group instruction. It may be true that we would want all pupils to learn *of* the same things, but never could all students learn the same amount in the same way. As for the learning time of pupils, one would hope that students can learn at times other than when in direct contact with the teacher.

Recall that the purpose of diagnostic instruction in content area classrooms is twofold: that the students' conceptualizations of what they study and their ability to read and learn will show concomitant growth. This is most feasible when opportunities for individual and small group instruction are provided as alternatives and supplements to total class instruction. Examine Figure 9-2, an overview of classroom organization presented to suggest types of activities appropriate to three instructional motifs. Total class activities are appropriate for some purposes; small groups may be best suited to other purposes; for yet other purposes, individual instruction may be best.

Total class activities

Under this heading are included three suggested purposes. Certainly there are more than these, but consider the *type* of activity that may be appropriate. Screening tests are easily and efficiently given to an entire class, be they of a standardized or an informal nature. The value of these tests stems from the necessity to ascertain what pupils generally know before planning specific instructional and learning strategies for them.

Likewise, a total class setting is often appropriate for an introduction to the rudiments of concepts to be emphasized. The purpose of units of study, explained

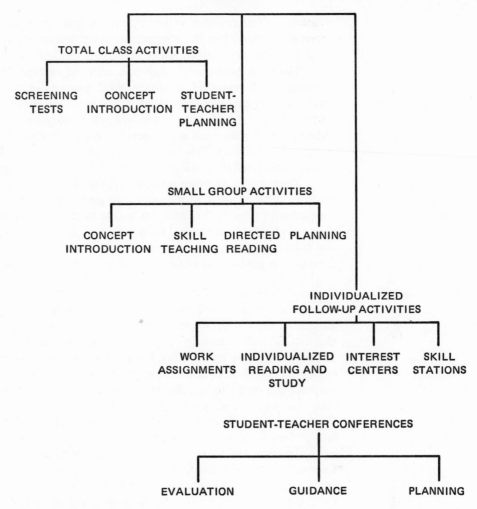

Figure 9-2   *Classroom organization.*

subsequently in this chapter, is to allow all pupils to come to different, but individually appropriate, understandings of similar concepts through different activities. At one level of instruction, however, the entire group or class may need to see the "big picture" of what they are studying. This picture would be necessarily sketchy but nonetheless important for the whole class to understand before proceeding to small group or individualized study.

Consider, for example, a familiar concept in the study of literature: "The short story is distinguished by unity of characterization, theme, and effect." A whole class discussion in a high school English class might, over the period of one or more days, bring into focus (for all pupils) the meaning of this rather erudite but essential concept. It would not be necessary, however, that everyone had read the same short story or, for that matter, any short story prior to such a discussion. The purpose of this discussion, to introduce the concept, would be to allow exploration of the terms *unity, characterization, theme,* and *effect.* Deeper individual understandings, made richer by a general introduction of the concept, would be developed in other organizational settings.

The third example of total class activities in Figure 9–2 is student-teacher planning. This is especially important. Much planning of time, space, and materials is necessary for the individualization desirable for effective instruction. Many problems of discipline and order are solved when everyone concerned knows when, where, and how individuals are expected to learn and what the consequences are for inappropriate behavior. This knowledge can best be introduced to the whole class at once and reiterated for small groups and individuals as necessary.

There are many other activities appropriate for the whole class setting. For example, films or guest presentations are often appropriate in such a setting. In some schools, trips to the library as well as field trips must be scheduled for whole classes at one time. Figure 9–2 is by no means definitive, nor is it meant to suggest that total class activities are undesirable. It should suggest, however, that activities other than in a total class setting may often be appropriate and necessary.

Small group activities   Four activities are listed in Figure 9–2 as appropriate for small group work. Again, consider the type as well as the specific activity suggested. For example, having introduced the concept of the short story to the total class at a previous time, the idea can be refined to a level appropriate to a smaller group. In the organization framework that we are building, the small group may occupy the majority of the teacher's time. With roughly three groups, which constantly change according to purposes and needs, the teacher might spend approximately two-thirds of his or her time with groups made up of a third of the class or less. At a given moment, then, the remaining two-thirds of the class must be engaged without direct teacher contact, perhaps in groups or individually.

To elaborate, let's examine how this type of instruction can be applied to a discussion of the elements of a short story. Pupils who have read a story can form a small group to discuss characterization, theme, and effect with respect to that story. As this is done, the individuals in the group are to clarify their understanding of the element of unity in relation to the story. They can thus come to a better understanding of the concept than they did from the whole class discussion, and they can then proceed to read other stories, individually or under teacher direction, as in a directed reading activity. In other cases, a group may be more advanced and have read several stories which, with a teacher's help, can be compared and contrasted with respect to defined elements. In each case, the discussion in the small group may be made more meaningful for the individuals in that group than would be possible in a large group discussion.

Skill teaching is another example of an activity for a small group. By "skills" we do not mean some endless list of only theoretically existent reading skills. As teachers are attuned to diagnostic teaching, however, skill weaknesses will reveal themselves, and the most appropriate place to diagnose effectively may be in the small group setting. The skills we mean would include "reading" the periodic table of the elements in chemistry which some students would not have mastered after a whole class introductory lecture. (For how many must *that* be true!) Equally appropriate would be the rule of 3-4-5 in geometry, a rule as apparent to some students as to Pythagoras, yet to others as elusive as to a five-year-old. For some, extended work with such ideas is critical and the small group is ideal for such extension. Generally speaking, any skill introduced to a whole class but not grasped by certain individuals can be reinforced when necessary in a class where small group work is organizationally possible.

The term "directed reading" used in Figure 9-2 may not be familiar to all secondary teachers. In chapter 11, *Information Search,* this will be taken up in much detail as we discuss the content reading lesson. As a preface to that discussion, we might at this point merely say that the small group of eight to twelve students is ideal for directed reading. The purpose of directed reading is to allow a group to engage in meaningful and directed reading and study of a relatively short selection. A short story is an example, as is a subsection of a chapter in a history or science textbook. Students in a small group setting can often get more from common discussion with others of similar interest and ability than they can from either large group or individual reading. As the teacher stimulates the discussion, students can set their own purposes and make predictions, read in selected bits, and weave the elements of the passage together as they search for information to verify or deny the ideas they have anticipated they would find.

Planning is as important a component of small group work as it is of total class activities. While total class planning may be directed to general operating procedures, small groups formed for interest and skill work may plan their common work together, even without the teacher's guidance. In this setting, plans may be made more specific than was possible in a total class setting. Indeed, often the small group may work with the teacher to plan certain activities that can be carried out while the teacher works with another group.

Individualized
follow-up
activities

The final element in the organizational paradigm presented in Figure 9-2 is individualized work. It is in this setting that students *may* spend as much as two-thirds of their time. One of the major purposes of the organizational plan is to allow for the most appropriate setting in which individuals may work at their own pace toward common goals. Realistically, the purpose of education, and let us emphasize that we might be speaking of any content area, is to allow all students to achieve individual levels of understanding of similar concepts. Individualized work is therefore essential as an extension of whole class and small group work.

In the individualized setting, pupils may complete assignments that have been explained in another setting. The number and kinds of activities which might be completed individually by pupils in a class are limited only by the teacher's, and, for that matter, the students' imagination. Reading and study may be individualized through teacher-assignment or self-selection by students. Every classroom should have a quiet library corner where one can find interesting things to read related to the study at hand. Some teachers have found it convenient to label this the "time-out" corner where students may retreat from pressure or frustration on days, or at times, when things are not going well. All of us need to get away or take a break now and then; students in a classroom are no exception.

Interest centers and skill stations are other places of focus for individualized work. In the small group setting, students will often mention special interests in a topic. Individual follow-up to this is valuable in allowing these interests to be developed. In like manner, skills instruction in the small group may require follow-up. Such work areas need not be elaborate; a place to work alone on individual skill deficiencies or areas of interest is all that is required.

Overriding all individualized work are student-teacher conferences. Because of the provision for self-directed and individualized work, the teacher is left free to engage with pupils in cooperative evaluation, guidance, and planning. The teacher who can manage up to two minutes of individualized time with each pupil in each class each week can accomplish at least two critical goals of instruction. First, there is the possibility of doing a lot of teacher "homework," reviewing work folders and performance, on school time and in a meaningful setting for pupils. Second, any individual contact with pupils may enhance the possibility of greater learning. In a world driven to impersonalization by sheer numbers, the classroom environment can be set up to avoid impersonalization despite the numbers. This effort in itself may often result in more positive feelings on the part of individuals, leading to a more stimulating and rewarding classroom environment for all.

Before continuing to another aspect of organization, let us suggest a pattern that accounts for varied activities over a five-day sequence. Ms. Sherry Vaughan, who designed this particular sequence, emphasizes that the structure should not be envisioned as rigid and, in fact, if more than one day were necessary to complete the work most suited to the pattern of a particular day, this schedule easily accommodates such an extra day. In addition, any day's pattern could also be inserted whenever it was most appropriate.

For an overview of this cycle of study, see Figure 9–3. The following excerpt describing this schedule is reprinted here with permission. The plan was designed for a tenth-grade English class and the references to specific activities are to that class.[1]

"The class was divided into three heterogeneous groups, but these groups did not remain constant and, in fact, often changed. At times, homogeneous groups were designed for specific interest or skill work. Our work schedule was organized on a five-day work cycle designed around six major work areas which were located at various places in the room.

1. *IR Independent Reading* was the focus of study for Day 1 of our cycle. Here the students read books they had selected from the required list or were free to choose articles or short stories related to the topic of study. During this period, I could meet with about half the class in individual conferences concerning their work. I divided the time among the groups and met with about half of each group during the first third of the period, half of another group during the second period of the class, and about half of the third group during the last third of the class period. There were twenty-

[1] Our thanks to Ms. Sherry Vaughan, tenth grade teacher at Marana High School, Marana, Arizona, for sharing with us her ideas and experiences.

	Time Period		
	9:00–9:15	**9:20–9:35**	**9:40–9:55**
Day 1:			
Group 1	IR*	IR	IR
Group 2	IR	IR*	IR
Group 3	IR	IR	IR*
Day 2:			
Group 1	RG	I	S
Group 2	S	RG	I
Group 3	I	S	RG
Day 3:			
Group 2	RG	I	S
Group 3	S	RG	I
Group 1	I	S	RG
Day 4:	W H O L E G R O U P C L A S S		
Day 5:			
Group 1	IW*	IW	IW
Group 2	IW	IW*	IW
Group 3	IW	IW	IW*

IR – Independent Reading
RG – Rap Group
  * – Teacher-Student Conference

S – Skills Work
I – Independent
IW – Individualized Work

Figure 9-3   *Schedule for a cycle of study.*

six students in the class and I allowed fifteen minutes per group. I kept a timer running to keep both me and my students on schedule.

2. *RG Rap Group* centered around teacher-student discussions of the concepts we had identified as important to our study and their application in the books that students were reading independently. On Day 2 we discussed the concepts and on Day 3 we had a follow-up assignment which emphasized that concept (e.g., role playing or improvisations involving characters from the materials the students were reading).

3. *S Skill Work* periods allowed time for students to work in skill stations in spelling, standard and nonstandard English usage exercises, and word study activities.

4. *I Independent Study* periods focused on students' work in independent response projects for which they contracted. This included such activities as creating mobiles, paintings, writing poetry, doing multi-media presentations, etc., as an attempt to communicate to

others something they had learned about the concepts we were emphasizing.

5. *Whole Group Class* During this period we reviewed the concepts discussed in RG the two days before and also re-emphasized the major concepts we had isolated as focal points of study at the beginning of the unit. Students made contributions to this by discussing these concepts in relation to the material they had read. Occasionally, new information was presented to the whole class on this day; on another day a guest speaker came to the class.

6. *IW Individual Work* was a clean-up day. While I met with the remaining half of the class in individual conferences, all students worked in the areas that needed most attention for each of them. The night before Day 5, I checked over the log sheets students had kept during the week. This gave them feedback on their work for that particular cycle."

LESSON ORGANIZATION

A lesson may be defined as a relatively brief, structured opportunity for the teacher to diagnose and for students to learn. It might be as long as one or two class periods or as short as fifteen minutes. It might be conducted with the whole class, a small group, or an individual. In any case, the organization of a daily lesson hinges on three factors: concepts, materials, and activities. The purpose of organizing a lesson should be to create a proper balance among these three factors so that learning occurs. Excellent discussions of the nature of reading lessons, in reading class or in content areas, appear in Stauffer (1969), Herber (1970), and Spache and Spache (1977).

A lesson should be designed to facilitate students' understanding of basic concepts. These concepts should be clearly identified so that both the teacher and the students can immediately discern why they are involved in a given lesson. The substance of the lesson must be directly related to the concepts and the lesson should be organized to foster students' understanding of the concepts.

Presumably, any lesson should be conducted with students in material which at least approximates their instructional level as defined in chapter 2. What this means is that the material and the skill required to handle it are within the grasp of the learner, given some teacher help.

The activities through which the lesson is to be channeled must also be appropriate. An activity can fulfill one of three purposes: 1) preparation for learning, 2) support for learning, or 3) reinforcement to learning. Given that, the teacher may structure any lesson in such a way that answers to the following types of diagnostic questions emerge.

1. What is the students' background of information with regard to the conceptual content of the lesson? Do they hold misconceptions that could interfere with their study?

Answers to these questions can be derived from informal discussions. As a preface to any lesson, the teacher can direct a discussion that calls for information related to the concepts being studied. The important thing to bear in mind, however, is that the questions all of us tend to ask are sometimes rather literal in scope. Sanders (1966) has provided guidance in questioning strategies in his book *Classroom Questions: What Kinds?* and it would be worth any teacher's effort to peruse this little book.

**, 1

> 2. Are the students interested in the content? If not, what might be done to build their interest?

One of the points we have made and will repeat is that teachers teach best what they themselves know best and in which they are interested. Likewise, students will best learn those things in which they are most interested and knowledgeable. That is not, however, tantamount to saying that students only learn in their interest areas, but that their learning will increase relative to their interest in the subject.

A good way to diagnose students' interest is to ask them what they know about the topic of the lesson. As group members volunteer information, it can be written on the chalkboard. This provides a good opportunity for students to share their interests and through discussion with one another they will often reveal interests and pique other students' curiosity. Peer approval is a powerful force and any use possible should be made of it to enhance learning.

In addition to the structured discussion which may reveal interests, the teacher can often provide interest-building activities as a preface to the study of a particular concept. For example, in introducing the study of "Death" in literature, the teacher can begin by reading a powerful poem, such as "Richard Cory," to the group. Students' reaction can be observed for clues to interest in the general topic. In a science class where the topic of "Chemical vs. Physical Change" is to be studied, a simple demonstration of the two phenomena might be made. The comments that emanate from the minor drama will often reveal and build interests.

The principle behind the matter of interest is simple: people tend to pursue study of things in which they are interested and to avoid study of things in which they are disinterested. Any time spent in diagnosis and building interest is likely to pay a greater return on the investment of time than any other single phase of the lesson.

> 3. What kinds of reading-study skills does the lesson require? How facile are the students with these skills?

A critical part of lessons in content areas is the development of information processing skills. To assume the possession of such skills by students is to deny them the opportunity to learn either the content of the lesson or the skills. The teacher-directed lesson is an excellent setting in which to diagnose such skills and to help students master them.

4. Qualitatively speaking, at what level do students' responses to the content of the lesson seem to occur?

This can be one of the best clues available to the teacher as he or she tries to guide students' thinking. Where responses in discussion tend to be specific and literal rather than conceptual and integrative, students may need help in higher level thinking. This can be provided in the form of study guides or, less formally, in discussion that stimulates such thinking.

5. Will the concepts covered in the lesson require extended study beyond the lesson per se? What resources will have to be made available for this extension?

Typically in textbooks, the last section is entitled "Suggestions for Extension and Reinforcement." It is a section too often ignored. Some of the best opportunities for learning can be provided in response to needs for extended learning that are generated in a specific lesson. A vital dimension of any lesson in content areas is the opportunity it provides for diagnosis of what extended learning can and should be pursued. Likely, most learning does not occur in the formal lesson setting; what can occur is a taste of success which whets the appetite for more of the same.

ORGANIZATION OF INSTRUCTIONAL UNITS

The unit is the ultimate organizational consideration in diagnostic instruction. As we will define it, a unit is systematized study where the teacher coordinates time, space, and activities around key concepts and understandings that the students are to acquire. It provides an atmosphere for the varying abilities and needs of all students and seeks to create the best possible opportunity for learning for each student. The effect of the organizational system in the unit will be to allow students of varying abilities and background to come to better understandings of similar concepts through individually tailored combinations of activities and learning experiences. That is not only a mouthful of a sentence; it is the desideratum of education! It can, however, be translated into practical terms.

Examples of units of study in various content areas appear in the appendix of this book. You might choose one of these examples, preferably one most appropriate to your content specialty, and examine its parts as we discuss the parts of units in more general terms.

There are five essential parts to the framework of any unit of study:

1. a definitive title

2. the list of concepts and understandings

3. a list of materials and resources

4. a list of learning activities

5. weekly log sheets

The title of the unit is important since it should describe in briefest terms the specific domain of inquiry that the unit will cover. While it is impossible to say how general the domain might be, this generality will determine the breadth of other parts of the unit, namely the concepts, materials, and activities. A title like "Biological Science" or "U.S. History before 1865" would probably be too broad since it is doubtful that such topics could be compressed into manageable form. More likely, some part of these would have to be chosen, such as "Amphibian Life Forms" or "The American Revolution."

One clue to the definition of a unit will often be provided by the textbook in use for the course, given that the book is reasonably appropriate for the grade and class with which it is used. Many texts in current use are divided into units, and often this is well done. In cases where the text is well organized, the definition of a unit's scope is facilitated, as the text can suggest the scope of the unit while the teacher defines the content of the unit. In effect, the text can be used as a baseline, and the other major components of the unit (concepts, materials, and activities) can be organized by the teacher to more fully develop and individualize that content baseline.

Composing the list of concepts and understandings for the unit is the second step in its development. The ideal number of concepts for a unit is impossible to define, but the number of concepts should rarely exceed ten. The assumption is that all students will be exploring the various concepts in sufficient depth to acquire reasonable understandings within a limited period of time. If too many concepts are projected, the depth of learning will certainly be diluted.

The choice of specific concepts to be included rests on two basic considerations. First, the concepts should be reasonably appropriate in sophistication and interest appeal for the students. To a degree, this must be determined by the level at which the unit is to be taught. In any case, it is a diagnostic decision the teacher must make in trying to match the sophistication of the students' thinking and their interests to what they are expected to learn. The information on which such decisions must be based can be obtained from simple, informal observations through daily contact with the students as well as through formal and informal pretesting. In such pretesting, when items are keyed to concepts being considered for inclusion in a unit, a rather good profile of students' existing understandings can be compiled. Those concepts about which the students seem to know least should be dealt with at a low level of sophistication, if at all. Conversely, concepts in which the students have a firm grounding can be treated at higher levels of sophistication.

Second, concepts should be chosen for their relative importance to an understanding of the overall topic of the unit. With respect to any topic, there are many concepts that might be understood. Those that are most basic and essential for understanding the essence of the unit topic are the ones from which choices must be made. It is the choice of a limited number of appropriate concepts that will form the foundation of a good unit of study.

Following the list of concepts comes the list of materials and resources. The textbook used in a course is often one good source to include, especially if divided into short sections rather than presented as a set of chapters. Textbooks, however often tend to be rather limited in their breadth of appeal and suitability of diffi culty. One major advantage of the units we are describing is that students are ofter freed from textbook limitations, freed from the fact that the textbook is insuffi cient in meeting either their needs or the goals of the teacher.

Other materials and resources may include supplementary readings, both fic tion and nonfiction; films, filmstrips, and records; guest speakers and field trips encyclopedias and other library resources; pamphlets and brochures; materials fo use in making collages, dioramas, displays, and the like; charts and maps; and th list goes on, limited only by imagination. The key to determining whether a sourc is appropriate is simply its value in helping students seek understanding of th concepts within the unit.

Each piece of material is then keyed to the concept(s) to which it bear relevance. As such a key is constructed, the teacher insures that sufficient material for each concept will be available. Where they are not, for whatever reason o resource limitation, the teacher must reconsider including the concept in the unit No concept for which little material is available can be well taught to students thus, the materials and concepts can be manipulated against one another as addi tions and deletions are made.

The unit title, the list of concepts, and the list of materials, then, form definition of what is to be learned and what means will be used for learning it. Th next element, the list of activities for the unit, will define *how* the content of th unit will be learned.

A question that frequently arises is, "How many activities do I need?" Arbi trarily, the number of activities for a given unit can be set at three to five times th number of teaching days to be devoted to the unit. For a three-week unit, exclud ing one day for pretesting and one for post-unit evaluation, one could think i terms of thirteen teaching days and, thus thirty-nine to seventy-five activities. Whil that number may not be realistic for a unit of study being created and used for th first time, each time a unit is taught, a backlog of materials and activities will ten to build. Within a few years, thirty-nine will seem almost insufficient and seventy five begin to loom as almost necessary. The object of a lengthy list of activities is t provide every student, regardless of background or ability, an appropriate combina tion of activities related to the concepts being stressed. Very likely, no two student would engage in exactly the same combination of alternatives for study. Not a would read the same textbook; not all would write term papers; not all would se the same film. But all *would* come to a better understanding of the same concept through the means most appropriate to their individual needs and skills. That thi might happen is the object of any unit of study.

As activities are listed, they are keyed to both materials and concepts t which they are related. This, in a similar manner to the materials/concepts key provides a visible account of the scope of the activities, across the various concepts Thus, it can be assured that each student engages in a combination of activities tha covers the range of conceptual content within the unit.

The fifth and final part of the unit is the students' weekly log sheets. Eacl student can be provided a folder that contains his or her personal log, available t the student daily. The log sheet provides both the teacher and the student with a running account of activities. Space can be provided for dates, activities, students' reaction, and teacher comment. Then, by frequent "quick-checks" and individual planning conferences with students, the teacher can strive for the best match between students and their activities.

Not all activities will be individualized. Where groups are to gather for teacher-directed lessons, this can be indicated by having everyone in the group assigned to a particular activity, e.g. "14. Small group content reading lesson, section III of chapter 4, text." At a time when the teacher is ready, he or she simply calls together all students who have activity 14 listed.

A NOTE ON INDIVIDUALIZED INSTRUCTION

There is a strong tendency toward individualized instruction in schools today. The use of learning centers, learning packets, and units such as those described in this chapter can be viewed as a positive sign. We do not want to dampen the spirit of this concept, but there seems to be some misconception associated with the idea of individualized instruction. The misconception is related to the heavy emphasis on "individualized" at the expense of "instruction." To establish a lesson, or a unit, or a program on the idea of individualized learning does not mean that instruction should suffer. Learning packets and skill stations do not an individualized program make! Learning occurs when students interact with students, teachers, and materials through well constructed activities. As you seek to provide individualized instruction, bear in mind that instruction is individualized only when students are doing things appropriate for them, not when each person does the same activity or worksheet separately from every other person. That is individualized Procrustean education, analogous to "lock-step" in disguise.

10

Prereading Anticipation

What the reader knows is more important to comprehension than is what the author says.

SUMMARY

Comprehension depends on what the reader knows that can be related to what is being read. That is, the reader attempts to find in memory anything related to the author's message; success in this search for relationships is the primary determinant of comprehension. It would appear, therefore, that in preparing a student for a reading task we should strive to create an interaction which establishes information in the memory of the reader to which the content of the reading selection can be related.

Several techniques for accomplishing this are available. Each is a method of helping students to anticipate intellectually what they are going to learn. Set in the framework of a content reading lesson, prereading anticipation techniques help students to develop strategies and to understand what they are studying.

SOMETHING OLD, SOMETHING NEW

Read the following paragraph and rate it on a scale of difficulty from 1 to 5, with 1 meaning very easy, 5 meaning incomprehensible.

Always begin from the left. Accomplishment requires balance, as well as the ability to stand on one foot cross-legged. You should, of course, hold on. The steps are these: push your left leg down, picking the right one up and over and down in one smooth movement. The propulsion which is caused will complicate the matter, so be careful!

If you are like most readers, you probably found the paragraph incomprehensible. But if we had said to you that the paragraph concerned mounting a bicycle, your comprehension would have been near perfect and on that basis you might have said the difficulty was 1 or 2, relatively easy.

A group of children were once asked to read the following paragraph, which they found very difficult. It is taken from a research article by Edward Thorndike (1917), entitled "Reading as Reasoning: A Study of Mistakes in Paragraph Reading":

> In Franklin, attendance upon school is required of every child between the ages of seven and fourteen on every day when school is in session unless the child is so ill as to be unable to go to school or some person in his house is ill with a contagious disease, or the roads are impassable.

You probably did not have difficulty with this item from a school board policy manual. In this case, and as was *not* true for the children in Thorndike's classic study, you could easily judge the topic of the paragraph and thus process the information. The readability levels of the two paragraphs, one about getting on a bike, the other about rules for attendance at Franklin School, are very similar. Why the difference in difficulty for the reader?

Susan Haviland and Herbert Clark (1974) have recently proposed an explanation that is intriguing. Much research has yet to be done on the matter, and these researchers are dealing with listening rather than reading, but consider what the following statement might mean for instruction in reading:

> According to a proposed Given-New Strategy, the listener, in comprehending a sentence, first searches memory for antecedent information that matches the sentence's Given information; he then revises memory by attaching the New information to that antecedent. (p. 512)

The key point here is that sentences contain information which the speaker (or author) provides not as "new" information but as "given" information, information which the listener (reader) already has. Thus the speaker cues the listener to that part of memory store to which the message may be properly attached.

Marvin Minsky (1976) has put this in slightly different terms with his notion of "frames." Whenever we try to understand anything, his model proposes, we do so by trying to relate it to a framework that we have previously constructed out of our experiences. Thus, if you had known that the earlier paragraph was about getting on a bicycle, you would have "pictured" certain expectancies for the paragraph before you began reading. Your "frame of reference," called to mind in anticipation of what the paragraph was to be about, would have given you a mental set for comprehension of what the paragraph said. Look again at the first sentence of the paragraph. Given a proper anticipatory frame, you would have known what you were to begin. As it was, you had no way to picture the event, and so you failed to understand the sentence. The same can be said for the second sentence; you couldn't picture what was to be accomplished. Your frame for getting on a bicycle was buried somewhere, and we weren't doing much to help you bring it into focus. A well written paragraph would be a help to the reader, and a good reader would constantly be modifying or adjusting his or her frame of mind on the basis of continually flowing information.

We confess we tried to write our bicycle mounting directions to *prevent* comprehension, done in fun and only to demonstrate a point. But for students in school, reading incomprehensible paragraphs is not such fun, though unfortunately what happened to you in the bicycle example happens frequently to them. Too often, when students are reading, they either aren't properly cued to an appropriate frame of reference, or their experiences have not led them to construct the frame they need. In either case, they don't understand what they read because they have no way to relate the message of what they are reading to what they already know.

In our view, the most important thing that could be said about reading is that it is the application of reasoning in an attempt to understand what is being read. In the sense that comprehension is the object of reading, reading is reasoning. In teaching reading, the task is to lead students through the method and logic of reading as reasoning. In other words, it is to help them to call to mind a proper frame of reference built out of their previous experience (something old) and, by a process of reasoning methodically and logically, to modify the frame in the light of understandings gained from reading (something new).

Any time a reader, despite best efforts, does not comprehend what he or she read, he has somehow failed to get the picture. It is possible that the vocabulary was too far removed from his experience, or that the logic of the writing was unfamiliar or too complex. It is also possible that the student didn't get quite the help needed in cueing to what was happening in the selection, didn't get quite enough help in "seeing" what the author was trying to say. The essence of reading instruction, we think, is to provide just such help as we will explain in terms of the content reading lesson.

THE CONTENT READING LESSON

The content reading lesson is founded on the idea of reading as reasoning. Lessons in content areas that require reading by students provide an excellent opportunity for teaching students about the reading process. That is, as students are directed and guided through the reading task, they can acquire a familiarity with reading strategies that will allow them to read better independently. The manner in which a lesson is organized, aside from what it includes, will determine its success in achieving its dual objective: acquisition of skill, understanding of content.

A content reading lesson can be organized to incorporate three basic parts, each of which is essential to maximal learning. These parts also reflect the integral components of the reading process, and as such they represent concurrently the theoretical and the practical aspects of reading instruction. These parts of the reading process and the content reading lesson are prereading anticipation, information search, and reflective reaction.

During prereading anticipation a reader actively seeks to remember all he or she knows relative to the topic of the selection to be read. Each of us knows a great deal about the world around us. What we know is stored in our mind, and it constitutes the frame of reference to which we must relate anything we try to learn. As we learn something new, we relate it to something we already know. The purpose of the prereading anticipation stage of a content reading lesson is to help students realize what they already know, and out of that to adopt an inquisitive mental set. Often students charge into a reading assignment without mobilizing their prior awarenesses. If they would first call to consciousness all that they know about the subject in a reading passage, that which will be "Given," they would vastly improve their chances of learning whatever "New" information they may find as they read.

Consider this concept another way. A student brings what he or she knows to a learning task, an entire cognitive structure. In this, there is little choice. There is much choice, however, about the degree to which that cognitive structure is organized and mobilized relative to the task at hand. If the student approaches a reading task without first thinking about what he or she already knows concerning the topic, learning will be minimized. On the other hand, if the student can have help in organizing his or her cognitive structure appropriate to the reading task, the chances of associating new information with prior knowledge will be maximized. Thus, comprehension will be much more likely to occur.

The purpose and value of the prereading anticipation component of a content reading lesson is to help students mobilize, call to consciousness, all that they have stored in their cognitive structure relative to whatever they are about to read. Without this component of a lesson, students will have to grope for bits and pieces of their cognitive structure as they encounter new information in their reading.

The second part of the reading process, information search, is unfortunately the only stage of the content reading lesson that students usually perform. Information search is, simply, reading. As you may have perceived by now, however, reading is not that simple. Different strategies for reading are required, depending upon the purpose of the reader and the nature of the material. Whatever the strategy, most students will benefit from guidance and direction. Exercises designed and used through the format of a content reading lesson will help students learn to choose appropriate strategies when reading on their own, will help in learning to form a proper frame of reference for questions.

The final stage of the content reading lesson, reflective reaction, is more elusive than either of the first two stages, but in some senses it is more critical. Passivity is the archenemy of comprehension. A very high percentage of what readers understand as they read is forgotten within a few hours. The exception often is that information to which the readers can react and upon which they can reflect. In effect, the purpose of this stage of the lesson is to help students reorganize their cognitive structure, adjust their cognitive framework, to assimilate the new information with the old information. That is why this stage is so crucial. Without it, new information may be only loosely attached in the cognitive structure and thus quickly forgotten.

For now, we hope you have gained a perspective of content reading lessons; what they are, why they are necessary, their purpose, and their parts. In the remainder of this and in the next two chapters we will focus on specific techniques of carrying them out.

As a final note, let us depict the content reading lesson in the form of a diagram:

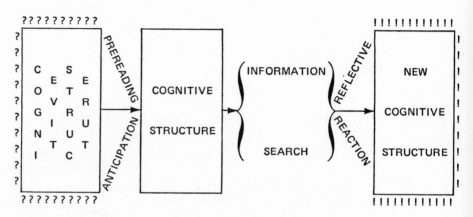

Figure 10-1   *Reading.*

ADVANCE ORGANIZERS

One man who has addressed the problem of how to bring readers to a proper mental set in anticipation of the reading task is David Ausubel. His idea is that we would facilitate comprehension by first providing readers with related information at a higher level of generality than the information in the selection that they are going to read. The device that he designed to supply that related information is called an advance organizer. The practical result of its use is to supplement, clarify, stabilize, and organize the readers' cognitive structure in anticipation of a reading task.

Translated into usage, the advance organizer is a short reading passage that precedes a longer selection and deals with the same topic on a higher level of generality. For example, Ausubel presented students with a short passage on "alloys" followed by a longer selection on "steel." His research showed that a clearer understanding of the general topic of alloys facilitated understanding of the narrower, hierarchically related topic of steel.

Under certain conditions, advance organizers may be helpful to students. Their use, however, would seem limited to situations where these conditions prevail:

1. The reader is at least passingly familiar with the topic of the reading selection.

2. There is good reason to believe that the advance organizer passage is clearly related to the learning selection in a higher to lower order of generality.

3. Students do see the logical hierarchical relationship.

It is not easy, however, to find short passages to serve as advance organizers to longer selections or textbook chapters. Furthermore, writing organizers is far too time-consuming to be feasible. The suggestion we offer is that teachers be on the lookout for passages that might be useful. That is, in your everyday reading there occur passages that can be used as advance organizers. Your awareness of the potential usefulness of the organizer technique will sensitize you to potentially applicable material when you come across it.

STRUCTURED OVERVIEW

Have you ever noticed how most students approach a reading assignment? If so, you probably know that the typical strategy consists of three steps. First, they open their books to the page where they are to begin; then they read once, often painfully slowly, to the end of the assignment; finally, they close the book. Because students approach a reading assignment this way, we chose to discuss the idea of the content reading lesson at a recent workshop we conducted for some content area teachers.

To introduce the idea of the content reading lesson, we began by discussing what we consider the essential ingredients of learning. We wrote the following diagram on a chalkboard:

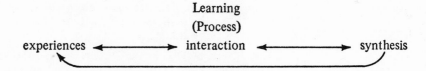

Learning
(Process)

experiences ⟷ interaction ⟷ synthesis

We said then that learning best occurs when the learner associates experiences to a learning task, interacts with the new information in the learning task, and then synthesizes findings with old experiences. That is the process of learning.

Next, we suggested that teachers often tend to utilize activities that are capable of stimulating learning in just this way, if used correctly. We then launched into the following discussion:

We: What strategies or activities do you use in your classroom to help students relate their experiences to a learning task?

Susan D. (science): I sometimes begin a unit by having the kids take a pre-test on the subject we're going to cover, but I tell them it's for fun. I mean, it's a competitive quiz sort of thing and some kind of prize is usually given to winners, but that way they'll get an idea of what they already know and what they'll have to learn.

Linda S. (math): Now I do something like that, only with vocabulary. When the kids are going to study about a particular theorem, I'll give them a crossword puzzle to work with terms they'll need to be able to use when applying or figuring out the theorem.

Betty H. (science): I do that too, but not in a crossword puzzle format. I list the new words on the board and ask if anyone knows them. When someone does, they'll tell us what it means, but the object is to see who can figure out what the new topic is that we'll be studying. That way all the kids can be involved.

Jody S. (art): I try to get kids to think about their experiences by showing slides sometimes. Recently, we were preparing to study post-impressionist artists, so I showed some slides of impressionistic paintings while the students identified characteristics of the impressionist period we had just studied. By doing this, they were better able to recognize the differences between those and the post-impressionists.

We: O.K., now. . . . Yes, Anne?

Anne R. (social studies): I just want to mention one other thing I often use for this—field trips or guest speakers. I know it's sometimes hard to work out all the details—with permission slips, busses, and all that, but I like to use these things to break up the monotony if nothing else. We just finished studying the legislative process in my government class so I set up a visit to our local courthouse where two of our state legislators showed us around, talked about their committees, and talked about the whole rigmarole of how they try to get a bill passed. When we got back to school, we talked about what we'd found out and the kids constructed several bulletin board displays (in teams) on how they thought it was all done. As we then proceeded to study the process, the kids made changes in their displays, but that initial experience really set them up.

We: Now, these are some of the things for our experience category. How about the interaction category we have here on the board? What activities do you use to help kids interact with new information in a learning task?

Susan D. (science): A lot of my students have trouble reading our textbooks so I try to have some experiments and that kind of activity for them to do. For example, in biology they just finished using big charts of the human body to figure out what parts of the body were involved in the digestive system and how they interacted with each other. Most of their learning about this came from examining the charts and then they went to read about some of the details in their text.

Clorien M. (English): I like to have lots of material around for kids to read. I'm teaching a unit now on propaganda, and I have students read articles from different columnists they select and then we discuss them in terms of their personal experiences versus facts, biases, and prejudices, radical ideas and so on. They try to identify methods and tricks authors use to influence others.

Fred L. (history): I have found that my students like some specific direction from me while they study so I give them a list of questions to answer while they study. That way I can steer them toward some of the major things I think are important. Sometimes I get the kids to help me make up the questions, too.

Donna T. (home economics): I have somewhat the same problem Susan has; my kids have trouble reading the textbook. I swear I think that book is written for Ph.D.s, but anyway I almost never use it. Instead I let kids go to the library or bring things from home. Sometimes I'll bring books and materials from the library to help them find information on things we're studying, but I always ask them to make up a list of places where they find good information so other kids can use that list to guide them toward information. That way they share their learning.

We: Good. Now, let's move on to the synthesis category. What might some of you do to help kids synthesize what they learn?

Susan D. (science): I use post-tests. That is, the same pretest I used with them. That way the kids find out how much they've learned.

Linda S. (math): Post-tests really do it for me too. That way kids work problems using what they've learned and they show what they've learned.

Tom C. (industrial arts): This is the whole focus in my teaching. This is where the kids make something or do something. It's the end product that's really the only important thing and they can see something tangible.

Carol B. (English): I ask kids to write reports or summaries of what they've read. Sometimes I ask them to pick a favorite character and explain whether they'd have done what he or she did and if not, what would they have done and why.

Tina C. (English): I prefer to have students synthesize by creating a collage or montage or something—or maybe to role play in a skit how someone would have done something. I agree with Tom, it's the utilizing and applying that's important in synthesis. Otherwise, how'll they ever transfer their book learning to reality?

While this discussion was going on, we listed the teachers' ideas on the board under the appropriate categories. When we finished this discussion, our diagram looked like this:

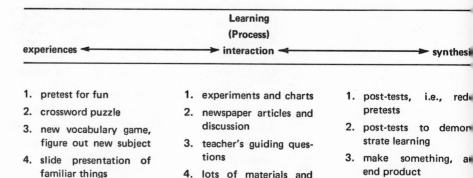

Learning (Process)		
experiences ← →	interaction ← →	synthesis
1. pretest for fun 2. crossword puzzle 3. new vocabulary game, figure out new subject 4. slide presentation of familiar things 5. field trip, followed by discussion and team-designed bulletin board displays	1. experiments and charts 2. newspaper articles and discussion 3. teacher's guiding questions 4. lots of materials and students list informational sources	1. post-tests, i.e., redo pretests 2. post-tests to demonstrate learning 3. make something, an end product 4. reports, summaries 5. collages, skits, role playing

It was then time for us to begin discussing the content reading lesson by applying the information collected during the construction of this diagram to the specific learning strategy of reading. To make this transfer, we introduced the terms *prereading anticipation, information search,* and *reflective reaction.* We did this by suggesting that when students read an assignment, they can enhance their learning by applying the three basic parts of the learning process. For example, they can think about what they already know about a subject by anticipating what they will find when they read. This is commensurate with the experience part of the learning process and can be called *prereading anticipation.* As students interact with print that is, as they read, they are trying to find and process information, so we might call that part of the process *information search.* After they have interacted with the print, they can then synthesize their learning by reflecting over what they have read and reacting to it. Thus, we can call this stage of reading *reflective reaction.*

Having discussed the ideas underlying the content reading lesson and the terms that apply to it, we then asked the teachers to get into small groups and to design a diagram that reflected the way that all these parts, including their ideas for doing it, were related. Once the groups had completed their diagrams, they shared them with other groups and then we constructed a diagram on the board which reflected the whole group's ideas. It looked something like Figure 10–2.

The diagram that was designed by this group of teachers with our direction is called a structured overview. Richard Barron, of Oakland University, conceived this idea, and research on it has continued now for several years. It is a process of associating students' prior knowledge with what is to be learned. In the case of this particular structured overview, the information to be learned was the concept of the content reading lesson, the ideas behind it, and various ways to use it. Having put together this structured overview, we then proceeded to discuss the ideas be-

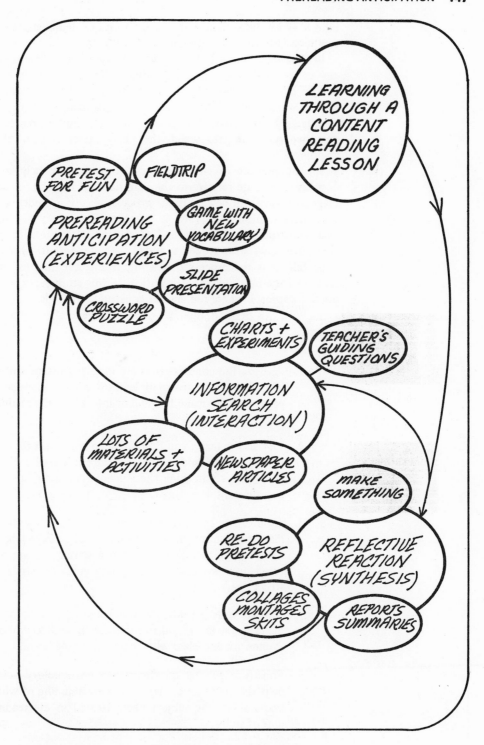

Figure 10–2   *A structured overview of the content reading lesson.*

hind it as we did earlier in this chapter and to demonstrate specific strategies that can be used to carry it out effectively.

The most important thing we can say about a structured overview is that the key to its effectiveness as a prereading anticipation device is that students participate in its construction. To the students, then, the structured overview is a process (notice we do not say "a product") of recognizing what they know and relating it to what is to be learned. It enables students to approach material with an organized cognitive structure into which they may integrate new information and understandings.

The purpose of the structured overview is to help students organize their cognitive structure relative to the material that is to be learned. The concept of a diagram is far from new, it is the *process* of getting students to relate old information to new information that is different from many teaching strategies. Rather than constructing a diagram and presenting it to students, a teacher must create these overviews *with* students, and it is to students to whom major responsibility must fall. It is the process that is important, not the product. It is the inductive nature of the procedure that is critical to this strategy, in contrast with a more deductive approach where the teacher constructs and tells.

With this in mind, then, we offer these general guidelines for the construction of a structured overview:

1. Analyze the concepts that are most important within a given reading selection or group of learning activities, especially those concepts most germane to the unit into which the reading and activities fit.

2. List all the terms you think may be important for students to know if they are to understand the material clearly. This list should include terms you think the students probably already know as well as important new words.

3. Arrange for yourself the terms you think students may not know. Place these terms in a diagram that reflects the relationships among the concepts being studied. (In a sense, you are building a structured overview that will help you guide the students as they construct one.)

4. Add to your personal diagram some terms that you think the students might know and might come up with as you discuss the basic framework and ideas with them during the lesson.

5. Construct guiding questions and introductory activities that will help the students come to an understanding of what they already know about the subject being treated in the reading selection or unit of study.

6. Inductively, help the students design a structured overview. You

might want to go back and reread the description of how we did this with the teachers in the workshop we conducted.

Having helped the students construct their structured overview, insert some of the new words into the final product where they make sense and where the students can see the relationship between the new terms and their own conceptual awarenesses. Once the final product is designed, it might be helpful to leave it on the chalkboard or to reconstruct it on a bulletin board enabling students to refer to it as they read and study. It may be you'll want to let students continually revise the overview to picture their understandings which come out in class discussion.

*, 3   As soon as possible, you should try this process with a group. Perhaps you'll want to begin with a small reading group. If possible, you might want to compare your results with other teachers who try it.

INSPECTIONAL READING

Good readers read for some purpose, of that there is little doubt. There is doubt, however, about how readers accomplish this, about how they manage to establish their purposes for different reading tasks. In any event, prereading anticipation is a definite part of purpose. Purposeful reading involves activity and expectancy. The reader searches for ideas with an expectancy of success. Therefore, we can state generally that any technique of introducing a reading task to students is a good technique if it facilitates activity and builds expectancy.

Adler and Van Doren devote a good deal of space to discussion of inspectional reading, and for good reason. This kind of reading is important since it is related closely to purpose and anticipation. To read inspectionally is to search for the form and structure of a selection, literally to inspect what might be read more carefully if the inspection reveals cause enough to read more deeply. A major part of development of good reading habits is development of the ability to decide whether and how to read a given selection. The content area classroom offers the finest setting available for this development.

The introduction of a chapter in a textbook to a group of students provides an excellent case in point. Preceding analytical reading, students can "thumb through" the text examining the illustrations, various headings, introductory and concluding paragraphs, and questions at the end of the chapter, all with an eye to establishing the mental set or frame of reference called for by the selection. Typically, this might take as much as twenty or thirty minutes. The fluent, independent reader can do this with no help and in less time than that. (You probably do so, for example, as you skim the newspaper looking for interesting articles. In every sense of the word, you are "inspecting" the paper to decide what you want to "read.") Students in a classroom, however, need help in the development of this important and highly sophisticated skill, inspectional reading. As they acquire facility with the strategy, they will become more and more able to actively anticipate as they read on another level. The information acquired from an inspectional reading heightens anticipation for more careful reading.

REQUEST

The topic of prereading anticipation would be incomplete without mention of the work of Anthony Manzo and his "ReQuest" technique (Manzo, 1969). Like many similar techniques, ReQuest is a procedure for getting readers to question before they read and to base their purpose for reading on questions. Unlike many techniques, however, ReQuest has built in a feedback and modeling feature which gives the student needed information. It works something like this:

1. Both teacher and students read the first sentence in the first paragraph of a selection.

2. The teacher closes his or her book and the students may ask any questions they wish related to that sentence. The teacher must answer. Where possible, comments (feedback) regarding question quality is given as well.

3. The students close their books and the teacher now asks any questions he or she wishes. These purposefully include 1) as many as might be useful to the students in terms of information and 2) the kinds of questions that students might emulate when their turn comes again.

4. The procedure is continued through a paragraph or two until students can be expected to reasonably answer the classic purpose question, "What do you think will happen (or be told) in the rest of the selection?"

ReQuest works and is to be recommended for one-to-one and small group teaching. Certainly it is useful for building anticipation and teaching students how to prepare themselves for reading, but there is more to ReQuest than just that. The procedure works, in our judgment, because it provides a chance for feedback and modeling. The students know when what they do is good and have an example of what to do. As you read through the Manzo article and/or try ReQuest, consider how these critical features might be incorporated into other techniques. The structured overview certainly lends itself to feedback and modeling. Can you see how other techniques might lend themselves also? How important is this, in your estimation?

*, 4

QUESTIONS: THE BUILDING BLOCKS OF ANTICIPATION

Notice that each of the techniques we have suggested related to prereading anticipation has somehow involved questioning. The structured overview and advance organizer imply, at least, the same questions as inspectional reading, and likewise ReQuest. Whatever else one might do to build prereading anticipation, the following three questions in some words or other would seem essential. The reader should ask himself or herself:

1. What is this selection about?

2. What do I know about this topic?

3. What might I expect to learn of the topic from this reading?

The importance of the idea behind these questions cannot be overemphasized. They are, in fact, construed here as the first step in the lesson framework we have defined as the content reading lesson.

ALLOW US TO SHARE

Before this chapter went to press, Ronaldo Cruz[1] shared with us his experiences in using the following handout. We think it's an excellent way to introduce students to the idea of prereading. You might want to consider adapting it for use in your classroom.

STEPS IN PREREADING

Prereading involves finding out what you are going to read about and making up questions that you want to answer when you read an assignment.

I *TEXTBOOK*

A. Find out what the subject of the assignment is
1. leaf through the pages of the assignment and find out what clues the visual aids (maps, graphs, pictures) can give you. Read the captions.
2. look in the table of contents to put this assignment in context with the entire course. What has gone before? What will come after?

B. Study the questions at the end of the chapter or section to see what the author thinks is important in the assignment.

C. Look carefully at the bold face type in the assigned pages. From this, make up logical questions that you can answer when you read.

[1] Our thanks to Ronaldo Cruz, of Adelante Institute, Tucson, Arizona.

II *NOVEL or PLAY (full length)*

  A. Read a plot summary (synopsis)
  1. *Masterplots*
  2. *Masterpieces of World Literature*
  3. *Oxford Companions*
  4. Front matter of most study guides
     a. Barron's Educational Notes
     b. Monarch Notes
     c. Cliff Notes

  B. Find a book in the library that contains critical commentaries about the book or the author. Look for something like *Twentieth Century Views Series.*

  C. Look through *Book Review Digest* for the year the book was first published. (Use only as a last resort or if you need critical commentaries by critics—especially good for contemporary plays and novels.)

  D. Use the study guide notes to preread each chapter or scene in the book.

  E. Make questions to answer as you read each chapter or scene.

III *SHORT STORIES OR POETRY*

Read the entire story or poem through once to determine the plot or characters. Pose questions about the dramatic actions and anything else you may need to know.

IV *NONFICTION MATERIAL*

  A. Look up subject in encylcopedia

  B. Read the first and last sentences in each paragraph

  C. Make up questions to answer

11

Information Search

In their search for information, students may find opportunities to practice a variety of reading strategies.

SUMMARY

Information search, the second step in the content reading lesson, is closely tied to the comprehension process. How people *learn* bears heavily on how and what to teach them; what comprehension *is* bears heavily on how to teach it. Comprehension is not a skill, it is not a list of skills. It is a practiced strategy of adaptation and flexibility exercised with the intent of understanding an author's message sufficiently well to satisfy the reader. The information search step of the reading lesson provides an excellent environment in which students may develop adaptiveness and flexibility under guidance and direction of the teacher.

Study guides are often useful in providing students with needed guidance and direction, though discretion must be exercised in their use. A study guide should be employed where 1) students perceive its worth as a help to them in understanding what they are studying; and 2) the guide has the potential to develop students' sophistication in comprehension of similar material.

Several types of guides suggest themselves on this basis. The three-level guide leads the reader to see comprehension as both a process and an outcome, varying in sophistication which begins with a literal understanding of the author's message. The organizational guide leads the reader to see the pattern of thought and logic of the author and to use the same in an attempt to understand. Concept guides are based on the idea that people remember what they can "chunk," or associate conceptually by categorizing within a cognitive structure.

153

WHAT IT WAS WAS . . .

Remember that football game we spoke of awhile back? What we said about it was that the object of the game is to move the ball and we drew an analogy between that and reading. Now, let's carry it one step further.

If we were to try to coach someone in how to play football, what would we need to know and how would we find it out? Offhand, several possibilities come to mind. We might view films of some of the great teams to analyze the way they work. We might talk to some football players, asking them how they play their position. We might play in a sandlot tag game at a picnic to get the feel of the game. But notice this: Football is a game understood only by an examination of the process of play. To know how to coach it, we would need to look closely at how it is done. Certainly, there are rules of football and strategies to consider, but they really only generally describe the play. They do not define it. Football is defined by its object, and knowing all the rules of football won't tell you how to move the ball or how to score points.

An almost precisely similar case can be made for the teaching of reading. And, as you will see, the content area classroom is the best place to teach reading, since the need to read is greatest there.

Consider this: What we know about reading is that its object is comprehension, and to teach people to accomplish the object, we must first look closely at what good readers do. It's like watching a great football player, a Jim Brown or a Gayle Sayers. By observing what they do, we can make conjectures about how they do it, about the way they do it. When we looked at Liz, Ron, Karen, and Mary, we asked ourselves what it was they accomplished when they read. Then we tried to make some qualitative judgments about their success in comprehending. Now, we want to look at what they actually seem to be doing as they try to accomplish the object of reading.

For example, the most important thing we know about how good readers read is that they read in different ways for different purposes. They seem hardly aware that they are constantly switching strategies. What's more, those purposes and strategies are highly individual and situational. And the essence of the strategies is not to be defined by a simplistic list of skills (reads for detail, reads for main idea, etc.) or by directives (skim, survey, etc.). Mature reading is best characterized by adaptiveness and flexibility, not by knowing the rules of reading. It is, among other things, a *creative* activity like any "languaging" behavior; it develops through practice and out of need.

In teaching reading, one must create situations in which maturing readers have a chance to explore and use appropriate strategies to suit different purposes. In content areas, this means using different sources dealing with a similar topic rather than relying on the same book for all students. This is part of the reasoning behind units of study as a motif for content area instruction.

What other characteristics can we observe in the behavior of a good reader? For one thing, the good reader seems to sort material by what it says and what it means. He or she reads for meaning. Often the reader will say, "The author said

_____, and by that I take him to mean _____." Or, "For *me,* the poet is saying _____." In both cases, the reader is reading beyond the literal message of the author. Robert Frost said, "Poetry is saying one thing in terms of another." The good reader knows that Frost did not mean *only* poetry.

Olive Niles, a luminary in the field of reading for many years, once said she thought there were three things that would distinguish the good reader. These were: the reader makes full use of previous understanding of the topic, reads with a definite purpose in mind, and, most importantly, looks for "various kinds of thought relationships which exist in reading materials" and uses these as an aid to understanding.

Yet another thing the mature reader will say he or she does is to process information by trying to understand and remember it in large chunks. Remembering a lot of detail is very cumbersome for most readers. What good readers try to do is to make groupings and associations based on concepts they are building. They deliberately sacrifice many details in the interest of deeper meanings.

In all of these strategies and behaviors, the student in the content area classroom can be helped. In giving that help, the teacher will be assisting the student in understanding what is being read and how to read better. The teacher does this when he or she identifies and provides strategies that facilitate the students' learning as they seek information in their reading. This is, in fact, the teacher's role in the second step of the content reading lesson, the step that we have called information search.

Before moving on, we feel compelled to repeat a particular point. What we have just done is to "diagnose" the reading act, examining the *general* behavior of good readers to determine what they do when they read. To teach reading, then, becomes a matter of creating an environment in which they have opportunities to practice good reading habits. But realize that *this step can be taken only when you know something about the specific reading behavior of your students.* Think again of the football coach. To teach football, he needs to know what good football players generally do and what his players specifically need to learn to do. He can know that only by looking at their specific behavior. Remember our earlier quote **, 2 from Frank Smith's "Twelve Easy Ways to Make Learning to Read Difficult, and One Difficult Way to Make It Easy." The one way to make it easy is *"Respond to what the child is trying to do."* Let us now extend the quote, if we may:

> Children learn to read only by reading. Therefore the only way to facilitate their learning to read is to make reading easy for them. This means continuously making critical and insightful decisions—not forcing a child to read for words when he is, or should be, reading for meaning; not forcing him to slow down when he should speed up; not requiring caution when he should be taking chances; not worrying about speech when the topic is reading; not discouraging errors . . .[1]

Now, how can we do that?

[1] F. Smith, 1973, p. 195

GUIDING THE SEARCH

This is the familiar scene. We have a group of students. They have something to read, and a reason to read it. If the material is close enough to their grasp, if what they have to read is approximately suitable, the reading will provide the practice that will make them better readers. What we need to consider are the specific ways in which we *can* respond to what the readers are trying to do. In other words, we need specific ways to provide the help students need in accomplishing the object of reading. Study guides of various sorts are one of those ways.

We will introduce three kinds of study guides which may be of value to students in different circumstances. We should emphasize, however, that what we are presenting are ideas, not prescriptions. The effective use of study guides in a classroom requires their creative adaptation to particular settings. Furthermore, study guides can be gratefully appreciated or resentfully rejected by students. Like Longfellow's child, when they are good, they are very, very good, but when they are bad, they are horrid. We therefore introduce study guides with the following cautions:

1. Study guides should not be used with every reading selection required of students. They should be reserved for reading selections that warrant careful reading and with students who need the special help a guide can offer.

2. Study guides should provide help in understanding specific content and should give direction in the application of appropriate reading strategies.

3. Format variety is essential. Don't let boredom with the procedure interfere with quality of the product.

4. Study guides must not be graded. To do so is to make tests of them when their purpose is to teach. They should, however, be checked and discussed with individual students when possible.

5. Study guides do not "run themselves." Certainly students may use them with relative independence, but guides work best when students share them in groups and are familiar with the way study guides work. Students feel better about study guides when teachers are available for help when needed.

THREE-LEVEL STUDY GUIDES

Among the characteristics of a good reader is the ability to go beyond what an author explicitly says to determine what was meant and how the message can be more generally applied. When diagnosing the quality of a reader's comprehension, a basic consideration is how well the reader can go beyond the explicit message to the inferential and applicative levels of understanding. Remember Liz, Ron, *et al*? When guiding a student's search for information, teachers can use a three-level study guide to call the reader's attention to higher levels of meaning within a selection. At the same time, exposure to these guides will help a student explore the processes through which he or she can understand the same thing in different ways.

**,3   The three-level guide was conceived by Harold Herber (1970). He bases the idea upon a hierarchical relationship among what he has defined as the literal, the interpretive, and the applied levels of comprehension. That is, a certain degree of success with the literal level would seem requisite to interpretation, and likewise success at the interpretive level is requisite to application. For example, almost any literate person can know what the authors of the Constitution said simply by reading the document. What the authors meant, however, let alone how it applies in a given instance, requires a comprehension eluding most people. The Supreme Court sits in judgment of exactly such questions: What does it mean? How does it apply? By providing students with three-level study guides and helping them work through them, a teacher can lead students to seek higher levels of meaning. While their attempts may not always be successful, readers are never successful without the search. Remember how turtles make progress: by sticking their necks out. Only by seeking can answers be found.

*,5   As an illustration of the three-level guide, work through the one which follows and, if possible, compare your responses to those of one or more other persons. By the differences in response to such a simple story, you may see that reading is quite a creative process!

LITTLE RED RIDING HOOD[1]

Level 1 — What did the author say? (check two)

_____ a.   Red Riding Hood met a wolf in the woods.

_____ b.   Red Riding Hood visited her aunt.

_____ c.   Red Riding Hood recognized the wolf immediately upon entering Grandmother's house.

_____ d.   The woodsman killed the wolf.

Level 2 — What did the author mean? (check two)

_____ a.   The wolf only wanted the goodies meant for Grandmother.

_____ b.   The wolf appeared a lot like Red Riding Hood's grandmother.

_____ c.   Red Riding Hood was a naïve little girl.

_____ d.   Red Riding Hood was a trusting little girl.

[1] *Our appreciation to John Childrey of Florida Atlantic University for sharing this one with us.*

Level 3 — How can we use the meaning?

_____ a. Don't walk in the woods alone.

_____ b. Don't speak to strangers.

_____ c. Look more carefully at sick grandmothers.

_____ d. All's well that ends well.

_____ e. Don't send a little girl to do a nurse's job.

This particular study guide is much more structured than most designed for classroom use. However, it does illustrate the kinds of thinking the three-level guide may stimulate. An important feature of the guide is that the higher the level of reaction, the more individual may be the responses. That is, at level 1, reactions are limited since either the author said what is indicated or did not say, and the question is easily resolved. At level 2, however, the reader is required to think a little harder in making judgments and at level 3, there are virtually no limits to the applications that could be argued. The *use* of what an author said and meant is highly individual and students' reactions at this level are often exciting and creative.

Notice also that where statements in the guide are inconsistent with the story, it is for good reason. For example, it is *not* true that Red Riding Hood recognized the wolf immediately upon entering grandmother's house. In fact, her failure to do so is one of the problems on which the plot of the story turns. The same can be said at level 2. Note that the inference that the wolf only wanted the goodies is contrary to the intrigue and danger of the story. As any child could tell, Red Riding Hood is in big trouble and more than her goodies are in peril. It is precisely such judgment that is critical to inferential reading of any selection, whether it be a children's story or a treatise on a philosophical topic or scientific inquiry.

**, 3   The idea of a study guide based on "levels" of comprehension is presented by Harold L. Herber in his *Teaching Reading in Content Areas* (1970) to which the reader is referred for a fuller description and many excellent examples. One of Herber's ideas is that the levels operate interdependently, that the applied level operates in relation to the product of the interpretive and literal levels and that the interpretive level operates in relation to the product of the literal level. Furthermore, Herber suggests that greater sophistication is required of the reader at succeeding levels and that differentiation for varied ability levels may properly be made by requiring each student to respond only at the level(s) commensurate with his or her ability.

In our own experience, differentiation of instruction is more successfully accomplished by variation in material used than by variation in understanding expected. In other words, better a student be given material he or she can read fully (at all levels) than that the student be restricted by the material to lower levels of response. Recall the basis we take for organizing units of instruction: that all students come to different but individually better understandings of the same concepts through study in different materials and activities. Thus, with every student working in material that is appropriate to his or her needs and abilities, all individuals are allowed opportunity to respond at equally sophisticated "levels."

The disparity of ideas we are exploring here leads us to a rule of thumb for the use of guide material. *Use study guides as aids to carry students' understanding to as high a level as the nature of the material and the ability of the students will allow.*

Steps in constructing the three-level guide

The construction of any study guide requires careful analysis of 1) the selection to be read; 2) the purposes of the lesson in which it is included; and 3) the needs of the students relative to that purpose. Construction of a three-level guide often begins at level 3. This is necessary where the underlying reasons for teaching the selection relate to the "transfer effect" the selection may have. The guide should build toward this transfer of learning, the application of new understandings to other settings. Thus, as the *first step,* you would consider possible generalizations of the basic ideas of the selection.

For example, a social studies teacher may be teaching a unit on *Practice and Principles of Democracy,* part of which includes the study of suffrage. The general application of the concept of suffrage leads into participatory government, equal rights of minorities, responsibilities of citizenship. Level 3 of a guide to comprehension of a selection on suffrage might focus on ideas of this type. By initiating his or her own thinking at the most general level, the teacher creates a mind set which tends to focus thinking at other levels on ideas that lead in the right direction, i.e., toward reasonable transfer and application of ideas.

The construction of a three-level guide moves from the general to the specific. This is necessary because the importance of a specific idea is derived from its relationship to a more general idea. Detail, or what the author said, will be judged important in terms of the inference it can generate, or in terms of what the author meant. Thus, when the purpose of the lesson is to foster an ability to generalize, the *second step* in constructing a three-level guide is to devise level 2. Think of level 2 as comprised of the possible inferences which might be drawn from what the author said. Include inferences that lead directly from the literal level to applications. In other words, allow inferences to stem from what the author said, but think simultaneously in terms of level 3, the application level.

Referring again to the example of the social studies selection on suffrage, perhaps the author has said much about suffrage for various groups—landowners, freemen, blacks, women, teenagers, other groups. What the author has *said* is that these groups gained suffrage at various stages of our history. What he or she might have *meant* to imply could be that "suffrage is earned, not given," or "people's right to vote is an inalienable right," or "those who can vote, should vote." Such inferences lead to *applications*—"persons' rights often must be fought for," or "participatory government requires participation of the governed," or "civil rights, like muscles, require exercise for their maintenance." Inferences that bridge the way from the literal to the applied levels are the ones you should include in a guide.

Part of the purpose of a guide is to help the student "tie things together," to see relationships of ideas within and without the context of what is being read. This interrelatedness of the levels of the three-level guide is critical to proper understanding.

The *third step* in constructing this kind of guide is to examine what the author said and to select only those details that are essential to making the inferences included in level 2 of the guide. Detail is important primarily as the foundation of inference. Part of many students' reading problem stems from an inability to sense the relative importance of general ideas and specific detail. Naive readers lack the ability to separate the chaff from the grain, the important from the irrelevant, in the face of the incredible detail of many textbooks.

Often as not, it will be necessary to vary the procedures we have outlined for three-level guide construction. The primary reason for teaching a particular selection may be to lead the student to "see" the author's implications. In such cases, the focus of concern will be on level 2, the inferential level of comprehension, and so construction of the guide would begin there. That is, you would begin your thinking with this level and balance the other levels on it.

Take a look at the guide on cigarette smoking, for example. What the teacher intended with this was to get the students to realize what the data on smoking are telling us, beyond mere facts and figures. You might think at first that the applicative level (level 3) was most important in this guide, especially where the interest was in getting high school pupils to take action about their own habits. On second thought, though, we know that no one just *quits*. People only quit smoking when something about the *meaning* of smoking finally overcomes their desire to smoke. Because the force of the article on which this guide is based is in the inferences which can be drawn from it, its construction would center on level 2.

We have found it convenient here to discuss the steps of construction of a three-level study guide in a one-two-three fashion. Actually, we do *not* mean to imply that one completes construction of one level, then moves to another and another. In practice, you will probably find yourself working on all parts at once in constructing a guide. Our point is that the product of your work will be best if your thoughts carry you, in general, from either level 3 or level 2, depending on your major purpose in the lesson. But, for example, you will often find that what you perceived to be a reasonable line of thought (in level 2 or 3) is not adequately supported by the facts (level 1). So you switch tactics midstream. Likewise, as you examine the literal level of the selection, you may be led to applications and inferences you hadn't before considered. So what you must do is to work back and forth between and among levels of comprehension, searching for a clear and precise guide which will lead students to understandings and thought processes which they can eventually take as their own.

"100,000 DOCTORS HAVE QUIT SMOKING CIGARETTES"

I. Answer these:

1. How does smoking one cigarette affect these body functions:
   a. circulation

Thanks to Juanita Hutton, health and physical education teacher at Sahuaro High School, Tucson, Arizona, for permission to use this guide as an example.

    b. respiration

    c. temperature

2. How do death rates and morbidity rates relate to smokers?

3. How many doctors have quit smoking?

4. Is the damage done to the body by smoking reversible? How?

II. Explain why you agree or disagree with each of the following:

1. Smoking is directly related to lung cancer.

2. There are more heart attack victims among smokers than non-smokers.

3. The more cigarettes smoked per day, the higher the death rate.

4. Cigarette smoking is an expensive habit.

5. There is no excuse or reason for smoking.

6. Smoking is a detriment to the quality of the smoker's life.

III. You may find it interesting to answer the following questions:

1. Does your family doctor smoke?

2. Does anyone in your family smoke?

3. How many of your teachers smoke?

4. Why do you smoke (or not smoke)?

       One final comment about this kind of study guide. The question often arises of how guides can be used without unduly limiting students' thinking. The paradox is one of how to stimulate thinking without telling people what to think: How can we teach but not tell, instruct but not indoctrinate? At the risk of oversimplifying an answer, we would say that guides should be as structured as necessary to stimulate thinking. As their familiarity with the procedure increases, students will adopt the process, will gradually stop looking for "right" answers, and will start thinking much more creatively. As this happens, loosen the structure of the guide. Let students have more freedom for open-ended response, at the application level at first but at all levels later. What you will see is that students themselves can write guides, can use the procedure, for example, as a notetaking system, as a motif rather than a model of thinking. When that happens, the guides will have served *, 6 their ultimate purpose, to habituate in students the process of comprehension they orginally sought to stimulate.

PATTERN GUIDES

       Often it is true that the manner in which a reading selection is organized is its most salient and useful characteristic. That is, where a reading selection has been written in a clearly discernable pattern, that pattern may help the reader understand in the same way it helped the writer compose. For the pattern to help, however, the reader will require, first, a knowledge that organization exists in composition and, second, practice in utilizing the organizational pattern of the text to good advantage.

There are several thought relationships an author may use. Most commonly, these are comparison-contrast, cause-effect, sequence (chronology), and simple listing. Also possible are other patterns such as categorization and taxonomy, logical argument (induction and deduction), general idea/specific detail and spatial arrangment. In fact, any form which a writer might employ could be included under the idea of "patterns of organization." What the good writer tries to express by the form chosen is the relationships among the ideas expressed. These relationships are as valuable to the reader as to the writer.

Let's consider now four ways in which students can come to know patterns of organization. Following this, we will offer suggestions for practice in using the patterns in reading.

First, perhaps the best way to teach what organizational patterns *are* is to show pupils various examples taken from their textbooks. Texts generally do have an overriding pattern in their organization, but within that will be embedded various other patterns used by the author to organize "single sentences, . . . paragraphs, . . . selections of various length," to use again the words of Olive Niles. Often these patterns are evident in the author's use of "signal" words which you can call to students' attention. For example, where an author is setting up a contrast, he or she will often use the conjunction *but*. A comparison calls for the conjunction *and*. A simple list may use the terms *first, second, third,* or *first, then, last.* Similar terms are used when an author has begun with a main idea and is listing supporting details. A cause/effect pattern will often be cued by terms like *because, as a result, if/then,* and *consequently.* Temporal organization is commonly distinguished by such terms as *after, before, by, within, since, until,* and *finally.* Students need help in seeing these terms and in using them as an aid to comprehension. Providing that help is often a matter of scanning the text with the students, searching for "organization words" which might be used in reading.

Second, the purpose of inspectional reading, suggested by Adler and Van Doren, is to answer the questions, "What is the structure of the book (or other reading matter)" and "What are its parts?" It would be helpful to all readers if they were to attempt to answer those questions of anything they read. With regard to teaching, it is almost always helpful, even necessary, to "walk" students through the process of inspecting what they are about to read as an assignment. As they perceive the logic of the organization of their book, chapters within that book, and key sections within those chapters, students' understanding is facilitated and their reading ability enhanced.

A third technique of teaching patterns of organization is to have pupils look for examples of various patterns in newspapers, magazines, and other sources they may find. One teacher's idea was an attractive bulletin board, entitled "How Do You Say?" and containing examples of different organizational schemes of sentences, paragraphs, and short selections. The examples were supplied by the students. It is also possible to construct games for learning centers on organizational patterns, where students compete in time and accuracy of categorizing examples of patterns.

From time to time almost all content teachers require writing assignments of their students. These may be short essays, term papers, observational records, extended answer exams, and so forth. When it is required, instruction in composition provides one of the best possible opportunities for teaching logical organization. Writing and reading are in some ways mirror images of one another. Organized writing is generally good writing, mainly because it is easy to follow and comprehend. But when you read a composition written by a student, what are you looking for and what have you done to help that student write? Anyone who makes writing assignments should at the very least remind and explain to students that he or she expects an introduction, a body, and a conclusion. Surprising as it may seem to some, however, the skills involved in outlining, arranging ideas before writing, revising before final copy, in short, the rudiments of composition are not the strict domain of English classes. They are a part of "languaging" and instruction in them is imperative wherever they are required. The pity is that so many opportunities for teaching writing and reading simultaneously are ignored! Our fourth and final suggestion of how to make pupils aware of organizational patterns is to give them help in organizing their own writing. Help them use organization words themselves, to organize from topic sentences, to arrange details in logical fashion, to "clinch" their ideas with a snappy ending. The result could easily be better writing and reading for everyone concerned.

**, 3

When students have at least a basic understanding of organizational patterns, study guide material which guides practice in using the patterns in reading will be useful. (Following ideas from Olive Niles and others, Harold Herber originally conceptualized guides for organizational patterns. Reference is again made to Herber's book as a source of further explanation and examples.) The patterns guide might be no more than a skeleton outline listing main ideas under which the students fill in detail. Other patterns guides might list causes and have pupils fill in effects, or list both causes and effects and have pupils match them as they read. List one half of various comparisons or contrasts, let students fill in the other halves.

*, 7

In the units section, you will find examples of pattern guides constructed by teachers for students' use. Using these examples as models and following the suggested steps listed here, you may wish to try your hand at constructing a pattern guide to accompany a textbook selection you are using.

Steps in constructing the pattern guide

The *first step* in constructing this guide, as any, is to carefully analyze the purpose of the lesson and the nature of the reading selection. Look for the overriding logic the author has chosen. Underline key words the author has used, if any. If you can classify the organization of the material, you may proceed to construct a guide based on that pattern. Not all writing yields easily to such analysis, however. *TAKE CARE:* use patterns guides only for material in which a clear organizational pattern exists.

The *second step,* once the pattern has been identified, is to look for key statements that reflect that pattern. At times, these key statements will have to be created from inference since they may be implied rather than stated. For example, consider this passage from Grace Halsell[1] in which she sets up a comparison be-

---

[1] Grace Halsell is author of *Bessie Yellowhair,* an account of life among the Navajos. Social studies teachers would find this sensitive book an excellent source in a unit on American Indians.

tween the way of life of modern man and that of the American Indian:

> You sleep on dirt floors, on sheepskins. When you wake up, you don't need to get dressed, because you have slept in your clothes. There are no windows in the hogan; it's dark as a dungeon. (*Excerpted from an address by Grace Halsell, reprinted in the* Washington Post, July 29, 1975).

The comparison/contrast pattern in this paragraph is implied. When *you* awoke this morning, you were probably in a bed covered with soft sheets. You got dressed, having slept in night clothes. And so forth, the comparisons and contrasts are implied.

Within the same selection, however, other comparisons may be stated directly. Examine the comparison in the following passage, from the same source:

> We've been taught the work ethic; we've been taught to want the good things in life, as we define them: good salary, good house, good car, a good carpet on the floor. None of us really wants to go back to sleeping on dirt floors.

> But the Indian, if he remains Indian, is tied to the land, which he calls his Mother Earth. He never attempts to conquer nature, but to live in harmony with it. He wishes to be like a fish in the sea, a bird on the wing: to pass by without leaving a trace of his existence. *Being,* not achieving, is important. (Grace Halsell, *ibid.*)

Now, examine part of a simple study guide for this selection. Grace Halsell's intent is to help the reader see how the life of the Indian is different from the life of the modern person. The guide will be set up to help in this.

LIVING AS A NAVAJO

Directions: The selection entitled "Living as a Navajo" on p. 16 contrasts the lifestyle of Bessie Yellowhair with the lifestyle we have. Listed below in *Column A* are things that apply to our life. Read these. Then read the selection and beside each item in *Column A*, list in *Column B* a contrasting aspect of Navajo life. Number 1 is done for you.

Column A	*Column B*
1. We sleep on beds.	Navajos sleep on dirt floors.
2. We wake up in light.	
3. Achieving is important.	

4. We want a good salary,
   house, car, etc.

5. Etc.

In the example, we have completed the *third step* in constructing a pattern guide. This step is to construct the guide in a way that reflects as clearly as possible the pattern you hope students will see. The best rule here is not to assume too much; give students all the help they may need. The patterns guide can be as simple or as complex as the nature of the selection, purpose of the teacher, or needs of the student may demand. The guide we began here, for example, gives the implied half of comparisons, asks for the stated half. More thinking would be demanded (and more creativity) if the opposite were true. A third or fourth column might be added which would set up a structure for syntopical reading with reference to previously studied cultures. Still more creativity and skill might thus be required. How much to demand and how much to assist with a guide is impossible to decide outside the context of a given situation. As you construct guides, however, attempt to make them as challenging as possible and as helpful as need be in reference to the abilities and needs of the pupils who will use them.

There is one more example we'd like to share with you before moving on to a third kind of guide. In some materials, the pattern of organization of material is absolutely critical to comprehension. This would call for extraordinary care in understanding the pattern, as many a home economics teacher knows.

READING RECIPES

If the oven is to be used, **locate temperature required.**
Think ahead! And at the appropriate time preheat your oven. Light your oven before assembling your ingredients. It will take about 10 minutes for it to reach the temperature desired.

PART I MATERIALS

READ through the **entire recipe** with special care.

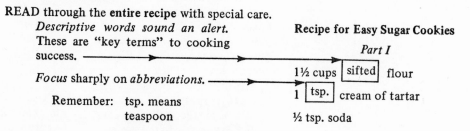

Descriptive words sound an alert. These are "key terms" to cooking success.

Focus sharply on *abbreviations.*

Remember: tsp. means teaspoon

Recipe for Easy Sugar Cookies

Part I

1½ cups sifted flour

1 tsp. cream of tartar

½ tsp. soda

Reprinted from Improving Reading in Every Class, a Sourcebook for Teachers, *Second Edition, by Ellen Lamar Thomas and H. Alan Robinson.* © *Copyright 1977 by Allyn and Bacon, Inc.*

Tbsp. means
tablespoon

¼ tsp. salt

Note carefully *quantities* you'll need. ————————————————→ ½ | cup | shortening

1 egg

Unknown terms say STOP! LOOK! LEARN!

½ cup sugar

A single word left unknown may ruin your batch of cookies. The index of your cookbook or its "List of Terms Used in Recipes" should give you "instant access" to the meanings.

½ tsp. vanilla

ASSEMBLE your **ingredients** and **utensils**.

STOP

Then doublecheck. Reread Part I of the recipe to be certain you have everything.

OVEN TEMPERATURE 375

PART II METHOD

Carry out all the **steps** one by one in the **order given**.

Notice that the ingredients are conveniently listed in the order in which you'll use them.

CAUTION

Watch for special *action words,* for example: ————————————————→

Part II

Sift   Beat
Cut in   Mix

1. Sift together flour, cream o tartar, soda, and salt

and perform the technique called for. Remember that specific words are used for a purpose. Though some words may *seem* to differ only slightly, there is a *decided* difference in the action called for and a world of difference in the way your cookies may turn out!

2. | Cut in | shortening until lik fine crumbs

3. Beat egg with sugar and vanilla

Focus on *descriptive words.* ————→

4. Add egg mixture to flour mix ture and mix well. Dampe hands with water and roll int balls the size of walnuts.

"Zero in" on *amounts, timings, temperature.*

Quantitative directions are "danger spots"

5. Place balls 1½ inches apart o an | ungreased | cookie sheet.

Carry out each step **with great care!** For example, add the egg mixture to the flour, **not** the flour to the egg mixture.

6. Flatten first cookie with bo tom of dampened glass tumble

7. Dip tumbler into the sugar an then press all the cookies.

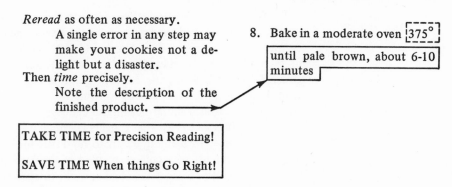

Reread as often as necessary.

A single error in any step may make your cookies not a delight but a disaster.

Then *time* precisely.

Note the description of the finished product.

8. Bake in a moderate oven 375°

until pale brown, about 6-10 minutes

TAKE TIME for Precision Reading!

SAVE TIME When things Go Right!

CONCEPT GUIDES

Concept guides are a third type of guide that often stimulates students' understanding. These guides are based on the proposition that for learning to occur, one must first be aware of an idea and then associate it with something already known. In other words, concept guides are based on a theory that learning is a two-step process. First, the learner becomes aware of an idea. The trigger step in successful learning is cognitive awareness. Second, the learner must categorize awareness by relating it to previous experiences or ideas. That is, once awareness is achieved, learning occurs when the idea is associated with something familiar through a categorization process. In that way, the learner places the new idea into cognitive perspective. Thus, stimulated by concept guides, learning occurs in somewhat the following way:

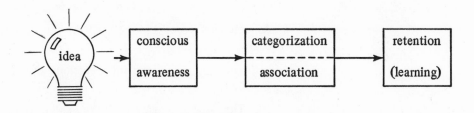

idea → conscious awareness → categorization / association → retention (learning)

The theory behind concept guides is related to a psychological process called "chunking." Derived from information theory, "chunking" is presumed to be what the human brain does to compensate for limitations in processing and storing bits of information. Consider this example. Say the following numbers aloud, one at a time: 194114921215. Repeat them several times, so that you might remember them two days from now. You will likely find, however, that it will be almost impossible for you to remember them in two days unless you saw that there are only three, not twelve, things to remember: the dates of Pearl Harbor (1941), Columbus' discovery (1492), and the Magna Carta (1215), all of which you probably know or could likely remember. What you would do with this information is to "chunk" the twelve numerals into three dates.

To retain information, then, a learner "groups the input events, applies a new name to the group, and then remembers the new name rather than the original input events" (Miller, 1967, p. 38). Ausubel (1968) has defined chunking as the "process of rearranging the stimulus input into a more efficiently organized 'sequence of chunks' " (p. 59). Thus, the concept guide is designed to make the learner consciously aware of discrete bits of information and then help chunk the facts, inferences, and ideas into more meaningful conceptual units through categorization and association. It is awareness that triggers learning; it is association that synthesizes it.

This theory of learning seems to hold true for much more complicated information than the list of numbers we used in the preceding example. People remember what they can associate into higher order categories. Students in a social studies class, for example, might find it easier to remember the conflicts between the North and South leading to the Civil War if 1) they studied characteristics of the North and of the South, and then 2) were guided in categorizing the information in terms of similarities and differences between the two cultures. Thus, they would be more likely to conceptualize the idea of conflicting ideologies as they chunked the bits of information about each.

Similarly, in teaching a unit on the parts of the body, a biology teacher would be particularly concerned that students understood the relationship of the various parts to one another and to the roles each plays in the process of living. By constructing a concept guide, these understandings can be fostered. For example, the first part of such a guide might be concerned with identifying the proper terms relative to their specific job. Thus, the first part of the guide might look like this:

PARTS OF THE HUMAN BODY

Concept Guide

I. As you read pages 114–121, fill in the right word from choices below.

1. The＿＿＿＿＿＿controls reactions of all parts of a human body.

2. The＿＿＿＿＿surrounds the pupil of the eye.

3. The＿＿＿＿＿is a part of the brain.

4. An＿＿＿＿＿pumps away from the heart.

5. The＿＿＿＿＿is a bone located in the leg.

6. The end of the nose is composed of＿＿＿＿＿.

7. The＿＿＿＿＿is a large muscle inside the mouth.

8. ＿＿＿＿＿protect the eye.

9. ＿＿＿＿＿protects the lungs.

10. The entire human body is a mass of＿＿＿＿＿.

1. artery	9. cartilage
2. tongue	10. bone
3. iris	11. femur
4. vein	12. eyelashes
5. muscle	13. pupil
6. cells	14. ribcage
7. cerebrum	15. skin
8. brain	16. cells

Having provided the students with a conscious awareness of the key "bits of information" in the selection, the next step might be to help them relate these "bits" to the higher order concepts of internal and external parts of the body. Thus, a second part of a concept guide might be:

II-B: Group each of the body parts which you used to fill in the blanks in Part I under one of the two categories below:

Internal Parts	External Parts

This will enable the students to associate the specific parts of the body to one another and to begin to associate each with their respective roles in the total process of living.

To extend the students' learning to the specific functions to which each body part is related, a third part of the guide could be designed.

II-B: Write each of the ten body parts under one or more of the following senses with which they are associated.

Sight	Touch	Taste	Hearing	Smell

Steps in constructing concept guides

Construction of a concept guide follows the same process inherent in the learning theory that it represents, except the construction process is the reverse of the theory. Briefly, the construction steps are:

1. Analyze the reading passage to determine the major concepts the students should acquire. List each in a word or phrase.

2. Reread the passage and select statements that underlie the major concepts chosen for emphasis.

3. Arrange the guide so that the statements from the selection become Part I of the guide and the categorization component becomes Part II.

The first step in constructing a concept guide is to analyze the selection *and* your purpose for having students read it. Determine the major concepts you want the students to learn. (Your unit objectives should provide some guidance in this determination.) List each concept in a word or, at most, a phrase. This will form Part II of the concept guide, the higher order categories under which informational bits may be organized and associated. The number of such categories should be limited, as the purpose is to facilitate learning, not tax it.

When the major concepts overriding the information in the selection have been determined, the second step in constructing this kind of guide is to reread the passage so that you can select (or reword) statements from it that underlie those concepts you want to highlight. Those statements you choose to use must be directly related to the concepts on which the selection focuses.

The statements from the selection form Part I of the guide; the categories, or overriding concepts, form Part II. In format, they occur as headings for columns. The first two steps completed, there remains only to arrange the guide's physical format. As the third step, then, place the information generated in step two (notice: *step two,* not Part II) in a format similar to the format used in level I or level II of a three-level guide. Insertion of distractors is sometimes advisable, but the distractors should be deliberately worded to be in error for good reason. When using true-false items in Part I of a concept guide, students can be asked to reword false statements to make them true, thus avoiding the danger of students' remembering a distractor as truth.

Now, consider the following example of a concept guide based on the novel *A Patch of Blue.* The teacher chose prejudice, love, intolerance, sincerity, and fear as the concepts the students might acquire. The quotations in Part I were then chosen because they, or parts of them, would lead to an understanding of the concepts. A reminder: The form of activity in Part I is limited only by the imagination of the teacher, but care must be taken to make the activity accurately reflect the content of the reading selection. In the example here, italicized portions of the quotations were used as the basis for transferring items to the concepts in Part II. Often the whole item would be used. In completed form, a concept guide derived from *A*

*, 8   *Patch of Blue* might look like what follows. (You might want to work through it yourself, if you've read the book or seen the movie.)

A PATCH OF BLUE

Concept Guide

Part I   In the space provided, identify the speaker. For the moment, disregard the italicized portions of each quotation; they will be used later. You will probably not remember who said these particular words directly, but thinking about what is said should help you determine the speaker.

_____   1.   *"I wear them* (dark glasses) so I will not have to *show people my true feelings."*

_____   2.   "Without *tolerance* there can be *no friendship."*

_____   3.   "I can *never be like you."*

_____   4.   *"I got to come home and clean up* after the *biggest slut of all."*

_____   5.   "You are not only beautiful, you are *brave and beautiful.* I never saw a braver one than a *blind girl sitting under an oak tree in a park."*

_____   6.   "You are my *much sinned against baby."*

_____   7.   "Leave Sleena be. You *God damned nigger."*

_____   8.   *"Pearl,* I love you, Pearl."

_____   9.   *"Niggers is black.* You want to have a *black friend?"*

_____   10.   "It was crazy to be *out of the room."*

Part II   Below you will find five terms related to this novel. Take each of the italicized words or phrases from Part I and write them under the term(s) to which they apply. Be prepared to justify your choices.

Prejudice   *Love*   *Intolerance*   *Sincerity*   *Fear*

Once a concept guide is designed, how might it be used? First, have the students respond by:

1. Identifying the correct responses to the items in Part I (in this case by identifying the speakers.)

2. Categorizing the statements or parts of statements from Part I under the proper concept(s) in Part II.

Second, provide the students with feedback. This may be accomplished in teacher-led discussions with the entire class and/or in student-directed, small group discussions. The students should be encouraged to express their own ideas and to support their opinions with references to the text wherever possible. They should also be urged to explain their responses to the guide.

Another example of a concept guide may help to illustrate its flexibility and possible extensions. In this case smaller bits of information, vocabulary, serve as the initial activity and the interrelationship of characters and concepts serve to extend the thinking process. This guide is divided into three parts, but each is based on the dual concept of cognitive awareness and association. (You may also wish to work through this one if you've read the novel.)

*, 9

THE OUTSIDERS

Concept Guide

Part I From the list of words below, choose the one that best fits the definitions given.

conscientious	vulnerable	lonely
tolerant	bitter	empathetic
sensitive	understanding	responsible
straightforward	naive	prejudiced
charming	amicable	haughty

_____ 1. responding or feeling acutely

_____ 2. standing apart from others; being isolated

_____ 3. attractive; fascinating; delightful

_____ 4. involves knowing right from wrong

_____ 5. sympathetic awareness

———— 6. a fixed notion or conception based on prior experiences

———— 7. direct; honest; open

———— 8. easily hurt

———— 9. ability to share another's feelings or emotions

———— 10. readily assuming obligations; dependable

———— 11. feeling and acting superior

———— 12. friendly

———— 13. not suspicious; foolishly simple; childlike

———— 14. being free from bigotry or prejudice

———— 15. a strong feeling of hatred, resentment, cynicism

Part II   "If the shoe fits . . ." If the words in the left column apply to the characters below, put a check in the proper box. Be prepared to justify your answers.

	Pony	Soda	Darry	Johnny	Dallas	Randy	Cherry
conscientious							
vulnerable							
lonely							
tolerant							
bitter							
etc.							

Part III   Below you will find several major concepts which were included in *The Outsiders*. List each character in the book according to the concepts with which they are associated. Be prepared to justify your choices.

Brotherhood   *Prejudice*   *Sensitivity*   *Maturity*

A concept guide can be used whenever it will help students understand the concepts in a passage and/or will lead to an improvement of students' conceptual skills. However, to maximize the potential success of concept guides, they should never be used as tests. The students should not be threatened by being "wrong," as it is the thought process that is right, not the answers themselves. In many cases, more than one answer can be "right." The *process* must be the focal point of the feedback.

*, 10   Having done all this, you are probably ready now to construct a concept guide for trial and evaluation. Pick a selection in which there are certain but limited concepts being developed by the author.

COMBINATIONS, PERMUTATIONS, ADAPTATIONS

An understanding of the three different guides we have discussed is only a bare bones beginning. The true value of study guides in learning is in the creation of them to fit the specific needs within a classroom, not to force the format of any one of them to a passage. Often a selection that you want your students to read does not lend itself to the purposes or format of any one of the specific guides we have discussed. Instead, you will discover that you need to pick and choose elements of two or all three of these specific guides if you are to provide the most appropriate guidance for your students.

Once you become comfortable with each of the guides separately, you will almost certainly feel the constriction imposed by each, and you will recognize the need to become more flexible and adaptive in creating guides. When that happens, you will have reached a milestone in becoming adept at using study guides for both

*, 11   diagnosis and instruction. Since combination guides must evolve from direct instructional needs, we suggest that you examine some of the examples included in the units provided in the final section of this book. Then, try your hand at constructing one.

As with the construction of each of the other types of study guides, we urge you to begin your construction of a combination guide with an analysis of your instructional objective and the overriding concepts in the selection. From there, the format and content of the guide should be limited only by the students' needs and your imagination. Happy permutating!

STUDY GUIDES: AN AFTERWORD

It is important for you to realize that study guides are but a part of a total lesson framework. Because it is important, we beg your indulgence with what may seem like repetition. The lesson framework we refer to includes prereading anticipation, information search, and reflective reaction. A study guide is neither necessarily nor sufficiently the central substance of any one of these parts. A particular danger with study guides of which you need to be aware is that they may be oversold and overused. They absolutely must be *adapted* to a set of circumstances, not *adopted* as a motif of instruction. What we have been able to present here and what you may find among the examples provided in the units included in the final section of this book will be useful as it can be modified to suit the purpose of a given setting. The guides that will work best for you are those you create, and that's why we believe that good teaching is dependent upon imagination and creativity.

On the other side of the coin, we should also point out that study guides are intended as more than just a set of chapter ending questions in disguise. For perspective, we can contrast the approach assumed by study guides with the approach often assumed by textbook questions.

TEXTBOOK QUESTIONS vs. STUDY GUIDES

Textbook Questions	*Study Guides*
1. Assume reading skill	1. Develop reading skills
2. Emphasize questions	2. Emphasize content/skills interrelationships
3. Tend to ignore individual differences	3. Can compensate for individual differences
4. Tend to test	4. Tend to facilitate learning
5. Focus on recall	5. Focus on conceptualization
6. Foster passive learning	6. Foster activity
7. Emphasize product of learning	7. Emphasize process as well as product (*how* as well as *what* was learned)
8. Promote memory	8. Promote problem-solving
9. Correct answer is the solution of differences	9. Reasoned premises and conclusions explore differences in search of understanding
10. Create dependence	10. Build independence

Textbook questions as an aid to information search

We do not intend to leave you with the impression that textbook questions are necessarily negative in effect. They are not, any more than study guides are a cure-all. It is quite possible that if the textbook being used is reasonable in terms of students' ability, then the questions at the end of a chapter or section can be of value. Their main value may be, however, in prereading anticipation. Not their answer, but the *asking of* good questions fosters comprehension. Thus, in discussion before and after reading, textbook questions can be used as guides to the germane parts of the textbook selection. If used in this way, they may act to guide students' reading in the sense of helping them see what to remember or consider most carefully.

12

Reflective Reaction

The opportunity to reflect and react to what one has read
solidifies learning.

SUMMARY

The purpose of reflective reaction is to allow readers to examine relationships
between what they know and what they have read. People remember what they can
relate; people comprehend what they can integrate into their cognitive structure.
Students need to understand that reading comprehension, if by that we mean
understanding what is read, does not stop with the end of the act of reading. It
continues as understandings are deepened in reflection.

Small groups of students are the logical classroom entity for reflective reaction. Most groups will require some teacher participation and direction, unless the
problem for which the group is constituted is very clear to group participants.

Guide material used in the information search phase of the reading process
can be a good stimulus to small group reflection. Students often need and appreciate the opportunity to explain and defend their reactions to guide material while
seeking to understand others' differing reactions.

The advance organizer is a short passage of content similar to but conceptually more inclusive than a longer reading selection. It is read in advance of the
main selection. But it may also be read in succession of the main selection, and
hence the term successive organizer. A group of students who have read the source
passage may read a syntopically similar but conceptually broader selection as a basis
for their reflective reaction.

The structured overview, similar in theory to the advance organizer, may also
be used as a stimulus to post reading reflection. The overview of a unit of study is a
benchmark to which students may refer repeatedly as their study progresses. They

may also construct their own overviews in different settings, both in reflection and anticipation of further study.

MEMORY, COMPREHENSION, AND REFLECTION

As the queen said to Alice, "It's a poor sort of memory that only works backwards." Those of you who are also friends of Alice and the queen, like us, will know that no one has the power of the queen to "know" the future. She, of course, could determine it in many ways. But so can readers when it comes to determining what they will learn. As the queen continued, good memories "work both ways." For the skilled learner this is certainly true. One of our recurring themes is, therefore, that what one knows determines what one can learn. That is, knowledge that can be transferred from one cognitive setting to another serves as the anchor for new knowledge. The pre-eminent concern of education should be to help students become learners, to help them develop skills and knowledge on which to base future understandings and attainments. Good learners need two-way memories.

The value of anything learned and remembered is determined by whether it 1) relates to and modifies or supplements previous understandings and 2) nurtures future learning by providing scaffolding on which memory and understanding may be built. As we have been saying all along, success in the search for relationships between what is known and what is read as new information is the major determinant of comprehension. This search, however, does not commence and cease simultaneously with the act of reading. The search begins in anticipation and continues through reflection, both of which involve tying what is being learned to what is already understood.

Comprehension is constructive. To understand, even to remember the most trivial fact, human beings must integrate what they learn into their cognitive structure. Comprehension is not to be confused with simple memory, however. Indoctrination requires only memory and belief; education requires, in addition, comprehension and understanding. Presumably, schools are in the latter business, that of education, of developing comprehension and understanding. If so, students must be given opportunities to carefully and critically construct those understandings which are appropriate to their individual cognitive needs and abilities. One of the best times for this is while one reflects and reacts to what is read or experienced.

*, 12   Mature readers often seek the opportunity to reflect and react with others about what they have read or learned. Discussion and criticism of the current bestsellers is common fare of conversations among adults. People can be heard everywhere talking about news stories they have read. This need to share and discuss is ubiquitous in a literate society, and it should be instructive to those of us who teach reading. When they are sharing, mature readers are reflecting and reacting, and are saying, in effect, "This is how it seems to me; how does it seem to you?" By comparing their reactions and reflections together, two or more people usually gain a deeper understanding than any one of them could accomplish alone. Because of its importance to them as mature readers, a major part of teaching read-

ing to young readers should include opportunities to develop and exercise the habit of reflective reaction.

THE VALUE OF SMALL GROUP INTERACTION

There are several reasons for our continued recommendation of small groups as the prevalent organizational pattern for teaching subject matter and reading skills. In the context of reflective reaction, perhaps we should address this topic most directly. We will discuss post-reading activities in this chapter with the assumption that students will have an opportunity to discuss what they are studying. We will further assume that the setting of that discussion will be in small groups involving five to ten students only.

The primary value of the small group is that it allows differentiation of assignment by interest and ability. By teaching a class of pupils in three or four subgroups, flexibly arranged with different individuals comprising the groups at different times, it is much easier to individualize with efficiency. A good rule of classroom organization is to teach to the largest subgroup possible given the nature of the subject and the needs of pupils. With the variation that inevitably exists within a class of pupils, most reading assignments will necessarily be made to subgroups of the class. Put another way, it is hardly possible that everyone in the same class be able and need to read the same thing. Fortunately, it is not necessary that they do so, given proper classroom organization.

If discussion groups are to work well, it is recommended that the teacher exercise control over who is in the group and that he or she participate with the group. This is easiest to accomplish where individual students receive assignments in the form of a weekly log, as described in chapter 9. This places the teacher in rather direct control of group composition. Students can quickly learn a routine of gathering in a small group activity as a part of the content reading lesson. This activity commences with prereading anticipation under teacher guidance; from there proceeds to information search, done by students more or less independently; and culminates with reflective reaction, again under teacher guidance for at least part of the time.

There are some conditions under which small groups may function well without direct teacher guidance. Such groups are those formed for solution of specific problems. In a classroom setting, these problems characteristically involve such activity as investigations in science, simulation exercises in social studies, problem solving in math and related subjects, and role playing or dramatization in literature. Many other examples might come to mind, but the problems that are best solved by self-directed groups are those with the following three characteristics: 1) the problem requires multiple-step solution, where each member can offer something to the solution and no member is likely to have all the steps at his or her command; 2) every member of the group understands the problem and values the group in the sense of believing that the solution will more likely be reached by the group than by an individual; and 3) the resources for solution of the problem are readily at hand.

Whether or not under direct supervision of the teacher, small group work is usually the best setting for reflective reaction. It provides the opportunity for pooling ideas, providing the basis for new associations that one person might never come to alone.

REFLECTIVE REACTION TO STUDY GUIDES

Where used as a part of the information search stage of the content reading lesson, study guides can easily serve as the stimulus for reflective reaction. For example, having completed a three-level guide, students can compare their individual responses to the guide in the setting of the small group, seeking to follow one another's reasoning through the levels of comprehension. Similarly, for other sorts of guides, students can compare and discuss their reactions in the context of reflective reaction. The teacher's purpose in this small group setting is to moderate the discussion, seeking to involve as many individuals as possible.

Students should not get the idea that the reaction group is formed to "check" or "grade" the study guide. The guide is a catalyst for thinking and discussion. It is not a test of comprehension. Every student in a discussion group does, however, have two major responsibilities. First, each should be able to explain and defend his or her reaction to a reading selection. Second, all students have a responsibility to understand their peers' opinions and reactions. They needn't accept contrary interpretations, nor should they be expected to. But if people can dare to be different from one another, they must feel that others will try to understand.

The rules for reflective reaction are therefore these:

1) Disagree with reason, not disputation.

2) Everyone deserves understanding, but no one should demand acquiescence.

Where everyone understands the meaning of these rules, discussion may be fruitful and reflective reaction productive.

Think back to your own reaction to the study guide for Little Red Riding Hood, for example. If you compared your responses to those of others, you may have found differences. In effect, this particular guide asks the reader to decide on the best use of the meaning of the story, forcing a qualitative decision. Your decision may have been different from another person's since people seldom see exactly the same meanings or applications of the same story. But many positions are arguable, many are understandable. The point is that having taken one or another position, each person has the responsibilities of 1) defending his or her own choice with reason and 2) understanding alternative choices made by others. The reflective reaction stage of the lesson is designed to let students do these things.

SUCCESSIVE ORGANIZERS

Typically, the lesson plan of the textbook includes suggestions for "extension" activities, activities appropriate as "follow-up" to a reading selection or group of related stories. Unfortunately, this part of the lesson is often given short shrift as time runs out on the teacher's best plans. One reason the suggestion is made for follow-up activities is to provide students the chance to reflect on and react to what they have read, especially in light of new but related activity and reading. Often, the suggested follow-up is for additional, topically similar readings that students complete individually and discuss in a small group.

It is possible that David Ausubel's theory of advance organizers bears implication for post-reading reflection as much as for prereading anticipation. That is, readers may profit as much from a "successive" organizer as an advance organizer, as much from an organizer that "succeeds" as an organizer which "precedes." Related information at a higher level of generality and inclusiveness than the information in the main selection to be read need not necessarily precede the reading to affect its comprehension.

For example, suppose a group of students in an earth science class has completed reading a chapter or selection on minerals in which the major emphasis was mineral identification. As it happens, minerals are defined by such features as luster, hardness, color, crystal, streak, and cleavage, all of which are related concepts. For example, hardness is measured in terms of whether one mineral will scratch another, color varies along a continuum of values, luster is reflected light judged against other materials regarded as standards, etc. A grasp of the idea of relational comparisons is prerequisite to fuller understanding of mineralogy and mineral identification. Following the reading about minerals, therefore, students might be asked to read a short selection on relational concepts and to move from that to discuss their reading of the selection on minerals.

Another idea, and this might be more appropriate for less advanced students, would be to succeed the selection on minerals with a shorter organizing selection on rock formation. Minerals compose rocks. Therefore, some understanding of rocks could lend perspective to the study of minerals. Discussed in the perspective of their occurrence in nature, minerals might be more easily understood. The successive organizer, the selection on rocks, would lend such perspective.

THE STRUCTURED OVERVIEW AND REFLECTIVE REACTION

The structured overview, introduced earlier as a stimulus to prereading anticipation, may find its most flexible and creative use in the setting of reflective reaction. There are several forms that the structured overview idea may take as a catalyst for reflective reaction.

In most cases, the structured overview may display graphically the interrelationships of concepts. It can provide a framework for interim discussion in the progress of a unit. Furthermore, it may serve different groups of students in their reflection over different readings related to similar concepts. This is possible because when units of study are organized around concepts for emphasis, all reading and study required of pupils by the unit is related to one or more of the concepts. It is these concepts that have served as the basis of the unit and that should serve as the focus of any reading selection in the context of the unit. Therefore, in their reflective reaction to a particular reading selection, students often find it helpful to try to relate what they have read to what they have anticipated *vis a vis* an overview of the unit or some part of it. In effect, they are thus setting what they have read in the context both of what they know and what they are studying.

The research of Richard Barron (Barron and Stone, 1974) who, as we mentioned before, first proposed the structured overview concept, bears directly on the question of using the structured overview *after* rather than *before* reading. His suggestion is that students may construct their own overview (now called a *graphic post organizer*) by arranging and rearranging 3 X 5 cards on which have been written terms related to the concepts underlying the reading selection. The attempt would be to devise an accurate, graphic account of interrelationships of ideas understood from the reading. Having done this, a group of students can then easily compare their display with that of other groups and with the overview of the unit.

A similar way of using the structured overview idea to stimulate reflective reaction was recently suggested by the work of a group of high school teachers in Petersburg, Virginia. As an introduction to a unit of study, these teachers assign a general reading to all groups, a reading that surveys the major concepts in the unit. The reading might, for example, be a chapter in the textbook. Group members read the selection the best they can in the setting of the content reading lesson. Following that, each group discusses the selection in terms of what seems to them to be its major concepts. In the form of a structured overview, they seek to graphically display the concepts and their interrelationships, and the relationships of the concepts to other ideas. Each group submits its overview for review by the teacher, who makes passing comments. At the next class session, each group is given ten minutes to display and defend its overview to the rest of the class. Discussion is lively! The result of all this is that students have a chance to read and reflect and to build out of that reflection an anticipation of the content of a unit of study. The concepts of the selection are the concepts for emphasis in the unit as a whole. What these teachers have done is to combine creatively the strengths of both reflective reaction and prereading anticipation through the use of student-constructed structured overviews.

CINQUAINS: SYNTHESIZING

The synthesis which may come from reflective reaction is a most powerful learning experience. Time spent reflecting about the meaning of something learned will often establish it in the learner's cognitive structure. We have tried to suggest ways in which to provide an environment conducive to that reflection. In closing, we want to make one further suggestion. We think it has unlimited possibilities and are excited about sharing the idea with you. It is certainly the most creative technique we've seen for getting students to reflect and react.

The cinquain (pronounced: sǐng · kā́n) is a five-line poem of this definite form:

The first line is a one-word title.

The second line is a two-word description of the topic.

Line three is three words expressing action of the topic.

The fourth line is a four-word phrase showing feeling for the topic.

The last line is a one-word synonym that restates the essence of the topic.

Here is one done by a girl after reading about geological disturbances:

> Volcanoes
>
> Red hot
>
> Erupting from within
>
> Nature's furnace of fire
>
> Inferno

Another example is one that one of our students did for us in reaction to what we call the Foxfire principle:

> Foxfire
>
> Fluid, active
>
> Participating, sharing, learning
>
> Glow in the dark
>
> Illuminating

*, 13

You try some now. Think of a topic, any topic. Say, someone you love. Your parents. Your children.

Next, do one on the subject or some concept you teach in school. Try it out on your students.

Then, ask them to do and share some with the whole class. First do one about any topic, then about school, then about something they've enjoyed learning.

To write cinquains requires thought and, usually, the deeper the thought, the better the poem. The deeper the reflection, the more permanent the image.

What we like to do is have individuals do cinquains on a common topic and then combine their thoughts into one poem. These group poems can then be shared on bulletin boards, or read to the class for discussion. The power of cinquains in reflection is axiomatic. The beauty of them is that they *require* the reflection they are supposed to stimulate. Their use knows no limit of content area, or intelligence level, or reading ability. Kids love them, and they work.

Reflection

Retrospective thinking

Requiring cognitive reorganization

Demanding a rewarding, growing

Reaction

13

Developing Meaningful Vocabularies

Knowledge of vocabulary reflects a stage of understanding.

SUMMARY

Vocabulary development, like vocabulary diagnosis which we discusssed earlier, is intimately tied to conceptual development. It is not a matter of teaching words but of providing the opportunity for students to develop understanding. Then, the expression of those understandings will require vocabulary to which students are systematically exposed as a part of vocabulary enrichment.

The major thrust of vocabulary development activity in content areas should center on understanding and meaning. Meaning exercises, recognition exercises, and word study exercises must be coordinated with one another and timed appropriately with students' growing conceptualizations. Matching exercises, categorization activities, and various word puzzles may focus on meaning. Word games such as cryptograms and word hunts, so popular with people of all ages today, are appropriate for building word recognition. Word sort activities, as we describe them, are useful for word study; basically, these activities involve exploration of *how* words mean.

Perhaps we could best introduce this chapter by saying that language is *essentially* ambiguous. What a word means to any two people must be different, for if it were exactly the same, their experiences and hence their conceptualization associated with the word, would need be the same. *Exactly* the same. And that is both impossible and undesirable if language (or anything else) is to work. Thus, the meanings which students have for words (notice that words don't have meaning; people have meaning for words) are essentially different. The purpose of vocabulary development is to allow people to share their individual experiences and to provide them opportunity to have common experiences out of which may grow a richer meaningful vocabulary for every person involved. Thus what they study may come to make better sense and find better expression in the students who come to understand it.

THE MÖBIUS STRIP, A CIRCUITOUS ENIGMA

No one would deny the importance of vocabulary to understanding anything. Much of what is written about reading suggests that the first step in teaching concepts is to teach vocabulary. Common practice in elementary schools is to "preteach" the "new" vocabulary before reading. Secondary materials often follow the lead and list important vocabulary at the beginning of each selection. So why don't we just take up the cadence and go directly to a discussion of ways to build students' vocabularies? Well, we think we hear a different drummer and want you to listen with us for a moment.

Vocabulary facilitates learning; it is neither a requisite for nor the final product of learning. It is inseparable from conceptual development, and to try to make the separation is to get trapped by the paradox of the chicken before the egg. At the risk of oversimplifying, we might say that a word is merely the label for a concept; without understanding the concept, students have little need for the label. As Lavoisier, the father of chemistry, said, "It is impossible to dissociate language from science or science from language, because every natural science always involves three things: the sequence of phenomena on which the science is based; the abstract concepts which call these phenomena to mind; and the words in which the concepts are expressed." (Antoine Laurent Lavoisier, *Traité Éleméntaire de Chimie.*)

The vocabulary/concept paradox creates problems for students and teachers alike. First, to think abstractly and to communicate effectively about content area subject matter, students need to know the labels (i.e., vocabulary) for the concepts. Second, before they can meaningfully assimilate the labels, students need to associate those labels with the concepts they represent. Thus, it appears that we've come full circle. Can we escape from this Möbius strip?

The thrust of what we are saying is that vocabulary instruction is not the teaching of words but the teaching of meanings. Perhaps even that oversimplifies it because meaning is of a variety of sorts, parts, and stages—always in stages, never a matter of fact. At any rate, what we are suggesting is no more than what James Michener was saying in *Centennial* when he described Potato Brumbaugh's acquisition of two words important to him,

> He was only a peasant, but like all men with seminal ideas, he found the words he needed to express himself. He had heard a professor use the words *imprison* and *replenishment* and he understood immediately what the man had meant, for he, Brumbaugh, had discovered the concept before he heard the word, but when he did hear it, the word was automatically his, for he had already absorbed the idea which entitled him to the symbol. (p. 678)

Can you hear that drummer yet?

VOCABULARY DEVELOPMENT IN THE CLASSROOM

Plans for a unit of study should include specification of concepts, description of phenomena to be experienced, and delineation of the vocabulary that may come to have meaning for students. The question this raises, then, is: What vocabulary should you specify for emphasis in a unit?

In some instances the question of what vocabulary to highlight in activities seems easily answered. In math and science, for example, technical terminology is often highlighted by textbook authors. But is this a good way for a teacher to identify vocabulary for emphasis? Actually, we think not. Our own rule of thumb is this: *Vocabulary important enough to teach is vocabulary required for students to understand the concepts being taught.* Since a single textbook provides only one avenue for learning major concepts, highlighted vocabulary in a text provides only a general clue to the words that should be emphasized.

The best way to determine the vocabulary for emphasis in a unit of study is to form a list of all the possible terms that you consider relevant to each of the concepts to be studied. In doing so, you can include terminology at various levels of sophistication. In effect, what we are suggesting is that you make a concerted inspection of the vocabulary of each unit of study. From that inspection, choose the vocabulary that should be included.

For example, when designing a unit on forms of government, a social studies teacher might list this and similar concepts for emphasis: "Democracy is government 'of the people, by the people, for the people.' " What are the important words that come to mind when we recite this idea? Equality, representative government, constitution, self-government, home rule, vote, Congress, law, populace, people, public, majority rule, common man, silent majority, plebian, proletariat, democrat, republican, etc. Dozens of words can be listed. In effect, a thesaurus can be built for the unit as terms relevant to each concept are listed. From this can be selected those words that, at various levels of sophistication, represent the kernel or basic ideas underlying the concept. Certainly not all the vocabulary relevant to a concept will come to have meaning for all students. However, from such a broadly inclusive list, a teacher can select words of varied sophistication and incorporate them into a variety of exercises designed to enhance vocabulary development for students of varying ability.

INTRODUCING THE LABELS

In our discussion of the content reading lesson, we emphasized that prior knowledge is a major contributor to new learning. It stands to reason that this principle would apply to learning new vocabulary as well as to anything else. Thus, when new vocabulary is introduced, it should always be done in the context of familiar ideas. Perhaps that means that structured overviews would be most appropriate where students actively participate in their creation. Perhaps word association activities or an informal discussion about a topic should precede students' intitial encounter with new vocabulary. The most effective, hence appropriate, strategy would necessarily be determined by the situation, but the principle holds true for almost all cases. Teach vocabulary and concepts as if they were part and parcel of the same thing *and* keep both in close proximity to ideas and terms with which students are already familiar.

VOCABULARY ACTIVITIES

Like Potato Brumbaugh, students will naturally "pick up" some of the vocabulary of anything they come to understand better, much as young children acquire words to express relationships that they come to understand. Through their experience with activities related to concepts, they will find some meaning for the words in which the concepts are expressed. Experience with words in specific vocabulary activities is essential, however. Vocabulary cannot be left to chance without considerable risk: risk either that words may have little or incomplete meaning for learners or that learners lack the proper terminology in which to express their understandings. Vocabulary activities must be designed to allow systematic exploration of words in relation to concepts, to phenomena, and to other words.

Vocabulary we will use to mean recognition and understanding of words and meaningful word parts. One may at times, in other contexts, see *vocabulary* used to refer rather loosely to word recognition and analysis skills, namely phonics, structural analysis, and use of context. Such skills, though necessary for reading, are only indirectly the concern of the content area teacher. Not only that, but each of the skills, phonics included, *presupposes* meaning. In other words, meaning is the primary object of vocabulary development viewed from any perspective. It would therefore probably be helpful to reserve the term vocabulary for reference to the idea of understanding and using words. Certainly, as students develop understandings of words, their skill at recognizing those words is enhanced by familiarity. But that skill and familiarity is incidental to an increase in understanding of word meanings. While there are recognition practice activities, which students may enjoy and from which they may profit, the major thrust of vocabulary development activity in content areas should center on understanding and meaning.

It is too often the habit, if not the intent, in content area instruction to incorrectly do one of two things in the name of vocabulary development. It is only too easy either to assume students have or will learn meanings for words "on their own" or to require that pupils look words up in the dictionary and "copy the meaning and use the word in a sentence." Meaning is not copied from a dictionary. Valuable as they are, dictionaries are notoriously circular in their definitions: their stock in trade is the synonym. A dictionary's main worth is realized only when the person who uses it already possesses a firm grasp on the concepts and phenomena to which a word is related. Where this is so, the dictionary can be a great help in refinement and nicety of *definition*. It is only definition, i.e., preciseness, and not meaning, however, which the dictionary can provide.

How many students have heard the terms sine, cosine, tangent, cotangent, secant, cosecant, and yet have not now or ever understood the concept of trigometric functions? How many have learned to spell and copied definitions for terms like tragedy, climax, denouement; or sonnet, epic, meter, verse, cadence, metaphor?

It would have been possible for these same students to have understood the concepts to which these words are related and to have only then met the words. Lacking the concepts, the words remain hollow shells in the recesses of the memories of most people who once "learned" them.

To insure that students do acquire the meaning of vocabulary in a way that honors the natural way in which meaning grows for individuals, the following principle must govern: Provide students the opportunity to explore word meanings concurrently and as a complement to their conceptual development. That is, where they are most effective, vocabulary activities are appropriately integrated and timed with concept development and experience of phenomena. Several different kinds of activities and exercises may be utilized, each of which we can now present with explanation and example.

**, 3 The three kinds of exercises that we will present may be classfied roughly as meaning exercises, recognition exercises, and word study exercises. These labels are similar to those used by Herber (1970) and several of the exercise types we discuss have their origin with him. Each will be described in its turn, but by way of introduction we should emphasize that our classification is more convenient than real. Perhaps they are seeds for a program of vocabulary development in content areas. Rooted firmly in the ground of meaning, we believe they can be developed into valuable learning exercises.

MEANING EXERCISES

These are exercises aimed directly at helping students firmly attach words to concepts. Their purpose is to expand the vocabulary of the learner to fit an improving conceptual framework, to provide the vocabulary demanded by a capacity for nicer distinction. This means that the words they focus on must be seen by the learner in the context of the phenomena under study. The observation, experiences, discussion, reading, writing, and all other activities designed to enhance students' conceptual development form the context in which meaning exercises may be effective.

Meaning exercises bear an important relationship to other vocabulary activities which we call recognition and word study exercises. These latter two should, as a rule, be followed by meaning exercises. Recognition and word study exercises may focus on dimensions of vocabulary other than meaning, or, that is, focus on meaning only indirectly. They will need follow-up, therefore, with meaning exercises if the primary goal of vocabulary activity is to be honored.

Perhaps it won't be taken as redundancy to make the point that meaning exercises can be difficult and inappropriate unless students are well on their way to understanding the concepts on which the terms in the exercise focus. If students do not have some grasp of the concepts, vocabulary exercises of any sort can be so difficult that they become mere drill, impossible to relate to anything. Any exercise must be simple enough for performance by most, if not all, students and must not assume the strength it seems to build. Furthermore, specific and detailed directions and examples should be provided regarding the proper performance of the exercise. This will usually guard against confusion.

Matching exercises   This type of meaning exercise seems very simple, and in fact it is little more than a recognition exercise. It does, however, concern meaning and is so categorized. Vocabulary items are listed in two columns on a sheet, in random order. They may be synonyms, antonyms, roots and derivatives, terms and definitions, etc. The task for the learner is to match the items in one column with those in the other. The form is familiar:

$$\underline{\hspace{2cm}}\ 1.\ \ldots\ldots\ \ \ \ \ \mathbf{a.}\ \ldots\ldots$$

$$\underline{\hspace{2cm}}\ 2.\ \ldots\ldots\ \ \ \ \ \mathbf{b.}\ \ldots\ldots$$

$$\underline{\hspace{2cm}}\ 3.\ \ldots\ldots\ \ \ \ \ \mathbf{c.}\ \ldots\ldots$$

$$\underline{\hspace{2cm}}\ 4.\ \ldots\ldots\ \ \ \ \ \mathbf{d.}\ \ldots\ldots$$

etc.

*, 14   Students are asked to place the lower case letters in the blanks before the arabic numerals to indicate a match between the items. Consider this exercise:

_____	1. diamonds	a. lowest suit
_____	2. spades	b. one suit higher than clubs
_____	3. clubs	c. one suit higher than diamonds
_____	4. hearts	d. highest suit

The novice bridge player who works this exercise may become more familiar with the relationships among suits. Notice that the exercise tends to be self-correcting. If a mistake is made, it is apparent in the failure of a subsequent match. In other words, a person can reason his or her way to the correct answer even if he or she has only partial understanding of the terms. This is a desirable feature of such exercises since it allows relatively more teaching and less testing. All exercises should have this feature built in whenever possible.

Here is another exercise of the same type, again set up so that errors are somewhat self-correcting. Match the symbols on the right (lettered a., b., c., etc.) with the definitions on the left (numbered 1., 2., 3., etc.) by placing letters in the blanks before the numbers. If you come to a definition that you cannot at first match with a symbol, skip it and go on. From those matches of which you are sure, you may be able to figure out the ones of which you are unsure.

*, 14

	Definitions	*Symbols*
_____	1. identical with	a. $>$
_____	2. not identical with	b. $=$
_____	3. not greater than	c. $\equiv$
_____	4. equal to	d. $<$

_____ 5. is to; ratio   e. $\neq$

_____ 6. greater than   f. $\geqslant$ or $\geqq$

_____ 7. greater than or equal to   g. $\approx$

_____ 8. not equal to   h. $\not>$

_____ 9. less than   i. :

_____ 10. congruent to   j. $\not\equiv$

Some of the symbols in this exercise may be unfamiliar to students, but almost all will know at least the equals sign. By deduction and elimination the others may be reasoned out if the student has even the vaguest idea of how the definitions and symbols fit. For example, if = means equals, the best guess for not equal might be $\neq$ which is correct. By deduction, | must mean not. If the student couldn't remember > and <, he could deduce it from $\not>$, not greater than. Notice that $\not<$, not less than, is not included since to have done so would have been to require complete knowledge of the symbols being taught.

Many exercises of the matching type are, unfortunately, better tests than teaching tools. It is admittedly more difficult to build the self-correcting (i.e., teaching) feature in, but it is that feature more than any other that makes such exercises worthwhile.

Categorization exercises

*, 14

One of the best and most flexible of meaning exercises, the categorization exercise may frequently serve as a good follow-up to matching and other types of exercises. The basic form of the exercise is the categorical column head based on concepts to which terms are related. For example, an exercise related to a unit on nutrition might look like this:

Directions:

The basic food groups are carbohydrates, proteins, and fats. Certain foods are known for their particularly high content of these substances. List the foods given on page 192 under the group with which each is associated. Then add other foods you think might be closely related to one or another basic group.

Carbohydrates	*Proteins*	*Fats*
_____	_____	_____
_____	_____	_____
_____	_____	_____
_____	_____	_____
_____	_____	_____
_____	_____	_____
_____	_____	_____

cheese, butter, cereal, fruits, corn oil, fish, shortening, flour, bacon drippings, eggs, sugars, milk, vegetables, milk, olive oil

Students should be allowed to discuss their categorizations in small groups following completion of this sorting exercise. The categorization exercise will be most effective when:

1. Students have completed reading something that discusses the concepts used as column heads.

2. Either before or after the reading, but preceding the categorization exercise, students have completed a recognition or word study exercise (to be explained presently) that used vocabulary similar to that in the categorization exercise.

3. As they complete their categorizations, students can refer to the reading selections in which the vocabulary and ideas used in the exercise appear.

4. Students are allowed to compare their responses to the exercise in small groups. The task of the group is to resolve any differences and to present the group's completed categorizations to the rest of the class or to submit it as a group effort.

In the atmosphere described by these conditions, the pressure for the "right" answer may be relieved. In fact, there may often be no right answer, only various defendable choices. Being able to make, defend, and *relent* choices in the face of good and better reasoning is the most important lesson anyone can learn about vocabulary. The categorization exercise can demonstrate this and that is its strongest asset as a vocabulary development tool.

Crossword puzzles   Long a favorite of word hounds of all ages, the crossword puzzle can be found on almost any topic through educational supply houses. Many people enjoy working them and there can be little doubt that they foster curiosity about words.

For classroom use, especially where the objective is to build students' familiarity with particular words, the teacher-made crossword may serve best. It allows the teacher opportunity to use words most closely related to concepts under study and to associate the words with most appropriate definitions. Despite their complicated look, they are also rather easy to construct. Using either graph paper or a scrabble board and tiles and working from a list of conceptually related terms, a crossword can usually be worked out in less than an hour. What it may lack in professional appearance will improve with practice and is more than made up for by the appropriateness of the activity for the context in which it is used.

Individuals or groups of students often enjoy making their own crossword puzzles. The reading and discussion necessitated by this activity is usually very productive. It can require a very close examination of the concepts under study and the terminology in which those concepts are expressed. More than this, if other students have a chance to work the puzzles their peers construct, chances are that the level of difficulty of the puzzles and the words in which definitions are expressed will be appropriate.

Central word puzzles

A variation and simplification of the crossword is the central word puzzle. These are very easy to construct and simple to work, but they are appropriate for students who might be unable to work the more complicated, traditional crossword.

*, 14

As an example, you might work the following puzzle. The central word expresses the major concept under consideration.

1. M __ __   __
2. __ __ __ A __
3. __ __ __ M __ __ __
4. __ __ M __ __ __ __ __
5. __ A __ __ __ __ __ __
6. __ __ __ L __

1. small powerful burrowers (pl.)

2. rabbit-like, small, and almost tailless, also called conies. (pl.)

3. the order that includes monkeys, apes, and humans

4. probably the oddest mammal, it carries a plate of armor.

5. meat-eating

6. the largest animal ever to inhabit the earth.

Quite a variety of these puzzles is possible, all related to one general subject. For example, **carnivore** could serve as a central word, around which would be arranged different members of this zoological order (raccoon, bear, otter, hyena, lion, civet, badger, and seal, for example),

Beginnings and endings

In this last meaning exercise we will discuss, a beginning or ending element is listed that is common to many words or to words that are conceptually related. Definitions for the words are listed in one column, the words in another, with blank spaces for all but the common element. Try this for an example:

LOGY QUIZ

*, 14

1. The scientific study of man.   _ _ _ _ _ _ _ _ logy

2. The study of fossils   _ _ _ _ _ _ _ _ logy

3. The ethnology of early man   _ _ _ _ _ _ _ _ _ logy

4. The study of ancient animals   _ _ _ _ _ _ _ _ _ logy

5. The study of the influence of heavenly bodies on human events   _ _ _ _ _ logy

6. The study of weather   _ _ _ _ _ _ _ logy

7. The study of the evolution of language   _ _ _ _ _ logy

   etc.

Another version of the same game lists common beginnings and asks for endings. You may find this easier:

ANTHRO QUIZ

*, 14

1. The scientific study of man   anthro _ _ _ _ _ _

2. Attributing human characteristics   anthro _ _ _ _ _ _ _ _

3. Resembling man   anthro _ _ _ _

4. Of or pertaining to man   anthro _ _ _

5. Study of the origin of man   anthro _ _ _ _ _ _ _

Or, try this one:

Par one, two, three, . . .

1. To peel   par _

2. A hooded fur jacket   par _ _

3. Equality in amount   par _ _ _

4. A model of excellence   par _ _ _ _

5. Being equal distance apart at every point   par _ _ _ _ _ _

6. A distinct division of written work   par _ _ _ _ _ _

7. Oval protozoans   par _ _ _ _ _ _ _

   etc.

RECOGNITION EXERCISES, GAMES, AND PUZZLES

When followed by the use of the word in meaningful context, simple word games may be useful. Basal reader manuals have traditionally called for recognition exercise in the recommendation that the teacher write "new" or "unfamiliar" words on the board and pronounce them with children. Seemingly, a bond between the sight (look) and sound (say) would be established by this look-say technique. The problem is that the technique teaches something else, that reading is saying words.

An alternative to the show-and-tell method of building word recognition is the variety of word games and puzzles that students like to play. Newsstands are full of examples that can be copied, and students who enjoy working them are usually happy to try their hand at building games and puzzles. When they are centered on vocabulary related to a unit of study or area of concern to the course, such word exercises may have real value, particularly to the student who makes them up! They cause and reinforce genuine curiosity about language, just as traditional crosswords have done for so many years.

Two common and popular examples of word games that can easily be adapted for class use are the cryptogram and word hunts.

Cryptograms   These are coded lists of words which may be related to the same topic. The code is such that letters stand for something other than themselves. In the same puzzle, however, letters are substituted for one another consistently. An example from the puzzle is given as a clue to the other words. Our sample cryptogram will strain your memory of history:

CIVIL WAR GENERALS

*, 14

example: **Grant**

M D L E V R Q

— — — — — — —

P H D X H

— — — — —

J U D Q W

— — — — —

OHH

— — —

VKHUPDQ

— — — — — —

MRKQVWRQ

— — — — — — —

ZRUUHVW

— — — — — — —

Word hunts   This is one of the most popular puzzles of the day, known by a variety of names—ring around the word, seek-a-word, search and find, etc. Newsstands carry multiple titles. Popular as the hula-hoop, they are almost as simple to make and use.

*,14   **FAMOUS ARTISTS**

A R T I R E M I N G T O N A
R E M B R A N D T I I S U W
E B P S D E G A S N J U D Y
Y M I C H E L A N G E L O E
N U C V E S A L N R P L B T
O S A L E B U V W E E Y O H
L E S R O B T I S S A N B C
D I S M O N D R I A N V L N
S S O E F G C E Z A N N E W
V T H D E L A C R O I X Y Z

The same purpose as that served by word puzzles and games can be served by the teacher in directing the content reading lesson. A part of the introductory moments of the lesson can be spent examining with students the words that are italicized in the selection, listed at the beginning or end of the selection, or otherwise highlighted by the author. As an initiating step, students can be directed to look at the words, answering questions such as these, posed more or less informally: Do any of these words look familiar? Who can pronounce the first word? the second, etc.? Does anyone know of other words that look the same as the third (or other) word? Who can find a sentence on the first page of the selection which contains the fourth word? Questions can be asked in this manner to stimulate students to examine closely the vocabulary items that will be important to their understanding of the selection. Of course, alternatives to a conversational format can be used for this. The purpose of the exercise, in whatever format, is to lead into an examination of word meanings.

Thus, as the introductory comments proceed, the meanings of some of the words may be brought to the fore with questions which begin to focus on meaning. ("Does anyone know a word with the same meaning as _____?" "What other words have the same stem as _____?" etc.) In this way a nice transition between recognition and meaning can be made. This strategy will also provide a good lead into purpose setting and hypothesis formation which are the purposes of the initial part of the content reading lesson.

WORD STUDY EXERCISES

The third category of vocabulary exercises which we will discuss includes some features of both the meaning and the recognition varieties just discussed. The major difference is that the word study exercise, as we will define it, is never limited to only the words taken from a selection or unit. Other exercises are limited in that way in order to focus directly on the vocabulary of the phenomena and concepts under study.

Word study exercises may be completed in a variety of formats. The common characteristic of all, however, will be a concentration on word "families" of various sorts. Students are asked to work with words of similar stem, specialized meaning, similar phonetic properties, similar affix, similar derivation, or other particular features. The choice of feature is based on the likelihood that its understanding might lead to increased sophistication with respect to the language of a particular content field.

The basic format of the word study exercise is called "hunt and sort." The exercise gives students a guiding pattern or model and asks them to find and sort other words with the same pattern which match the model. This must, of course, be varied to suit the task.

One such exercise gives the student a word that is described by its meaningful parts, and asks him or her to search in newsprint, texts, reference sources, and other printed matter for words that are related to the model word. The relationship will be found in similarity of the meaningful parts which occur in other words of the same "family." To take an obvious example, the word "biology" divides into "bio" and "logy," "life" and "study of." Words of this family can be categorized into two columns suggested by the two parts. (The format is similar to the categorization exercise discussed before.) There are many such words to be found in common speech, among them the popular "bionic," which students will know on at least one conceptual level.

To take another example, a similar exercise, though perhaps a bit more erudite, would have students explore and categorize the examples they found of words related to sine, cosine; tangent, cotangent; and secant, cosecant. These words have a variety of interesting relationships to one another and to other words. Given a rudimentary understanding of trigometric functions, it is helpful to see that the "co-" in each paired word means "complementary," which itself is an interesting word. Further hunting, properly structured, will reveal to students that "sine" is related to sinusoid, sinus, sinusoidal projection, and sinewave, among others, and that all are related to fold, curve, and hollow. Tangent, it can be found, is in the "tag" family, words whose relationship is related to "touching," such as "contact," "tact" (i.e., just the right touch), "tangible" (i.e., capable of being touched), and so forth.

The study of any new field opens wide the door for an exploration of how words are related. Rhyming words can be sorted easily, which can be shown to relate to poetry. Various meanings of the same words can be sorted to highlight their special meaning in relation to a given concept. "Similar," for example, means something different in biology and social studies and math. Part of any content area study is study of the specialization of vocabulary. The number of "families" that are possible is determined by the number of ways in which words have come to have a place in the study of any concept. The word study or hunt and sort activity is a way of giving students part of the opportunity they need to have words come to have meaning for them.

14

Changing Attitudes

Attitudes toward school are changed by experiences in school.

SUMMARY

Schools seem to exist for the cognitive domain of learning. The affective domain, students' attitudes, beliefs, interests, and values, is often a weak step-sister to other objectives. The irony of this is that attitudes toward what they learn are strong determinants of what students choose to study or learn in the future. (If schools, for example, were to teach people to read but to hate reading, need they bother?) As Karl Menninger has said, "Attitudes are more important than facts." —Or skills, we would add.

There are several things we do know about attitudes and their change and development. We know that attitude and achievement are not synonymous, so that to assume good attitudes will result from high achievement, or the reverse of this, is a mistake. On the other hand, grades based on achievement do tend to reflect attitudes. At times, this can be unfair unless proper attention to attitudes has been given. Classroom climate and the teacher are critical factors in attitude development. Somehow, children's attitudes toward school grow worse with successive years in school.

The implications of what we know about attitude change are none too clear. However, certain factors are both important and amenable to change. These include curriculum factors, the physical setting, pupil characteristics, and teacher characteristics. With attention to the details of these factors, directions of pupil attitude change may become more positive.

ATTITUDE CHANGE AS AN EDUCATIONAL GOAL

We wonder how many people have ever considered the implications of this: Research studies on attitudes in the world of business and politics outnumber those in education 100 to 1. The businessman and the politician depend for their professional lives on how people *feel* about what they have to offer. They seek what they call AIDA, which stands for *attention, interest, desire,* and *action.* If a product or political idea can get AIDA, it will survive. Otherwise, it will be rejected and forgotten, and when people aren't buying, somebody's going to want to know why! Why aren't people buying? Find out and change it and you've got a success on your hands. Ignore it and you've got an Edsel. We think there's a lesson in this somewhere.

Are schools looking for AIDA? It's hard to imagine a curriculum guide which doesn't include affective objectives: interests, values, attitudes, and the like. The question is whether schools are investing heavily enough in the things that cause good attitudes, or whether they are sacrificing attitudes for knowledge by caring more about what kids learn than about how kids feel.

Think of your own experiences. Most people sooner or later come up against a teacher whose philosophy seems to be "I don't care whether you like it or not; I know it will be good for you to learn this and some day you'll thank me." But the idea that learning in school need be painful is at best anachronistic and at worst damaging to the future learning experiences of students. The affective result rather than the cognitive product of learning will likely determine those experiences.

A case in point: For reading to become a lifelong habit, a person must *know how* to read and must *like* to read. A similar argument would hold for any content area. And in this light, students' attitudes toward what they study are more important than what they learn. "No profit grows where is no pleasure ta'en,"[1] and Shakespeare was right again; people study what they learn to like.

SUSPICIONS REGARDING ATTITUDE CHANGE IN SCHOOLS

There simply isn't a great deal known for sure about why students' attitudes toward school and school subjects form or change. There are, however, some firm suspicions about attitudes which experience and common sense would suggest. Before we get to specific suggestions about what can go on in school to make attitudes better, let's look at these points:

1) *Attitude and achievement are not the same thing,* which means that learning and feeling good about school don't fit quite like the hand and glove people sometimes take them to be. Many of you were probably very good students, yet it would come as no surprise to us if many of you have strong negative feelings about school. Knowing that you were a good student simply wouldn't say much about your attitude toward school. (You see, even being a good teacher doesn't mean you like school. Why, some of our best friends abhor school but love kids,

---

[1] *The Taming of the Shrew,* Act I, scene 1.

and they're excellent teachers!) So, if anyone wants to change students' attitudes for the better, he'll have to take that as a specific goal and do things to make it happen rather than hope that attitude will slide along on achievement's coattails.

2) *Teachers allow students' attitudes to influence grades.* We noticed this when we were studying attitudes and achievement and found their relationship to be weaker than the relationship between attitudes and grades. On the surface, that may seem reasonable; any humane teacher would tend to give better grades to cooperative class participants than to hellish troublemakers, even if the achievement of both were the same. It's a way of rewarding good behavior, which counts in school. But it is also a way of punishing bad attitudes. Below the surface of things, though, one could ask whether it is fair unless everything possible had been done to change the attitude of the troublemaker.

3) *Classroom climate is a very important factor in determining pupil attitudes.* Have you read the introduction to *Foxfire 2* yet? Remember Carlton and what Eliot Wigginton had to say about him?

> I was in the office and Suzy was in the outside room and I heard her laughing—as usual—except she was really cracked up this time, and so naturally I had to go out and see what was happening, and she said just be quiet and listen. And Carlton, one of the tenth grade kids, had been in the darkroom alone for an hour and I had forgotten—and God he was missing his English class—and this string of muffled swear words suddenly drifted through the darkroom door. Yep. Carlton was still in there—oh, hell, that English class—trying to make a double exposure print for Karen's and Betse's burial article. And he was trying to figure out how to do it and burning up all this printing paper and coming closer and closer to getting it just right and talking to himself explaining what was wrong like there were seventy-eight people watching. And Suzy had been listening to the struggle, laughing, when—Bam—out he came with a dripping wet print and a *There how does that grab you* —and it was beautiful, and we used it on the cover of the magazine that had that article in it (and in the book). And Suzy and I were both laughing, and then Carlton cracked up, too. And we laughed some more. And then he went to English.
>
> And when he got to English, he had to write five hundred times, "I will not be late to class any more."
>
> And the teacher read some poems aloud that nobody listened to, so she spent the whole hour reading to herself while the kids hacked off—or slept. Sort of like us in church five minutes into the sermon. You know.[2]

4) *Student's attitudes toward school get worse the longer they're in school.* Somehow, for many pupils the longer they're there the less fun school gets to be, until they finally drop out one way or another. (For evidence of this, see research

[2] Wigginton, Eliot. *Foxfire 2*, p. 9.

by Johnson, 1965; Neale, 1969; Anttonen, 1967.) For one thing, what they are required to read may appeal less and less as their tastes in reading enter the adolescent phase of development. As Robert Carlsen put it, ". . . this is the crucial period when many potential readers stop reading. Paradoxically this is also the period when the young person may devote more time to reading than at any other period of his life, provided his interest is not killed."[3] We think the quote would be equally justifiable if you changed the word "read" to "learn" in all three places. In the interest of "quality," schools have in the last few decades moved more and harder subject matter into earlier grades. The result is not only that pupils may understand set theory but not know how to do long division, but schools can become nonsense to them. Why the furor to teach everyone everything in twelve years? After the loss we suffered in Sputnik, we won the race to the moon, but some people are wondering what the prize was to begin with. The effect on schools was not altogether healthy, especially where we forgot that

> "To everything there is a season, and a time to every purpose under heaven."[4]

*, 15   5) *The classroom teacher affects attitudes of students more than does anything else in school.* College students especially find this little activity interesting. First, write on the left-hand side of a sheet of paper your favorite subject (or subjects) when you were in school. Then, on the other side, list the teachers who were your favorites. (Do they match?) Next, list all of the things you think made those subjects and teachers your favorites. (If possible, compare your list of reasons with someone else who has done the same activity.) We think the results will tell you a lot about the effect of teachers on attitudes in school.

*, 16   Here's another one. Think about the two best experiences in your life and describe them briefly. Now, by "best" we mean experiences that affected your life, your personal development, in a positive way. Then, think about and describe the two worst experiences in your life, ones that retarded your personal development, experiences you had to overcome later.

If what you put down in this activity is anything like that found in a study by Banan (1972), the overwhelming number of experiences (86 percent according to this researcher) involved other people. And of that 86 percent, the largest group of other people were teachers. Banan asked only for negative experiences, but our experiences in replicating the study suggest that results hold for positive experiences as well. Teachers have a lot to do with the attidues of students.

In the eyes of the student, it is the teacher who is democratic or authoritarian, interesting or boring, fair or unfair, student-centered or subject-centered. And those eyes make the student feel whatever he or she feels about what is happening to him or her in school. What the student sees is up to the teacher.

[3] Carlsen, Robert, *Books and the Teen-Age Reader,* p. 23.

[4] Ecclesiastes, 3:1.

IMPLICATIONS FOR CLASSROOM PRACTICE

What is known or supposed about affect is useful only if it can be translated into practical implications and suggestions. "Practical" means "capable of being put into practice" and we will limit our discussion to suggestions that have practical possibilities. (For example, if parents have bad attitudes toward school, so will the children, more than likely. But changing the parents' attitudes is all but impossible, and it might serve little purpose to discuss the problem and its unlikely solutions by teachers or schools.) Factors that are under control of the teacher and that have bearing on student feelings may be divided into four categories: 1) curriculum factors, 2) classroom setting, 3) pupil characteristics, and 4) teacher characteristics.

CURRICULUM FACTORS

The term "curriculum" may be taken to mean, collectively: what is taught, how it is taught, and what is used to teach it. Generally speaking, if what is taught is taught in a way that is appealing to students through materials that are appropriate for them, the chances of their liking it are increased. If learning is pleasant and successful, then students' attitudes toward what they learn are likely to be positive. Conversely, if learning is unpleasant, students will reject what they are taught. They simply won't buy.

There are always determinations to be made regarding curriculum, particularly what to teach. Whatever the choice, one result will be that students' attitudes will be touched. Therefore, choices of what to teach should relate to consideration of interest, appeal, and usefulness to students. In other words, what is taught in a course should relate in some way to students' present or future needs and be taught at a time appropriate to those needs. In no course can *everything* be taught about *anything*. To better the chance that students may continue to learn more of what they can be taught, what they are taught must be chosen to emphasize what is potentially interesting and useful.

Not only what is taught, but how it is taught must be considered in relation to affective change. For example, attitudes are likely to be more positive where students are allowed to express their thoughts freely. A classroom characterized by an open and honest atmosphere that stimulates creative and critical thinking is conducive to positive attitudes. Students, like all people, feel good when their ideas are considered worthy. They tend to feel bad when the atmosphere of their learning is autocratic and threatening. The outcome is practically axiomatic: if students associate good feelings with what they learn, they will likely continue to learn more of it; if they associate negative feelings, they will likely avoid learning of it. Classroom atmosphere plays a big role in this outcome.

The manner in which assignments are made to students is another example. To be successfully completed and for students to feel good about their assignments, directions and purpose for the task must be made very clear. Where they see little reason for what they must do, students' attitudes suffer. However, where assignments are made very clear, with the purpose explained and suggestions given for efficiently completing the task, students will more likely enjoy their accomplishments. And attitudes toward what is accomplished will be better.

The materials of the curriculum, what is used to teach whatever is taught, also bear on students' attitudes. Textbooks selected for a course should be carefully chosen for a pleasing, readable style. Moreover, a variety of texts and other materials should be used in a course. Surely an economist must have invented the single-text approach; teachers know that no textbook can serve all pupils equally well. We might also add that big books with hard backs tend to be intimidative rather than elucidative to many students. Materials of teaching are tools of learning and if the tools suit the needs of learners, their attitudes toward what they experience will be more positive.

CLASSROOM SETTING

The effect of physical surroundings was the object of study in the classic "Hawthorne Experiments," from whence derives the term "Hawthorne effect" heard so often. Actually, these were industrial experiments conducted by the Western Electric Corporation. One of the significant findings of those studies was that variety and change in surroundings had a positive effect on workers' production. All people seem to react badly to boredom and sameness in their surroundings.

Some characteristics of the physical surrounding may be out of the teacher's control. The thermostat for the room may be in an office down the hall, lights may need replacing but budget won't allow proper upkeep, desks may be old and dilapidated. Nevertheless, there are always so many factors about the teaching setting that *can* be controlled or changed that those that can't are made bearable. There are many striking exceptions, but the brightness, the activity, the receptiveness of so many classrooms of grades one through three are often a contrast to typical classrooms of grades ten through twelve. (By the way, those striking exceptions of high school classrooms invariably contain students whose attitudes are also exceptional.)

Wall space and bulletin boards can be used creatively for instructional and aesthetic purposes at any grade level. Where possible and appropriate, facilities and settings other than the classroom can be used for instruction. Within the classroom, desks and other furniture can be arranged and rearranged in a manner to serve a variety of instructional needs. (Straight rows of desks are good for two things: listening to lectures and sweeping between. Avoid lecture and seek custodial blessing, and your life in school will be easier.) These suggestions are meant as examples of the kinds of features of the learning environment that affect moods and attitudes toward learning. Learners invariably associate attitude toward what they learn with attitude toward how and in what surroundings they are asked to learn.

The classroom setting is defined not only by physical surroundings but also by that intangible element called "atmosphere." For example, where quiet is maintained at high expense, the atmosphere can be oppressive. Where the classroom is active and buzzing with purposeful activity, the atmosphere is stimulating. To hold interruptions to classroom activity to a minimum is to pay respect for the importance of what kids are doing. Conversely, if, and this by recent actual count, the interclass P.A. systems interrupts thinking and learning fifteen times a day, students may believe that there are very many things much more important than their study and learning. The effect on students' attitudes is painfully predictable.

PUPIL CHARACTERISTICS

If it were possible in schools to teach young people what they can learn instead of what they should learn, they would learn more and feel better about it.

Pupils might, for example, be allowed to group themselves on the basis of interest in topics relevant to the course curriculum and then to pursue those topics under the aegis of the course. For example, a group of social studies students could put together an interpretation of the early 1900s through music, focusing on Scott Joplin. The research they do on the time period would bring them to an understanding that is expert. Contrast their resulting attitudes with those of pupils who read a small portion of their dry text with a dryer title like "America Turns the Century."

Individuals in a class can and should be given freedom to choose a maximum depth to which they will study. So many texts and so many courses are superficial surveys from which pupils learn little. But school can be a place to study in depth under teacher guidance, even inspiration. Where this is so, pupil attitudes flourish.

The most important pupil characteristic to consider, however, is the "self" each student brings to the learning setting. What education comes right down to is *kids*, young people. If they are given a voice in the decisions affecting them, if the "system" seems to care for them, if they are helped to see their needs in perspective of the needs of the larger group, then they will often return the respect in the form of cooperation. The curriculum of a course, and the way it is "taught," can be cooperatively chosen by pupils and their teacher. The result will assuredly be more positive attitudes on the part of students.

TEACHER CHARACTERISTICS

As we discussed before, ask a person to name his favorite subject and his favorite teacher in school, and chances are very good the two will go together. The overwhelming influence of the teacher on pupil attitudes can hardly be overstated. There is no more potent force in the classroom; the teacher above all other factors affects student attitudes and achievement. This is true, we believe, because of the influence the teacher has on various dimensions of the school experience. But it is also true because of the teacher as an individual, the things he or she is or seems to be to students.

For example, a teacher's effectiveness in influencing attitudes toward a course is undoubtedly related to that teacher's own interest in the course and his or her conviction regarding its value in the curriculum. If the teacher approaches a course with enthusiasm and excitement, the students will often catch the feeling and begin to share it. Pity the teacher (and pupils of) who is assigned a course no one else wanted and doesn't like simply because no one else would take the assignment. The price of such expediency is staggering. Whatever the course, whoever the teacher, the image and practice of the teacher is an important determiner of pupil attitudes. Pupils need a resource in teachers, not a taskmaster. They appreciate fair grading and discipline, realistic expectations, adequate attention to detail. It is all of these characteristics that cause students to judge a teacher as good, and the corollary to that judgment is a better attitude toward the course and, in turn, learning.

In closing, we are reminded of the king of asteroid 325 whom the little prince met on his journey. The prince has just plucked up enough courage to ask a favor of the king:

> "I should like to see a sunset. . . . Do me that kindness. . . . Order the sun to set. . . .".
>
> "If I ordered a general to fly from one flower to another like a butterfly, or to write a tragic drama, or to change himself into a sea bird, and if the general did not carry out the order that he had received, which one of us would be in the wrong?" the king demanded. "The general, or myself?"
>
> "You," said the little prince firmly.
>
> "Exactly. One must require from each one the duty which each one can perform," the king went on. "Accepted authority rests first of all on reason. If you ordered your people to go and throw themselves into the sea, they would rise up in revolution. I have the right to require obedience because my orders are reasonable."
>
> "Then my sunset?" the little prince reminded him: for he never forgot a question once he had asked it.
>
> "You shall have your sunset. I shall command it. But, according to my science of government, I shall wait until conditions are favorable."[5]

[5] de Saint-Exupéry, Antoine. *The Little Prince.*

15

Design for Activities

Learning activities provide the conduit through which learners may make contact with educational objectives.

SUMMARY

Learning activities are the operations and, for practical purposes, the definitions of the curriculum. They must be designed in view of the developmental needs of learners. On that desideratum rests the quality of activities for learning.

There are dozens of types of activities possible. But not all are of equal quality, as teachers have attested in research we have done. Still, as the same teachers will hasten to add, the quality of a particular activity will depend on the student for whom it is intended.

The way in which quality activities can be insured for a unit of study is to include many different types of activities for each concept to be developed. Thus, each student may have a better chance at the activity that is appropriate for him or her. Care must also be taken to insure that learning activities provide opportunity to develop learning skills as well as content understandings. An example of how all this can be done is presented here, followed by suggested sources of activities for learning in various content areas.

LEARNING ACTIVITES: THE CRUCIAL CONNECTION

Our hope is that we have established clearly and consistently our position regarding the aim of education. We believe that aim is the nurturance of satisfactory development at the learner's particular level of attainment. We would now like to clarify and extend this idea.

Intellectual attainment, like physical growth, is natural. Given time and sustenence, attainment will occur. The quality of the attainment, however, like the quality of physical growth, depends on proper nutrition. (It is interesting to find that one meaning of "nurture" is "to educate.") In a very literal sense, quality of intellectual attainment depends on what might be called "nurturant education."

We see it this way: Attainment of sequential stages of growth is inevitable and irreversible in virtually all children. Analogously, a seed placed in warm, moist earth will germinate to attain the next stage in the life cycle of the plant. Attainment, however, represents only one of two dimensions of growth, the vertical dimension. The other dimension of growth, the horizontal dimension, is development. As depicted in Figure 15-1, development is distinguishable from attainment. The main difference is that quality does not depend on nature; rather, this dimension of growth relies on nurture. And for much of the nurturance of a child's cognitive, psychomotor, or affective development, responsibility falls to public schools and teachers. To extend the analogy we began earlier, it is to the gardener that falls the responsibility for the quality of the plants.

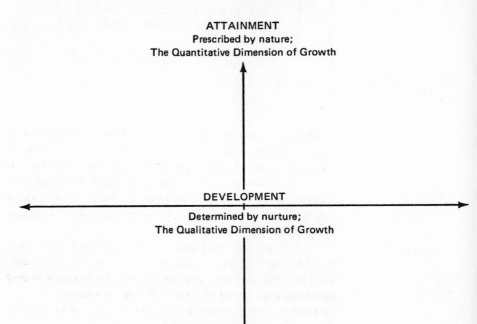

Figure 15-1   The dimensions of growth.

The reality of this in the classroom is clear. Educational objectives, whether behavioral or cognitive, product or process objectives, must be cast in the light of developmental needs of students. And, to the practical point of things, the learning activities in which students engage need be of the sort that stimulate and nurture horizontal development. One mark of a good classroom, one in which learning activities are suited to students' needs, is that students can answer these three questions: What are you doing? Why are you doing it? What are you going to do next? From the students' point of view, learning activities must have purpose. The goal of the learner and the purpose of his or her activities must be complementary if development is to be enriched by education.

Recall our earlier discussion of the organization of units of instruction. In that context (see p. 136) we suggested that activities will define *how* learning will occur, in the same sense that conceptual and behavioral objectives provide a definition of *what* will be learned. At that point, however, we chose not to discuss activities in any depth beyond saying that a sufficiently large number would be required to provide every student with a set of activities appropriate to his or her ability. We will say now that units of study require more than numerous activities. Quality of activities is an even more important consideration than number.

The purpose of this chapter is to provide suggestions and help in devising, selecting, and evaluating activities for learning. The discussion will be divided into three parts.

First, we will discuss the types of activities that are possible to use. We will present results of some of our own research on quality of activities along several dimensions which have been proposed. Our purpose here will be to establish a basis for judgment of quality of activities, to develop criterial attributes of quality activities. We want to provide a framework in which quality activities may be developed for a unit of study.

Second, we will demonstrate the application of our model by showing how a unit of work can be developed around the ideas we have suggested. We will try to exemplify activities that provide simultaneous development of learning skills as well as understanding of particular content.

Third, we will provide a bibliography of selected sources of ideas for learning activities.

TYPES AND QUALITY OF ACTIVITIES

There are always different means (i.e., activities) to accomplish any instructional end (i.e., objective). In fact, different activities are necessary for different pupils to achieve better understandings of the same concepts. At the outset, then, we are assuming that any unit plan will incorporate a range of different kinds of activities from which students may choose or be assigned. Our first question is, therefore: What are the types of activities that might be used in schools and what are their pertinent characteristics? From the answer to the question, we will be able to proceed to the question of what types of activities are preferable among those possible. Eventually, a third question emerges in the classroom, concerning which activities are best for the accomplishment of a given objective for a given pupil. That question is addressed to a circumstance where pupil and teacher are relatively free to choose among many types of activities. This will help insure that the quality of a specific activity is appropriate to the developmental needs of the learner.

To return now to our initial question, we sought an answer by consulting teachers and textbooks. Over time, we were able to compile the following list of twenty-five categories of activities commonly (and uncommonly) used in schools.

*, 17   As you study the list, we want you to partake in an activity we have asked of many other teachers. Following that, we will discuss results we have obtained previously so that you can compare your ideas with those of other teachers.

Think of the activities listed here in terms of children of upper elementary and secondary grades. Your task is to rank the activities on the basis of your judgment of their effectiveness. The following steps should make this easy to do.

First, place a I in the spaces before the five most effective activities. Place a V in spaces before the five least effective.

Second, for the remaining fifteen activities, place a II in the spaces before those which are the most effective of these. Place a IV in the spaces before those which are least effective of this group. The remaining five activities are in the middle range of effectiveness in your judgment and should be marked III.

Third, sort each of the groups of five activities from most to least effective, indicating this in the spaces to the right of the activities. Number your I activities 1, 2, 3, 4, 5; number your II activities 6, 7, 8, 9, 10; etc. When completed, you should have all twenty-five activities ranked from most effective to least effective, 1 through 25.

ACTIVITIES

Use these
spaces to rank
I, II, III, IV, or
V.

Use these
spaces to rank
1–25.

_____   1. Watch a demonstration.   _____

_____   2. Do an experiment or put on a demon-_____
stration.

_____   3. Take part in role play or dramatization.   _____

_____   4. Answer questions as the teacher calls on _____
you.

_____   5. Construct artifacts, models, diaramas, etc.   _____

_____   6. Complete vocabulary activities: matching, _____
puzzles, sorts, etc.

_____   7. Listen to a record or tape.   _____

_____   8. Write a report or research paper.   _____

_____   9. Read a selection and answer questions at the _____
end.

_____   10. View a film or filmstrip.   _____

_____ 11. View still pictures.   _____

_____ 12. Listen to reading or lecture.   _____

_____ 13. Use a study guide as an aid to reading and _____
        skills practice.

_____ 14. Find pictures or other examples to illustrate _____
        a concept.

_____ 15. Participate in discussion led by teacher.   _____

_____ 16. Participate in a debate.   _____

_____ 17. Take part in content reading lesson.   _____

_____ 18. Look up vocabulary words in dictionary.   _____

_____ 19. Go on an organized field trip.   _____

_____ 20. Do something (cook a meal, dissect an ani- _____
        mal, etc.) in class.

_____ 21. Listen to a guest speaker.   _____

_____ 22. Participate out of class in some concept- _____
        related activity (clean-up campaign, com-
        munity committee, etc.)

_____ 23. Participate in simulation of experience in _____
        class.

_____ 24. Do an exercise in which you sort and catego- _____
        rize ideas, words, etc.

_____ 25. Join a group to construct a structured over- _____
        view.

Now we would like you to do one more thing. Reflect on the reasons for your decisions. What is it that you think distinguishes effective from ineffective activities? If you think this question through before going on to see what other teachers have thought, you'll probably see that your ideas are similar to other teachers'.

When other teachers have evaluated this list of activities and ranked the items on effectiveness, we have noted that four major categories of activities emerge:

1. Those involving physically and mentally active participation.

2. Those involving mental activity of a creative nature.

3. Those involving solely watching and/or listening.

4. Those involving mental activity of a rote nature.

The rankings of effectiveness of activities tend to be highest for activities involving both physical and mental participation and successively lower for each of the other types of activities in 2, 3, 4 order, as listed. In other words, we can list the activities from most to least effective across major categorical placements. This is generally how the picture looks to most teachers with whom we have worked on the problem:

CATEGORY: *Physically and Mentally Active*

Out of class concept-related activity

Do something

Construct artifacts, models, diaramas, etc.

Simulation

Do experiment, investigation, or demonstration

Role play or dramatization

Join a group to construct a structured overview

Field trip

CATEGORY: *Creative*

Participate in debate

Complete directed and independent readings with various study guides

Illustrate concept with pictures or examples

Content reading lesson

Participate in a discussion

Write a report or research paper

Categorization exercise

Complete vocabulary activities

MOST EFECTIVE

CATEGORY: *Watching and Listening*

Watch a demonstration

Guest speaker

View still pictures

View films or filmstrips

Listen to a record or tape

Listen to oral reading or lecture

CATEGORY: *Rote Mental Activity*

Question-answer session

Read and answer questions

Look up vocabulary words

LEAST EFFECTIVE

What this means is that within each of the major categories, which we labeled when we saw how the activities were "grouping" themselves, the activities tended to be ranked close together in effectiveness. However, looking at activities in one category and comparing them to activities in another, we find clear qualitative differences. Grouped as they are, there is no doubt in most teachers' minds that the more physically and mentally active, the better; the more passive and rote, the worse. Does any of this ring true with the kinds of thoughts you were having as you ranked the activities?

Aside from consideration of the major categories of activities, there seem to be three other general considerations, each of which implies several subquestions, which are undoubtedly a part of the judgment of effectiveness. These form a sort of checklist when listed as questions:

1. Is the purpose of the activity apparent?
   a. Are activities logically related to objectives?
   b. Are activities thematically related to each other?
   c. Does the activity allow development of skill and understanding of content?

2. Does the activity provide opportunity for student involvement and participation?
   a. Does the activity demand thinking?
   b. Does the activity require creativity?

3. Does the activity possess inherent appeal?
   a. Does it appeal to student interests?
   b. Does it appeal to students' personal and intellectual needs?
   c. Is the activity likely to be enjoyable to students?

Before moving to the next section, we should comment briefly on one more point. The qualities of activities we have gathered in research with teachers do distinguish activities on the basis of *general* effectiveness. We are reminded repeatedly, however, that effectiveness is not inherent in an activity as such, but resides in the relationship among the learner, the activity, and the learning objective. With the possible exception of rote drill, but perhaps including even that, the *specific* effectiveness of an activity depends on a delicate set of connections between learners, activities, and objectives, as we illustrate in Figure 15-2, modeled after the semantic triangle of Ogden and Richards (1923).

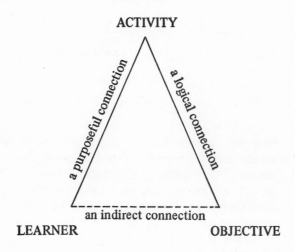

Figure 15-2   *The relationship between learners, activities, and objectives.*

It is hoped the learners can see the purposeful connection between what they need and what they are doing. The learner should also see the relationship between what he or she is doing and the objective of that activity. Both of these connections are direct. But notice that the connection at the base of our triangle is indirect. Learners achieve, that is *connect with,* objectives in school by the activities they engage in. *If a given activity provides a proper connection between a learner and an objective, that activity is effective.* In other words, effectiveness is a general term which takes on various definitions in specific instances.

A MODEL FOR THE DEVELOPMENT OF ACTIVITIES

We now wish to take a step-by-step walk through the construction of a unit of work, with particular attention to the development of activities. We are often reminded by our own experience that teachers' time and resources are limited. You may well wonder how a variety of activities can be most efficiently planned and practically offered in the classroom. While few teachers would disagree with the principles of individualized instruction or with the need for variety and effectiveness in activities, many have yet to find a satisfactory way to put it all together in classroom practice. Yet, it can be done, as we witness time and time again. We want to suggest some things that make it possible to individualize and vary activities in the classroom.

The unit framework suggested in chapter 9 provides a structure around which activities can be developed and used. After a domain of study has been identified and concepts within that domain selected, the teacher turns attention to planning the means to that end. The means are the resources and activities which must be organized and designed. The end is the specific understandings and skills that learners need to develop and to which the domain of inquiry lends itself. Perhaps another way of putting it is to say that the job of the teacher is to make as many different connections as possible in the triangle of Figure 15-2.

Everyone knows Rome wasn't built in a day, and perhaps you will accept the parallel that development of good units of study takes time. A unit evolves with use; it is never really complete. It requires trial and error. It benefits from cooperation and student input. In fact, we think it is fair to say that units are essentially a process of teaching rather than a product of planning. They do require initial planning to insure the desired process, however, and this we can give an example of presently.

We find these initiating steps helpful:

1. Across the top of a large sheet of paper, write the concepts you plan to emphasize in your unit.

2. Down the left side of the paper, write the activity types similar to those on pp. 210-211, which you plan to use. You may want to add more types to this list, and to omit those you feel would be least effective or inappropriate. (Notice we've added to and omitted from the list we were using earlier.)

3. Brainstorm. Think of activities of each type that you might be able to use. Try to think of activities that are suggested by your resources. Think of activities that will help develop students' skills as well as content understandings.

4. Seek help. Discuss your unit with other teachers and certainly with your students. A couple of weeks before a unit begins, announce it to students. Ask what they have that they might want to share. Ask what they might like to study in the unit. If students have a vital part in the planning of a unit, they will be more likely to participate in its operation and outcome.

5. Go to your school's or school system's professional library and search for ideas in periodicals, curriculum guides, and various books of ideas for activities. (We will list several at the end of this chapter.) Also, make your needs known to your school librarian and other resource and supervisory personnel. They are often eager to help, waiting only to be asked.

6. Add to and improve your unit from year to year. Be ever ready to take advantage of opportunities as they arise.

What we are pointing to, you may realize, is the teacher as organizer and guide rather than teacher as sage and dispenser of knowledge. There's nothing wrong with being sage, if that means judicious and wise, but few people can be all things to all others. Students need from teachers opportunities and guidance in learning. Organized units of work can help provide that.

It has been our experience that few teachers are fully acquainted with the resources available to them in their own school libraries or school system media centers. Making such acquaintance seems to be one of those things all too easy to put off until another day. This is unfortunate because most librarians today are well trained in information and research methods and, as we said before, are eager to share their expertise with interested teachers and students. Know your library and media center personnel and seek their assistance in planning resources and activities of your units.

Your librarian will likely be able to show you indexes of available printed and audio-visual materials. It is a good idea to peruse these and keep for yourself a "wanted list" of things that appear useful, even if not currently available. You will then be in a position to respond immediately when suggestions for materials to be ordered are requested.

With these preliminary steps and ideas in mind, we can walk through the development of the protocol of a unit of study in science. The title and domain of our unit is *The Seasons*. Particularly, we are interested in teaching the causes and effects of seasons. This will lead us directly into some of the most difficult of all the basic concepts in earth science, those of earth-sun relationships. Many of the problems here are similar to problems encountered in teaching units in other subject areas that deal with topics difficult for students to understand. The thinking demanded by such understanding, the reading ability and imagination required by texts on the subject, the sheer scope of the implications of what must be studied all add up to the fact that a wide variety of activities of different sorts will be required by such a unit. We hope that by showing what we did to pare things down to size to coalesce concepts, activities, and resources, you may get ideas for developing a unit of your own.

Step 1.
The concepts
We decided on seven concepts for this unit. In some way or another, each is vital to an understanding of the seasons. There are two questions that must be asked in this step. First, one must ask whether a concept could be eliminated without sacrificing a basic understanding on which the unit is being built. If not absolutely necessary, it is possible to eliminate many concepts that might clutter rather than help clarify. Second, one must ask whether each of the concepts listed is understandable to the students being taught. That is, given the needs and abilities of pupils and the resources available to the teacher, is the concept within the scope of what we earlier called "what can be learned of what might be taught?"

We thought the following were necessary to an understanding of the seasons:

and potentially comprehensible by students in earth science at the junior high school level.

1. The seasons affect all life and are everywhere apparent.

2. The earth revolves around the sun in an elliptical orbit once every 365¼ days, approximately.

3. The earth's axis is tilted at an angle of 23½° to the plane of its orbit around the sun.

4. The combination of the earth's revolution around the sun and the tilt of its axis causes the seasons.

5. The solstices occur at the times when the earth's axis comes as close as it ever does to pointing directly at the sun. (These times mark the beginning of summer and the beginning of winter on the calendar.)

6. The equinoxes occur at the times when the earth's axis is perpendicular to the plane defined by the earth and sun. (These times mark the beginning of spring and fall on the calendar.)

7. Seasons are opposite and different in the northern and southern hemispheres.

Table 15-1   Activities of various types for concepts of unit on "The Seasons"

CONCEPTS / ACTIVITY TYPES	I. The seasons affect all life and are everywhere apparent.	II. The earth revolves around the sun in an elliptical orbit.	III. The earth's axis is tilted at an angle of 23 1/2° to the plane of its orbit around the sun.	IV. The combination of the earth's revolution around the sun and the tilt of its axis causes the seasons.	V. The solstices occur at the times when the earth's axis comes as close as it ever does to pointing directly at the sun.	VI. The equinoxes occur at the times when the earth's axis is perpendicular to the plane defined by the earth and sun.	VII. Seasons are opposite and different in the northern and southern hemispheres.
1. Out of class concept related	a. Join and participate in school or community astronomy club.						
2. Do something	a. Make a record of changing temperatures at different latitudes during spring and fall.	a. Construct an "astrolab" with which to collect data on star positions.		a. With light and tilted globe fixed in plane, move globe around light to show where light hits.	a. Using a clear plastic hemisphere attached to board, record path of sun.		
3. Construct artifacts, models, dioramas, etc.				a. Construct model of sun and earth's relationship. If possible, power with small motor. b. Construct a gnomic cylindrical map to show position of earth relative to sun. (Directions at work center to be followed.)			
4. Simulation		a. Devise a scale to represent distances and simulate travel of planets around sun.					
5. Experiment, investigation, or demonstration	a. Demonstrate principle of Foucault's pendulum.						
6. Role Play or dramatization							

Table 15-1 (Continued)

7. Construct a structured overview	a. Groups work together to construct structured overviews for unit and its various parts.			
8. Field Trip	a. To observe progressively different life forms at different altitudes or seasons.	a. To planetarium for program on earth's movements. b. To observatory.		a. Man is best (least) suited for life in the northern hemisphere.
9. Participate in debate	a. In a modern world, the seasons affect us very much (little).	a. The earth is (is not) the center of the universe. (Ptolemy vs. Copernicus)	a. Man's life on earth is (is not) affected by the tilt of the earth.	
10. Complete directed and independent readings with various study guides	a. Study guide material is provided for reading of various selections listed here.			
11. Illustrate concept with examples	a. Montage or collage of appearances in seasons.	a. Construct chart to compare seasons on the planets b. Using a projector, trace picture of earth in relation to sun at different times.	a. Construct a chart to indicate exact times of solstices and equinoxes from now to year 2000.	a. Chart average temperatures of cities in northern and southern hemispheres at comparable longitudes.
12. Content Reading Lesson	a. Groups are called together at various times for reading in text and other selections.			
13. Participate in discussion	a. Small group or whole class discussions of the various concepts held occasionally. b. Various structured overviews serve as stimulus for discussion of concepts in unit.			

Table 15-1 (Continued)

CONCEPTS	I. The seasons affect all life and are everywhere apparent.	II. The earth revolves around the sun in an elliptical orbit.	III. The earth's axis is tilted at an angle of 23 1/2° to the plane of its orbit around the sun.	IV. The combination of the earth's revolution around the sun and the tilt of its axis causes the seasons.	V. The solstices occur at the times when the earth's axis comes as close as it ever does to pointing directly at the sun.	VI. The equinoxes occur at the times when the earth's axis is perpendicular to the plane defined by the earth and sun.	VII. Seasons are opposite and different in the northern and southern hemispheres.
ACTIVITY TYPES							
14. Library research for mini-paper on specific questions:	a. What would life be like on each of the other planets? Consider length of days, years, seasons.	a. How far is earth from the sun (avg.) in miles? light minutes? b. How did man discover that earth moves?	a. What is angle of axis of other planets?		a. What are main effects of solstices?	a. What are main effects of equinoxes?	a. Why is it colder in southern than northern hemisphere? b. What is the "midnight sun"?
15. Vocabulary activities	a. Games, puzzles, and vocabulary exercises provided at special word-study learning center.						
16. Report or research paper	a. What would be the effects of a 10-day change in length of earth's year?		a. Trace development of concept of solar system from ancients to present.	a. How would seasons be different if axis were at 0°? 45°?			a. How do life forms differ in two hemispheres?
17. Watch a demonstration	a. Whole class and small groups view demonstrations performed by teacher and pupils.						
18. Guest Speaker	a. If and when possible or appropriate, guests will visit to discuss one or more concepts.						
19. View still pictures or transparencies	a. "Because the Earth Rotates around the Sun" (UNC) (T) b. "Seasonal Star Clock" (West Pub. Ed. Ser.) (T)	a. "Light Rays and the Seasons" (West. Pub. Ed. Ser.) (T) b. "Revolution of Earth" (Encyc. Brit.) (P)		a. "Seasons on the Planet Earth" (West Pub. Ed. Ser.) (T) b. "Seasons of the Year" (Hammond) (T)	a. "Solstice and Equinox" (Ward's Nat. Sci.) (T) b. "Solstices and Equinoxes (3M) (T) c. "Summer Solstice" (Ed. A-V) (T)	c. "Winter" (3M) (T)	a. "Seasons: No. Hemis." (3M) (T) b. "Winter Sky–South" (Creative Visuals) (T) c. "Summer and Winter in No. and So." (4 pictures) (Encyc.

Table 15-1 (Continued)

20. View films, filmstrips, or filmloops	a. "Seasons" (Hubbard Scientific Co.) (FL) b. "Summer and Winter" (Pottors Photographic Applications Co.) (FL)	a. "How we know the Earth Moves" (Film Associates of Ca.) (FL) b. "Planets in Orbit—The Laws of Kepler (Encyc. Brit. Films) (F)	a. "The Earth in Motion" (Cenco. Educ. Films) (F)	a. "The Earth in Space" (Nat. Ed. Television) (F) b. "How Earth's Movements Affect Us" (Soc. for Visual Ed) (FS)	a. "Earth: Rotation and Revolution" (Hubbard Scientific Co.) (FL) b. "Day and Night" (Hubbard Sci. Co.) (FL)
21. Listen to record or Audio Tape	a. Passages of text recorded by teachers and/or students can be used in lieu of reading by some students.				
22. Listen to oral reading, lecture, or explanation	a. For example, in conjunction with transparencies, concepts can be given general explanation; poetry of seasons can be given interpretive reading, etc.				
Suggestions for Independent Reading	a. Smith, *The Seasons.* Harcourt Brace, 1970. (hdbk)	a. Knight. *Let's Find Out About Earth.* Franklin Watts, 1967. b. Ravielli, Anthony. *The World Is Round* (rev. ed.) Viking, 1970. c. Gallant. *Exploring the Planets*, Doubleday, 1967. d. Asimov. *The Kingdom of the Sun.* Collier, 1962. (paper) e. Dexter. *A Field Guide to Astronomy without a Telescope.* Houghton-Mifflin, 1971. (paper) f. Moore, Patrick. *The Picture History of Astronomy,* 3rd ed. Grosset & Dunlap, 1967.		d. Ohring. *Weather on the Planets,* Doubleday, 1966. (paper) e. Sutton. *Planet Earth.* U. Mich. Press, 1959. (paper) f. Bramley, Franklyn. *The Earth, Planet Number 3.* Crowell, 1966. (hrdbk)	b. *Farmer's Almanac.* c. Polgreen. *Sunlight & Shadows.* Doubleday, 1967.

Step 2.
The activity
types

As you can see in Table 15-1, we listed twenty-two activity types for the unit. We combined some, eliminated others, and made some additions as seemed to suit what we were trying to do. At that, we knew we were unlikely to list activities of all types for all concepts. It is quite unnecessary to do so. But listing the possible activity types in a chart such as shown here provides an excellent perspective in which to view the unit of study.

Notice that we have a special category of "activities" at the bottom of the chart, labeled "Suggestions for Independent Reading." This provides a way to list supplementary readings that can be used in the completion of various activities of the unit.

A chart like Table 15-1 can be displayed in class before and throughout a unit. Students can begin to pick and choose among activities, and can make suggestions of additional activities of various types under various concepts. They may also suggest selections for independent reading. The chart should evolve and always represent the current but changing stage of the development of the unit.

Step 3.
The activities

The choice of activities is the heart of any unit. As suggested earlier, we brainstormed, talked to librarians and media personnel and students. We checked all kinds of sources, some of which we will list for you later. The guiding principles of the search for activities can be extrapolated from the checklist of qualities which is discussed earlier. Study Table 15-1 in detail as we now discuss how activities were chosen and developed for this particular unit.

Activities 1 through 8 are the "Physically and Mentally Active" types. These activities require a minimum of reading, usually, though often the reading they do require is very important and highly functional. For example, constructing the "astrolab" or the solar path tracking device made from a clear plastic hemisphere or the gnomic device will require reading directions which are prepared by the teacher. The scale model simulation, probably to be done on a football field, will require reading in an encyclopedia or the like; similarly for the Foucault pendulum demonstration. The point to be emphasized is that you should not assume that because of the physical nature of these activities, students need do no reading. On the contrary, availability of sources in learning stations in the class or library is almost certain to be required. The reading practice these types of activities require is of a functional nature. It is in association with just such activities as these that school may provide opportunity for this very important kind of reading practice.

Activities 9 through 16 of this unit are those involving "creative" mental activity. Almost all these activities entail reading of some kind. Among these activities, we place the content reading lesson and the use of study guides in directed and independent reading. Obviously, these activities, too numerous to be listed individually here, will require reading. So also will preparation for debates, library research, and the construction of illustrations and charts. A special comment should be made about the nature of Activity 14, the mini-papers. Often, some students are overwhelmed by the task of a long research paper, Activity 16. They can, however, tackle specific questions by using various library sources. What this means is that the teacher uses the resources of the school library to find answers to specific, important questions. This insures that answers are available. Any resource available to students can be used. The task of the student, then, is to go on a kind of "library treasure hunt" in search of answers to specific questions. Answers they find may be summarized in a sentence or two, a paragraph at most. The point of the activity, though, is to give practice in using library resources without having to require more of students than they are capable of handling.

Activity 15 also deserves special mention. Many teachers like to set up learning centers or "skill stations" in the classroom. A table in a corner will do nicely. A word study center is appropriate for almost any classroom. Here crosswords, word searches, word games, and exercises can be used and constructed by students. As a certain unit is in progress, words associated with the different concepts of the unit can be used. Word activities tend to be very popular among students and probably deserve to be highlighted by a separate learning center, a "special place."

The last category of activities is the watching and listening types. These types tend to be rated relatively low on effectiveness by teachers. Actually, they needn't be ineffective at all if carefully chosen for use by students for whom they are appropriate. For example, if students are the ones who are putting on the demonstration (Activity 17), it can have much meaning and reinforcement value. Guest speakers must be chosen with care, surely, but this kind of break in the routine is often very worthwhile. Audio-visual types of activities (19, 20, 21) can add much meaning to a unit if used with descretion. Students need to be prepared and helped in the use of these activities. Too often, audio-visual materials are misused, the click of the switch their only introduction, the filling of time their only purpose. No activity will work like that, but when given proper introduction and with a clear purpose, audio-visual materials can often present content in ways that require little reading skill. This is a boon for students who are weak in reading. We might also add, in this same vein, that since such material will be a primary source of information during the adult life of many pupils, proper training and experience in its use is critical if schools are to meet their essential goal: To help students become better able to learn.

The last section of Table 15-1 is meant as a supplement to the body of the chart. In the final form of the unit, you may recall, activities will be listed down the left side and keyed to materials and readings as well as concepts. Table 15-1 is the working draft that would take a final form similar to those included as examples in the last section of this book. The main purpose of the preliminary form is to insure a variety of types of activities, to provide activities for simultaneous development of learning skills and conceptual understandings. Then, in final form, students of various interests and abilities can engage in the best possible combinations of activities.

1. Prepare a chart similar in format to Table 15-1, again listing concepts for emphasis across the top of the page.

2. List activities down the left side of the chart. (These are transferred from the body of Table 15-1.) Key these to concepts by placing Xs at intersections of rows (activities) and columns (concepts).

3. You may wish to list materials separately now and to key activities to materials by entering another column heading. Notice by our examples, however, that a variety of formats is possible.

In whatever way it is put together and organized, the unit of study as we see it is a system for coordinating what you want to teach with what students might do to learn. It is a viable alternative to more common procrustean models which attempt to adapt the child to the curriculum. We hope you agree that the only possibility for success in education is to adapt the curriculum to the learner. To do this without sacrificing the integrity of either curriculum or learner is the purpose of our units of study. Moreover, they provide a means whereby students may learn as much about how to learn as about whatever content they are studying.

SOURCES OF IDEAS FOR LEARNING ACTIVITIES

Recently, there have appeared many good sources on activities for learning in the classroom. "Learning centers" and "skill stations" are becoming common fare of instruction and, as we said earlier, this trend seems quite healthy. Quality of activity remains critical however, and this means the right activity at the right time for each child. It's not enough that everyone be doing something different (that's a questionable goal from the start) but that everyone be doing whatever is most appropriate for him or her at a given time. The following sources are valuable in helping to find appropriate activities for learners:

GENERAL SOURCES

Colburn, C. William. *Strategies for Educational Debate.* Boston: Holbrook Press, Inc., 1972.
Educator's Progress Service, Inc., 200 Center Street, Randolph, Wisconsin 53956 (guides revised annually)
    Educator's Guide to Free Films
        —Free Filmstrips
        —Free Tapes, Scripts, and Transcriptions
        —Free Science Materials
        —Free Social Studies Materials
        —Free Health, Physical Education and Recreation
            Materials
    Educator's Index of Free Materials
    Educator's Grade Guide to Free Teaching Aids

Free and Inexpensive Learning Materials
      Division of Surveys and Field Services
      George Peabody College for Teachers
      Nashville, Tennessee 37203 (published biennially)
            —16 mm Educational Films
            —Educational Audio Tapes
            —Educational Video Tapes
            —Educational Records
            —8mm Cartridges
            —Educational Overhead Transparencies
Index to 35 mm Educational Filmstrips
National Information Center for Educational Media (NICEM)
      University of Southern California
      University Park
      Los Angeles, California 90007
Newman, Dana. *The Teacher's Almanack.*
      The Center for Applied Research in Education
      521 Fifth Avenue, New York, New York 10017

Sources of Activities in English

Berger, Allen, and Smith, Blanche H., Eds., *Classroom Practices in Teaching English.* 1974. National Council of Teachers of English.

Brogden, J. *Developing Communications Skills in Non-Committed Learners.* Englewood Cliffs, New Jersey: Prentice-Hall, 1970

Brooks, Charlotte K. *They Can Learn English.* California: Wadsworth, 1972

Brown, Thomas, et al. *Teaching Secondary English: Alternative Approaches.* Columbus, Ohio: Charles E. Merrill, 1975

Carlson, Ruth. *Writing Aids through the Grades: One Hundred Eighty-Six Developmental Writing Activities.* New York, N.Y.: Columbia University, Teachers College Press, 1970

Decker, Isabelle M. *One Hundred Novel Ways with Book Reports.* Scholastic Book Services, 1969

Gerbrandt, Gary L. *An Idea Book for Acting Out and Writing Language K-8.* National Council of Teachers of English, 1974

Goddard, Arthur, and Hurwitz, Abraham B. *Games to Improve Your Child's English.* Simon and Schuster, 1973

Jenkinson, Edward B., and Seybold, Donald A. *Writing as a Process of Discovery: Some Structured Theme Assignments for Grades 5–12.* Bloomington, Indiana: Indiana University Press, 1970

Moffett, James A. *Student-Centered Language Arts Curriculum K-13.* Boston: Houghton Mifflin, 1973

Purves, Alan C., Ed. *How Porcupines Make Love: Notes on a Response-Centered Curriculum.* New York: Wiley and Sons, 1972

Reference List of Materials for English as a Second Language. Center for Applied Linguistics. 1611 N. Kent St., Arlington, Va. 22209 (These lists are updated periodically.)

Schrank, Jeffrey. *Teaching Human Beings:* 101 Subversive Activities for the Classroom. Boston: Beacon Press, 1972

Shuman, R. Baird, Ed. *Creative Approaches to the Teaching of English: Secondary* Peacock Publishers, 1974

Spann, Sylvia, and Culp, Mary B., Eds. *Thematic Units in Teaching English and the Humanities.* National Council of Teachers of English, 1975

The Whole Word Catalogue. Teachers & Writers Collaborative, P. S. 3, 490 Hudson Street, New York, N.Y. 10014 (newsletter of practical ideas and diary accounts of particular classroom experiences also available)

Sources of Activities in Math

Kidd, Kenneth P.; Myers, Shirley S.; and Alley, David M. *The Laboratory Approach to Mathematics.* Chicago, Ill.: Science Research Associates, Inc., 1970

Kohl, Herbert R. *Math, Writing, and Games in the Open Classroom.* New York: Vintage Books, 1974

Olson, Alton T. *Mathematics through Paper Folding.* Reston, Va.: The National Council of Teachers of Mathematics, Inc., 1975

Rising, Gerald R., and Wiesen, Richard A. *Mathematics in the Secondary School Classroom.* New York: Thomas Y. Crowell Co., 1972

Sawyer, W. E. *Mathematician's Delight.* Baltimore, Md.: Penguin Books, 1959

Sources of Activities in Science

The AAAS Science Book List, 3rd Ed. 1970, Washington, D.C.: American Association for the Advancement of Science, 1970 (for secondary schools and adults)

Barnard, J. Darrell. *Ideas for Teaching Science in the Junior High School.* Washington, D.C.: National Science Teachers Association, 1963

Deason, Hilary J. *The AAAS Science Book List for Children, 3rd Ed.* Washington, D.C.: American Association for the Advancement of Science, 1972

Gross, Phyllis, and Railton, Esther P. *Teaching Science in an Outdoor Environment.* Berkeley, University of California Press, 1972

Joseph, A.; Brandwein, P.; Morholt, E.; Pollack H.; and Castka, J. F. *A Source Book for the Physical Sciences.* New York: Harcourt Brace Jovanovich, 1961

Klopfer, Leo E. *History of Science Cases.* Chicago: Science Research Associates, 1966

Matthews, William H. III. *Helping Children Learn Earth-Space Science.* Washington, D.C.: National Science Teachers Association, 1971

Porter, T. R. *Earth-Space Science Teaching Tips from the Science Teacher.* Washington, D.C.: NEA Publications Sales Division, 1967

Schwab, Joseph. *Biology Teacher's Handbook.* New York: Wiley and Sons, 1963

Stone, A. Harris, Geis, Fred; and Kuslan, Louis. *Experiences for Teaching Children Science.* Belmont, Ca.: Wadsworth, 1971

Taylor, John, and Walford, Rex. *Simulation in the Classroom.* Baltimore, Md.: Penguin Books, Inc., 1972

Utgard, Russell O.; Ladd, George T.; and Anderson, Hans D. *Sourcebook for Earth Sciences and Astronomy.* New York: The Macmillan Co., 1972

Sources of Activities in Social Studies

Charles, Cheryl, and Stadsklen, Ronald. *Learning with Games: An Analysis of Social Studies Educational Games and Simulations.* The Social Science Education Consortium, Inc., 855 Broadway, Boulder, Co. 80302

Clark, Leonard H. *Teaching Social Studies in Secondary Schools, A Handbook.* Macmillan, 1973

Kohn, Clyde F., Ed. *Selected Classroom Experiences: High School Geography Project.* Normal, Ill.: William C. Brown Publications Center; National Council for Geographic Education, Illinois State Normal University, 1964

Fraenkel, Jack R. *Helping Students Think and Value: Strategies for Teaching the Social Studies.* Englewood Cliffs, New Jersey: Prentice-Hall, Inc., 1973

Miller, Bernard. The Humanities Approach to the Modern Secondary School Curriculum. New York: The Center for Applied Research in Education, 1972

Periodicals

The Arithmetic Teacher.
    National Council of Teachers of Mathematics
    1906 Association Drive, Reston, Va. 22091
Elementary English.
    National Council of Teachers of English
    1111 Kenyon Road, Urbana, Ill. 61801
English Journal.
    National Council of Teachers of English
    1111 Kenyon Road, Urbana, Ill. 61801
The Gifted Child Quarterly.
    The National Association for Gifted Children
    RR 5, Box 630A, Hot Springs, Ark. 71091
The High School Journal.
    University of North Carolina Press
    Box 2288, Chapel Hill, N.C. 27514
Instructor
    P.O. Box 6099, Duluth, Minn. 55806
The Journal of Creative Behavior.
    State University College at Buffalo
    1300 Elmwood Avenue, Buffalo, N.Y. 14222
The Journal of Geography.
    The National Council for Geographic Education
    115 North Marion Street, Oak Park, Ill. 60301
Journal of Learning Disabilities.
    5 North Wabash, Chicago, Ill. 60602

Journal of Reading.
    800 Barksdale Road, Newark, Del. 19711
The Mathematics Teacher.
    National Council of Teachers of Mathematics
    1906 Association Drive, Reston, Va. 22091
Media & Methods.
    134 North 13th Street, Philadelphia, Pa. 19107
NEA Journal.
    1201 16th Street, N.W., Washington, D.C. 20036
Reading Improvement.
    Academia Press, P. O. Box 125, Osh Kosh, Wisc. 54901
Reading Teacher.
    800 Barksdale Road, Newark, Del. 19711
School Science & Mathematics.
    School Science & Mathematics Association
    P. O. Box 1614, Indiana University of Pa.
    Indiana, Pa. 15701
Science and Children.
    National Science Teachers Association
    1742 Connecticut Avenue, N.W., Washington, D.C. 20009
The Science Teacher.
    National Science Teachers Association
    1742 Connecticut Avenue, N.W., Washington, D.C. 20009
Social Education.
    National Council for the Social Studies
    1515 Wilson Boulevard, Arlington, Va. 22209
The Social Studies.
    Heldref Publications
    4000 Albemarle St., N.W., Washington, D.C. 20016
Teacher.
    P. O. Box 800, Cos Cob, Connecticut 06807

REFERENCES

Adler, M. J., and Van Doren, C. *How to Read a Book*. New York: Simon & Schuster, 1972.

Alexander, J. E. and Filler, R. C. *Attitudes and Reading*. Newark, Delaware: International Reading Association, 1976.

Anttonen, Ralph G. *An examination into the stability of mathematics attitude and its relationship to mathematics achievement from elementary to secondary school level*. (Doctoral dissertation, University of Minnesota) Ann Arbor, Mich.: University Microfilms, 1968. No. 68–01528.

Ausubel, D. P. *Educational Psychology: A Cognitive View*. New York: Holt, Rinehart & Winston, Inc., 1968.

Banan, J. M. Negative human interaction. *Journal of Counseling Psychology*, 1972, 19, 1, 81–82.

Barron, R. F., and Stone, V. F. The effect of student-constructed graphic post organizers upon learning vocabulary relationships. In P. L. Nacke (Ed.), *Twenty-third Yearbook of the National Reading Conference*. Clemson, S.C.: National Reading Conference, Inc, 1974, 172–175.

Bormuth, J. *Readability in 1968*. New York: National Conference on Research in English, 1968.

Bormuth, J. Readability: a new approach. *Reading Research Quarterly*, 1966, 1, 3, 79–132.

Buros, O. K. *Mental Measurements Yearbooks*. Highland Park, New Jersey: Gryphon Press, 1938 and subsequent editions.

Buros, O. K. *Reading: Tests and Reviews*. Highland Park, New Jersey: Gryphon Press, 1968

Buros, O. K. *Tests in Print*. Highland Park, New Jersey: Gryphon Press, 1961, 1974.

Combs, A. W. *Helping Relationships: Basic Concepts for the Helping Professions*. Boston: Allyn & Bacon, Inc., 1971.

Dale, E., and Chall, J. *A Formula for Predicting Readability*. Educational Research Bulletin XXVII, Ohio State University (Jan. 1948).

Edwards, A. L. *Techniques of Attitude Scale Construction*. New York: Appleton-Century-Crofts, 1957.

Elam, S. The age of accountability dawns in Texarkana. *Phi Delta Kappan*, 1970, LI, 10, 509.

Estes, T. H.; Johnstone, J. P.; and Richards, H. C. *Estes Attitude Scales: Manual for Administration and Intepretation*. Charlottesville, Va.: Virginia Research Associates, 1975.

Estes, T. H.; Roettger, D. M.; Johnstone, J. P.; and Richards, H. D. *Estes Attitude Scales: Elementary Form*. Charlottesville, Va.: Virginia Research Associates, 1976.

Fry, E. A readability formula that saves time. *Journal of Reading*, 1968, 11, 7, 513–516.

Gates, A. T., and MacGinitie, W. H. *Gates-MacGinitie Reading Tests*. New York: Teachers College Press, Columbia University, 1965, 1972.

Goodman, Y. M.; and Burke, C. L. *Reading Miscue Inventory*. New York: The Macmillan Co., 1972.

Guthrie, J. Reading comprehension and syntactic responses in good and poor readers. *Journal of Educational Psychology*, 1973, 65, 294.

Guthrie, J.; Seifert, M.; Burnham, N. A.; and Caplan, R. I. The maze technique to assess, monitor reading comprehension. *The Reading Teacher,* November, 1974, 28, 2, 161–168.

Harman, D. Reading tests. *The National Elementary Principal,* 1975, 54, 6, 81–87.

Haviland, S. E., and Clark, H. H. What's new: acquiring new information as a process in comprehension. *Journal of Verbal Learning and Verbal Behavior,* 1974, 13, 512–521.

Herber, H. L. *Teaching Reading in Content Areas.* Englewood Cliffs, New Jersey: Prentice-Hall, Inc. 1970.

Hoffman, B. *The Tyranny of Testing.* New York: Collier Books, 1964.

Homans, G. Group factors in worker productivity. In H. Proshansky and B. Slidenberg (Eds.), *Basic Studies in Social Psychology.* New York: Holt, Rinehart, and Winston, 1965, 592–604.

Johnson, L. G. *A description of organization, methods of instruction, achievement, and attitudes toward reading in selected elementary schools.* (Doctoral dissertation, University of Oregon) Ann Arbor, Mich.: University Microfilms, 1965. No 65–05739.

Johnstone, J. P. *Convergent and Discriminant Validity of a Scale to Measure Attitudes toward School Subjects.* (Doctoral Dissertation, University of Virginia.) Ann Arbor, Mich.: University Microfilms, 1974, No. 72–32.

Klare, G. Assessing readability. *Reading Research Quarterly,* 1974, 10, 1, 62–102.

Kohlberg, J. W., and Mayer, R. Development as the aim of education. *Harvard Educational Review,* 1972, 42, 449–496.

Kohn, S. D. The numbers game: How the testing industry operates. *The National Elementary Principal,* 1975, 54, 6, 11–23.

Likert, R. S. A technique for the measurement of attitudes. *Archives of Psychology,* 1932, 140.

Lyman, H. B. *Test Scores and What They Mean.* Englewood Cliffs, New Jersey: Prentice-Hall, Inc. 1963.

Mager, R. F. *Preparing Instructional Objectives.* Palo Alto, Ca.: Fearon Publishers, 1962.

Manzo, A. V. ReQuest procedure. *Journal of Reading,* 1969, 13, 123–126.

McLaughlin, G. H. SMOG grading—a new readability formula. *Journal of Reading,* 1969, 12, 8, 639–646.

Miller, G. A. The magical number seven, plus or minus two: Some limits on our capacity for processing information. *Psychological Review,* 1956, 63, 81–97.

Miller, G. R.; and Coleman, E. B. A set of 36 prose passages calibrated for complexity. *Journal of Verbal Learning and Verbal Behavior,* 1967, 6, 851–854.

Minsky, M. Framework for representing knowledge. In P. H. Winston (Ed.), *The Psychology of Computer Vision.* New York: McGraw-Hill, 1975, 211–276.

Neale, D. C. The role of attitudes in learning mathematics. *The Arithmetic Teacher.* 1969, 16, 631–640.

Niles, O. S. Developing basic comprehension skills. In J. K. Shert, Jr. (Ed.), *Speaking of Reading.* Syracuse, New York: School of Education, Syracuse University, 1964, 62–74.

OEO's performance experiments will test seven instructional approaches. *The Nation's Schools,* 1970, 9, 86, 3, 55.

Ogden, C. K., and Richards, I. A. *The Meaning of Meaning.* New York: Harcourt, Brace & World, 1923.

Preston, R. C., and M. Botel. *Study Habits Checklist.* Chicago: Science Research Associates, 1967.

Robinson, R. D. *An Introduction to the Cloze Procedure.* Newark, Delaware: International Reading Association, 1971.

Rogers, C. R. *Freedom to Learn.* Columbus, Ohio: Charles E. Merrill, 1969.

Ruddell, R. A study of the cloze comprehension technique in relation to structurally controlled reading material. *Proceedings of the International Reading Association,* 1964, 9, 298–303.

Sanders, N. M. *Classroom Questions: What Kinds?* New York: Harper & Row, Inc. 1966.

Shaw, M. E., and J. M. Wright. *Scales for the Measurement of Attitudes.* New York: McGraw-Hill, 1967.

Shepherd, D. *Comprehensive High School Reading Methods.* Columbus, Ohio: Charles Merrill, 1973.

Smith, F. *Understanding Reading.* New York: Holt, Rinehart, and Winston, 1971.

Smith, F. Twelve easy ways to make learning to read difficult. In Frank Smith, Ed., *Psycholinguistics and Reading.* New York: Holt, Rinehart, and Winston, 1973, 183–196.

Smith, F. *Comprehension and Learning.* New York: Holt, Rinehart, and Winston, 1975.

Spache, G. D., and Spache, E. B. *Reading in the Elementary School,* 4th Ed. Boston: Allyn and Bacon, 1974, 1977.

Spache, G. D. *Good Reading for Poor Readers* (Rev. Ed.). Champaign, Ill.: Garrard Press, 1968.

Stauffer, R. G. *Directing Reading Maturity as a Cognitive Process.* New York: Harper & Row, Inc. 1969.

Taylor, W. Cloze procedure: A new tool for measuring readability. *Journalism Quarterly,* 1953, 30, 415–433.

Thomas, E. L., and Robinson, H. A. *Improving Reading in every Class: A Source Book for Teachers.* Boston: Allyn and Bacon, 1975.

Thorndike, E. L. Reading as reasoning: A study of mistakes in paragraph reading. *Journal of Educational Psychology,* 1917, 8, 323–332.

Valmont, W. J. Creating questions for informal reading inventories. *Reading Teacher,* 1972, 25, 6, 509–512.

Weber, G. *Uses and abuses of standardized testing in the schools.* Occasional Papers No. 22. Washington: Council for Basic Education, 1974.

Wigginton, E. (Ed.) *The Foxfire Book.* New York: Doubleday, 1972.

Wigginton, E. (Ed.) *Foxfire 2.* New York: Doubleday, 1973.

Wigginton, E. (Ed.) *Foxfire 3.* New York: Doubleday, 1975.

Units of Study
in Content Classes

Self-Development and Self Awareness

SUBJECT: *Reading*
GRADE: *10*
TEACHER: *Helen M. Friedman*

The following is a list of materials to be used in this unit. The ways they are to be used are indicated in the activity key.

I. *Reading*

A. Books
1. *Jonathon Livingston Seagull* by Richard Bach
2. *The Catcher in the Rye* by J. D. Salinger
3. *Huckleberry Finn* by Mark Twain
4. *Soul on Ice* by Eldridge Cleaver
5. *Black Like Me* by John H. Griffin
6. *The Autobiography of Malcolm X*, chapters 2, 4, 8

B. Short Stories
1. *The Secret Sharer* by Joseph Conrad
2. *Alexander and the Terrible, Horrible, No Good, Very Bad Day* by Judith Viorst
3. *The Young Man Who Flew Past* by Arcadii Averchenco
4. *First Confession* by Frank O'Connor

C. Plays
1. *Death of a Salesman* by Arthur Miller

    2. *Othello* by William Shakespeare
    3. *Antigone* by Sophocles
    4. *Medea* by Euripides
    5. *Hedda Gabler* by Henrik Ibsen

  D. Poetry
    1. *Song of Myself* by Walt Whitman, parts 1, 5, 6, 20
    2. "I Cannot Be Ashamed" by Emily Dickinson
    3. *Poetry* by Juan Ramon Jimenez
    4. "Ah, Are You Digging on My Grave?" by Thomas Hardy

II. *Films*
    1. *A Doll's House*
    2. *Conscience in Conflict*
    3. *Heroes and Cowards*
    4. *Man and Woman*
    5. *Black and White and Shades of Gray*
    6. *The Cherry Orchard Pt. 11—Comedy or Tragedy?*
    7. *How Close Can You Get?*

III. *Music*
    1. Beatles—selections
    2. Carol King—"Tapestry," selections
    3. Neil Diamond—"Jonathon Livingston Seagull," selections

IV. *Miscellaneous*
    1. Value Survey
    2. Oral Interpretations of Literature (children's)
    3. Cloze and Maze Tests and Discussions
    4. Vocabulary Exercises and Discussion
    5. Group Interviews
    6. Panel Discussions
    7. Reaction Statements
    8. Cave-In Simulation
    9. "I urge" Messages
   10. Labeling Game
   11. Role-Playing Game

Readability Check

	S.M.O.G.	FRY
The Secret Sharer	9	8
The Catcher in the Rye	8	7
Jonathon Livingston Seagull	9	7
The Autobiography of Malcolm X	9	8

Othello	8	7
Death of a Salesman	8	7

UNIT OUTLINE AND ACTIVITY KEY

Self-Development and Self-Awareness

Concepts to be developed

1. Becoming old enough to realize you have changed.

2. Will you act like you want or the way everyone else does?

3. Sometimes acting as an individual means being left out.

4. Everyone has good and bad experiences, all of which can contribute to personal growth.

5. Setting goals for yourself and realizing they are attainable. You can do it!

ACTIVITY	CONCEPT				
	1	2	3	4	5
Jonathon Livingston Seagull	X	X	X	X	X
The Catcher in the Rye	X			X	
Huckleberry Finn	X	X		X	
Black Like Me			X	X	
Soul on Ice		X		X	
The Autobiography of Malcolm X	X	X	X		X
The Secret Sharer		X	X		
Alexander	X		X	X	
Death of a Salesman			X		
Othello		X	X		
Antigone	X	X		X	X
Medea		X	X	X	
Song of Myself					X
"I Cannot Be Ashamed"		X	X		
Hedda Gabler		X			
First Confession		X		X	
Poetry		X			
"Ah, Are You Digging . . ."			X	X	
A Doll's House	X	X			
Conscience in Conflict		X	X		
Heroes and Cowards		X		X	

ACTIVITY	CONCEPT				
	1	2	3	4	5
Man and Woman					X
Black and White and Shades . . .		X	X	X	
The Cherry Orchard		X			
How Close Can You Get?	X	X			
Beatles	X				
"You've Got a Friend"				X	
Neil Diamond	X	X	X	X	X
Value Survey	X			X	

	CONCEPT				
	1	2	3	4	5
Oral Interpretations	X				X
Cloze and Maze Discussions	X	X	X	X	X
Group Interviews	X	X	X	X	X
Panel Discussions	X	X	X	X	X
Reaction Statements					X
Cave-In Simulation				X	X
"I urge" Message to One's Self		X			X
Labeling Game	X	X			
Role-Playing Game			X	X	
Vocabulary Exercises	X	X	X	X	X
The Young Man Who Flew Past		X		X	

ACTIVITIES SCHEDULE

Name _____

*Activities are required
°Activities available only at these times
All other activities are optional and can be done at times you chose.

ACTIVITIES	DAY				
March 8–12	Mon.	Tues.	Wed.	Thur.	Fri.
Jonathon Livingston Seagull		*	*	*	*
Alexander			°		
The Secret Sharer					
Medea					

March 8–12 (*cont.*)	Mon.	Tues.	Wed.	Thur.	Fri.
Song of Myself			*		
Conscience in Conflict				o	
Man and Woman			o		
Oral Interpretations					
Cloze Test and Discussion				*	
Vocabulary and Discussion				*	
Value Survey				*	
Neil Diamond					o

March 15–19	Mon.	Tues.	Wed.	Thur.	Fri.
Huckleberry Finn (parts)					
Black Like Me					
First Confession	*				
Othello			*	*	
"I Cannot Be Ashamed"		*			
A Doll's House	o*				
Black and White and Shades of Gray			o		
Tapestry (selections)				o	
Group Interviews				*	*
Maze Test and Discussion				*	
Reaction Statements	*	*	*	*	*
Labeling Game					

March 22–26	Mon.	Tues.	Wed.	Thur.	Fri.
The Catcher in the Rye		*	*	*	*
Soul on Ice (all)		*			
The Young Man Who Flew Past					
Antigone					
Hedda Gabler					
Poetry					
Heroes and Cowards		o			
The Cherry Orchard Pt. 11					o
Panel Discussions		*	*		
Reaction Statements	*	*	*	*	*

March 29–April 2	Mon.	Tues.	Wed.	Thur.	Fri.
The Autobiography of Malcolm X	*				
Death of a Salesman		*			
"Ah, Are You Digging on My Grave?"			o		
How Close Can You Get?				o*	
Beatles (selections)					
Reaction Statements	*	*	*	*	*
Cave-In Simulations		*			
"I urge" Messages					
Role-Playing Game					

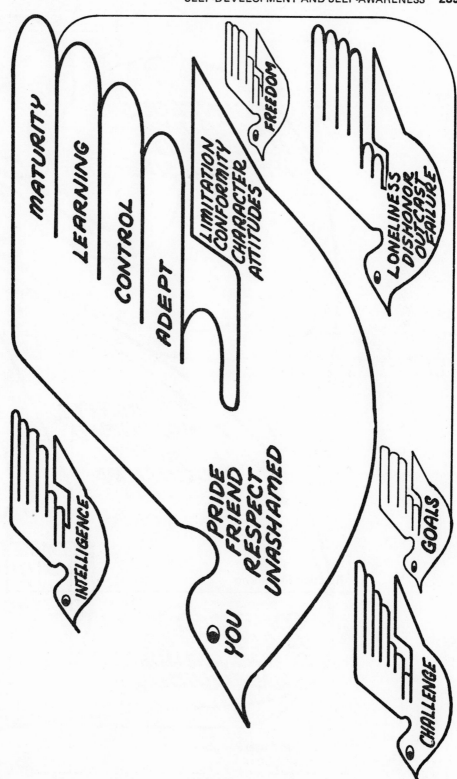

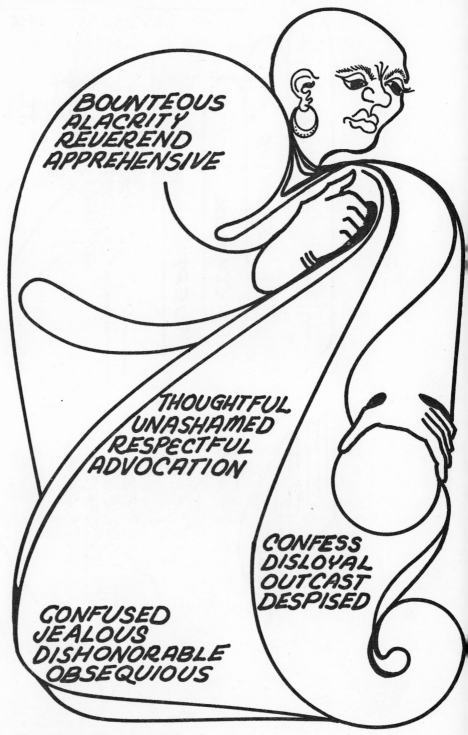

Structured overview for Othello

THREE-LEVEL STUDY GUIDE:
Othello (Act III, Scene III)

I.   Give the name of the character who is speaking.

    1. Who steals my purse steals trash; 'tis something, nothing;
        'Twas mine, 'tis his, and has been slave to thousands;
        But he that filches from me my good name
        Robs me of that which not enriches him
        And makes me poor indeed.

        ————————————

    2. I'll see before I doubt; when I doubt, prove;
        And on the proof there is no more but this—
        Away at once with love or jealousy!

        ————————————

    3. I am glad of it; for now I shall have reason
        To show the love and duty that I bear you
        With franker spirit. Therefor, as I am bound,
        Receive it from me. I speak not yet of proof.

        ————————————

    4.   This may do something.
        The Moor already changes with my poison.
        Dangerous conceits are in their natures poisons
        Which at the first are scarce found to distaste,
        But with a little act upon the blood
        Burn like the mines of sulphur.

        ————————————

II.   Othello went through many changes during Scene III. Indicate which of the statements below apply *only* to him.

    ———— 1. Iago's relationship to Othello improves as he continues to flatter Othello.

    ———— 2. Because of lack of proof, Othello at first is willing to doubt Desdemona's guilt.

———— 3. When Iago speaks of his own good name, Othello becomes convinced of his reliability.

———— 4. All it took to make Othello believe Desdemona was guilty was Iago showing him her handkerchief.

———— 5. Iago pretends that he is going to keep his inner thoughts from Othello.

III.   Briefly state to which characters and circumstances the following statements relate:

1. You shouldn't believe everything you hear.
   Who?_____ How?_____
   _____
   _____

2. Beware of false flattery!
   Who?_____ How?_____
   _____
   _____

3. Innocent until proven guilty.
   Who?_____ How?_____
   _____
   _____

4. If you are weak, you will be easily influenced by others.
   Who?_____ How?_____
   _____
   _____

CONCEPT STUDY GUIDE:

Othello (Act III, Scene IV)

I.   Indicate which of the statements below are true or false. If the statement is false briefly explain why. The underlined words are not important now.

———— 1. Othello faints because he cannot bear the thought of Desdemona being a disloyal wife.

———— 2. Cassio is not regarded as an outcast and is well-liked by Iago and Othello.

_____ 3. If there were not some <u>truthfulness</u> to Iago's stories then Othello's state of mind would not be so <u>confused</u>.

_____ 4. Iago is <u>jealous</u> of Cassio because he wants Bianca for himself.

_____ 5. Bianca is very <u>thoughtful</u> when she invites Iago and Cassio to dinner.

_____ 6. Iago is <u>dishonorable</u> because he tricks Othello into thinking Cassio is speaking of Desdemona.

_____ 7. When Desdemona tells Lodovico "I would do much t' atone them, for the love I bear to Cassio," she proves that she is <u>unashamed</u> of her affair with Cassio.

_____ 8. Othello's actions in this scene demonstrate that he is a <u>failure</u> both as a husband and a ruler.

_____ 9. After Desdemona is struck by Othello she says "I have not deserved <u>this</u>," because she feels she has been a <u>respectful</u> wife.

_____ 10. Iago is <u>deceitful</u> when he tries to convince Lodovico that Othello has changed for the worse.

II.   In the sentences above there are many underlined words. Each refers to one of the characters below as we, the readers, know him or her. Place the underlined words that best describe the character under that character's name.

Othello   *Desdemona*   *Iago*

COMBINATION STUDY GUIDE:

The Secret Sharer

Concepts   1. Recognizing your own needs.

2. Way to fulfil those needs once you recognize them.

I. In the story, we are told four different versions of how the sailor on the Sephora was murdered: the Captain's (C), Leggatt's (L), Archbold's (A), and the narrator-captain's (NC). Indicate by using the initial or initials of the person that you think is making the statement below. Read all of them through before answering.

_____ 1. "I had become so connected in thoughts and impressions with the secret sharer of my cabin that I felt as if I, personally, were being given to understand that I, too, was not the sort that would have done for the chief mate of a ship like the Sephora."

_____ 2. "God's own hand in it. Nothing less could have done it. I don't mind telling you that I hardly dared give the order. It seemed impossible that we could touch anything without losing it, and then our last hope would have been gone."

_____ 3. "I tell you I was overdone with this terrific weather that seemed to have no end to it. Terrific, I tell you—and a deep ship. I believe the fellow himself was half crazed with funk. It was no time for gentlemanly reproof, so I turned round and felled him like an ox."

_____ 4. ". . . I was in time to catch an evanescent glimpse of my white hat left behind to mark the spot where the secret sharer of my cabin and of my thoughts, as though he were my second self, had lowered himself into the water to take his punishment; a free man, a proud swimmer striking out for a new destiny."

_____ 5. "God only knows they locked me in every night. To see some of their faces you'd have thought they were afraid I'd go about at night strangling people."

II. Carefully read *all* of the events below and then put them in their proper order, 1–8, with number 1 being the first thing that happened.

_____ The captain of the Sephora arrives and tells his tale expressing disgust that it happened on his ship.

_____ The captain takes Archbold on a tour of the ship to try to convince him Leggatt is not on board.

_____ The captain was able to maneuver the ship out of the crevice because of his new-found confidence.

_____ Leggatt left the hat in the water and took his punishment.

———— The captain discovers a man resting beside his ship and helps him aboard.

———— Leggatt kills a sailor on the Sephora because he can no longer tolerate the man's inefficiency.

———— The captain suddenly changes course because Leggatt wants to leave the ship near the Cambodje Islands.

———— When the steward puts the captain's coat in the bathroom, the captain is terrified Leggatt will be discovered.

III. What were some of your impressions about the story? Briefly answer the following questions. We will discuss everyone's thoughts later.

1. Did Leggatt exist?

2. At the end of the story the captain took a chance and succeeded. In the beginning of the story Leggatt took a chance but would you say he succeeded?

3. What do you think of the captain as compared to Archbold?

4. Was Leggatt right in killing the sailor?

LESSON PLANS

Each day consists of one 55-minute period.

Monday, March 8

The entire period would be devoted to explaining the activity schedule and answering questions about it. An explanation of the contract of agreement, student log, and self-evaluation form would also take place. The teacher would proceed to explain that for the next nine weeks, the students would each be a member of two different groups—one group would be for reading-discussion activities, the other for interaction activities (games). They would also be responsible for some activity (ie of their choice to be completed on their own in conjunction with the teacher.

Tuesday, March 9

8:30 – 9:25	Entire Class
	Complete contracts, set up appointments. Discussion led by me, then students; develop unit concepts, construct structured overview; *Jonathon Livingston Seagull.*

Wednesday, March 17

8:30 – 8:55	*Jets*	*Reefers*	*Peros*	*Slicks*	*Freaks*
	Maze test—discussion	Maze test—discussion with the Jets	See "Black and White. . .'"—discussion	Discuss this week's reaction statement	See "Black and White. . ."—discussion
	T	T		T	

8:55 – 9:00	Entire class: questions-answer to teacher or complete student log.

9:00 – 9:25	*Rositas*	*Satans*	*Crows*	*Blackbirds*	*Bluejays*
	Discussion of short papers—"I cannot be ashamed"	Discuss first half of *Othello*—Cloze test	Read last half of *First Confession*	Discuss first half of *Othello*—structured overview	Finish *Black Like Me*—discussion
	T			T	

Friday, March 26

8:30 – 8:50	*Jets* Discussion of *Soul on Ice*—combination study guide	*Reefers* Finish reading *Antigone*—3-level study guide	*Peros* Act out scene from *Hedda Gabler* T	*Slicks* Discussion of *Soul on Ice*—structured overview T	*Freaks* Discuss short papers on *The Man Who Flew Past*
8:50–9:05	Individual Silent Reading				
9:05 – 9:25	*Rositas* Panel discussions—topics unknown to teacher T	*Satans* Panel discussions—topics unknown to teacher T	*Crows* See *The Cherry Orchard*	*Blackbirds* Panel discussions—topics unknown to teacher T	*Bluejays* See *The Cherry Orchard*

T—*teacher takes part in activity.*

Contract of Agreement

I _____ , after carefully examining and fully understanding the Activities Schedule, hereby agree to complete the following activities by April 30 in order that I may earn a grade of _____ .

Notarized by:

———————————   ————————
Teacher   Date

STUDENT LOG

Date	Which activity?	Did I learn anything about myself?	Student and/or teacher's comments. If you want me to comment put an X in the box.
Monday, March ———			
Tuesday, March ———			
Wednesday, March ———			
Thursday, April ———			
Friday, April ———			

My Overall Performance

I have just spent nine weeks looking at myself through literature, music, and various other activities. I think my performance throughout . . .

The student will be told that this will be looked at by the teacher and discussed individually.

CONCEPTS

1. Recognizing good and bad qualities about myself.

2. Getting my head together to cope with them.

3. Applying my new-found knowledge to the world around me.

A VOCABULARY GAME
(Extension Exercise)

The words below are written on the blackboard. The class is divided up into two teams. The teacher has written on pieces of paper all of the 256 possible combinations for these words and they are put in some kind of container. Round one begins. Each person chooses one piece of paper. Naturally, all of the combinations won't work. However, each student must try to make a coherent sentence from the combination of words indicated on the paper. The other team has a right to challenge if the members feel the sentence is absurd. The teacher acts as referee. In case it is impossible to make a sentence from the combination, that team neither gains nor loses a point. A dictionary can be used if the students would like one.

Column 1	Column 2	Column 3	Column 4
0 irrepressible	0 noisily	0 freedom	0 question
1 aware	1 underneath	1 imperfection	1 accommodate
2 desolate	2 incessantly	2 knowledge	2 blunder
3 brotherly	3 thoughtfully	3 master	3 be unproductive

This game would be both a good vocabulary exercise (they would not be able to use the words in sentences if they do not know what they mean) and a good grammar exercise (they would have to know what part of speech the word is so they would know where to put it in a sentence).

REACTION STATEMENTS

Examples   1. "I am you and you are me and we are all together."

2. "The gull sees farthest who flies highest."

A poster would be made containing a statement like one of the preceding examples. A different one would be displayed once or twice a week, depending on student responses. A group may decide to express its views on that week's statement or an individual may choose to have a conference with the teacher about it. The students would be encouraged to bring in their own "Reaction Statements."

LABELING GAME

Goal   To discuss the kinds of labels we give to people

To discuss the effect a label has on a person's opinion of self and behavior

To discuss the difficulty in changing a label and ways to do it

Procedure   1. The class meets in assigned groups. A label is placed on each group member without his or her knowing what the label says.

2. The labels are:

like me	listen to me
praise me	ridicule me
admire me	interrupt me
ignore me	one label is blank

3. The groups are assigned a topic to discuss for ten minutes. During the discussion each member must treat the others according to the labels on them and try to determine what his or her own label is.

Questions   1. What do you think your label was?

2. Describe your feelings about the way people treated you.

3. Describe your feelings about the way you had to treat people because of their labels.

4. Did any members in your group begin to act differently because of their labels?

5. Do we ever give people labels in real life?

6. What are some of the labels we give to people in the classroom?

7. Do teachers ever give students labels?

8. How would an inaccurate label affect a person?

9. Could a label determine or influence a person's behavior or self-concept?

10. Can a certain kind of label work to your advantage? Your disadvantage?

11. What if you had a label you did not like? Could you change it?

12. How does this activity relate to real life? (Group expectations—powerful force to producing behavior, self-identity, the way I think others see me will influence my behavior).

ROLE-PLAYING ACTIVITY

Family Quarrel

Four basic types of manipulative roles are:

1. The *Placater:* Pacifying, smoothing over differences, being nice, protective, defending others gently, covering up. "Oh, that's not so bad, really," "We agree, basically," "Everything will turn out all right."

2. The *Avoider:* Being quiet, pretending not to understand, changing the subject, playing weak, playing helpless. "I can't help it," "I didn't hear you," "I forgot."

3. The *Blamer:* Judging, bullying, comparing. "It's always your fault," "You never _____ ," "Why don't you _____ ." :

4. The *Preacher:* Lecturing, using outside authority. "You should _____ ," "You must _____ " proving that you are right by explaining, calculating, using logic, etc.

Form groups of 4 or 5 people, and balance sex as evenly as possible. Quickly form a "family," and decide who is Ma, Pa, Brother, and Sister. Keep these family roles throughout the improvisation.

Begin by playing the manipulative role (identified by the number above) in the first row of the table below for about five minutes. After about five minutes, look at the next number in your column and play that role for five minutes, and so on. For instance, for the first five minutes Ma will be placating (1), Pa will be blaming (3), etc. And for the second five minutes Ma will be avoiding, Pa will be preaching.

	Ma	*Pa*	*Brother*	*Sister*
First five minutes	1	3	2	4
Second five minutes	2	4	3	1
Third five minutes	3	1	4	2
Fourth five minutes	4	2	1	3

Additional members of the group may be relatives.

To the student   When you are assigned to be a Blamer, start blaming: "Ma, it's your fault I got bad grades this semester, because you don't wake me up in the morning." Make up any problems you like, and drop them when you want to move on to something else. Do not wait for someone else to stop talking—arguments are not like that. Put a lot of energy into this and enjoy yourself. If you are a blamer or a preacher, do not let the avoider sit back and avoid without being challenged. Make sure that he or she has to actively avoid.

Possible subjects   Grades (bad grades), car (dent in the fender), telephone, money, sleeping habits, eating habits, neatness, household chores, use of television, parties, dating, clothes, drugs.

Which of the four roles was easiest? Which was the hardest? Which was the most comfortable and felt the most spontaneous? Which was least comfortable and felt most strained and uptight?

BRIEF FILM DESCRIPTIONS

A Doll's House Henrik Ibsen's literary classic of 1879; Nora, the doll-wife who wakens from her dependent relationship and slams the door on husband and family as she leaves.

Conscience in Conflict Sir Thomas More chooses to hold to his own conscience rather than accede to King Henry VIII in his divorce and subsequent marriage to Anne Boleyn. More went to his death as others have in obedience to his own beliefs, a recurring theme in literature.

Heroes and Cowards Young naval officer Jim had always pictured himself as brave, even heroic, but in a moment of fear he abandons his ship and passengers. Conscience-striken, his life a shambles, he wanders aimlessly.

Man and Woman The battle of the sexes between the willful Kate and the wild Petruchio is a headlong uproarious conflict.

Black and White and Shades of Gray An open-ended film about a black boy in an all-white school, who invites a white girl to a school dance. Controversy ensues in her family.

The Cherry Orchard Pt. 11—Comedy or Tragedy? Is it comic or tragic when people are lost in fantasy yet seemingly unaware they are lost? Houghton shows why the controversy persists as he probes Chekhovian characterization and reveals the dramatist's conviction that words are often mere cover-ups for real feeling.

How Close Can You Get? "That 'No man is an island' bit really makes me laugh. That's a bunch of bull . . ." "The gift of self is just too much: it's a burden to the person you give it to . . ." "You can't live with someone if you can't live without him. . ." Such are the challenging problems wrestled with in this thought-provoking discussion.

Oceans of Fun

SUBJECT: *Science*
GRADE: *5*
TEACHER: *Peggy Donaldson*

SCHEDULE

This unit is designed for fifth graders, to last for approximately three weeks. The class schedule will be as follows:

Monday	whole class concept discussions, speakers, field trip
Tuesday	class divided in thirds rotate among word activities/independent projects
Wednesday	class divided into groups according to interests group projects, movies
Thursday	same as Tuesday
Friday	whole class presentations by groups: puppet show, role playing, demonstrations

Week 1	concentration on concepts 1 and 2 activities 1–21

Week 2 concepts 3 and 4 will be the focus
activities 22–42

Week 3 concepts 5 and 6 will be discussed
activities 43–57

Each child will participate in the designated "required activities." He will also complete at least three word games during the course of the unit, and two other activities each week.

Additional suggestions for activities from the children are encouraged, and additional resource materials are available.

CONCEPTS

1. Oceans support a wide variety of plant and animal life.

2. We have always explored and travelled the ocean.

3. Many ocean products provide livelihoods for people.

4. Oceans and their shorelines offer many recreational opportunities.

5. Oceans are a limited resource. People must learn to use them without misusing them.

6. Future uses of the ocean will affect our existence.

STUDENT LOG

	What I did today	*What I learned* *Things I thought* *Questions I have*	*Comments from [name of teacher]* *Ideas* *Suggestions*
Monday			
Tuesday			
Wednesday			
Thursday			
Friday			

MATERIALS AND READINGS

		CONCEPT KEY					
		1	2	3	4	5	6
Books, Fiction							
1.	Bamman, H. and Whitehead, R. *City Beneath the Sea.* Benefit Press, Chicago, 1964						X
2.	Latham, J., *Carry On Mr. Bowditch.* Houghton Mifflin Co., Boston, 1955		X	X			
3.	MacGregor, E., and Pantell, D., *Miss Pickerell Harvests the Sea.* McGraw-Hill, N.Y., 1968						X
4.	O'Dell, S., *Island of the Blue Dolphins.* Houghton Mifflin Co., Boston, 1960	X	X	X			
5.	Selden, G., *The Garden Under the Sea.* Viking Press, N.Y., 1957	X			X		
6.	Sperry, A., *Call It Courage.* Macmillan Co., N.Y., 1940	X	X				
7.	Yolen, J., *Greyling.* World Publishing Co., Cleveland, 1968		X	X			
Books, Nonfiction							
8.	Adler, I. and R., *Oceans.* John Day Co., N.Y., 1962	X	X	X		X	X
9.	Buehr, W., *World Beneath the Waves.* W. W. Norton, N.Y., 1964	X	X	X			X
10.	Carson, R., *The Sea Around Us.* (Young Readers) Golden Press, N.Y., 1950	X	X	X	X		
11.	Kovalik, V. and N., *Undersea World of Tomorrow.* Prentice-Hall, Englewood Cliffs, N.J., 1969	X				X	X
12.	May, J., *The Land Beneath the Sea.* Holiday House, N.Y., 1971	X	X				X
13.	Ray, C., *Wonders of the Living Sea.* Parents' Magazine Press, N.Y., 1967	X		X			
14.	Stephens, W., *Science Beneath the Sea.* G. P. Putnam's Sons, N.Y., 1966	X	X			X	
15.	Weiss, M., *Man Explores the Sea.* Julian Messner, N.Y., 1969		X				
16.	Woodbury, D., *Fresh Water from Salty Seas.* Dodd, Mead & Co., N.Y., 1967					X	X

CONCEPT KEY

	1	2	3	4	5	6
Poetry						
17. Bogan, L. and Smith, W., *The Golden Journey* (Anthology). Reilly and Lee, Chicago, 1965	X	X				
18. Cole, W., (Ed.), *The Sea, Ships, and Sailors.* Viking Press, N.Y., 1967	X	X	X	X		
19. Nash, O. *The Eel, The Octopus, The Squid, The Pocket Book of Ogden Nash.* Pocket Books, N.Y., 1972	X					
Movies						
20. *What Is Under the Ocean?,* FA, 1963	X				X	X
21. *Gray Gull the Hunter,* EBF, 1967	X		X			
Filmstrips and Tapes						
22. *Life on the Sea Floor and Shore,* R. Johnson, 1965	X				X	
23. *Oceanography,* Guidance Associates, 1968		X				
24. *Understanding Oceanography,* SVE		X				
Teacher-Made Materials						
25. Study Guide—*Island of the Blue Dolphins*		X	X			
26. Study Guide—*Call It Courage*		X	X			
27. Study Guide—"Sea Fever" by John Masefield		X		X		
28. Study Guide—*The Sea Around Us*						
29. crossword puzzle	X					
30. Structured Overview—Fishing: Not Just for Fun!			X			
31. word game—Alphabet Soup	X					
32. word game—Double Trouble	X					
33. vocabulary game—*Sealab 2020*						
Content Reading Lessons						
34. Dixon, Peter L., *Sealab 2020* Scholastic Books, N.Y., 1975	X	X	X	X	X	X
35. Barclay, G. T., "The Great Wave" *Ideas and Images* American Book Co. READ Series	X	X	X			
36. Helfman, E., "Water All Over the World" *Joys and Journeys* American Book Co. READ Series	X	X	X	X	X	

CONCEPT KEY

	1	2	3	4	5	6
37. Seigler, R. J., "Outgoing Tide" *Kings and Things*. American Book Company READ Series	X	X	X			
38. Sperry, A., "Ghost of the Lagoon" *Arrivals and Departures*. Allyn and Bacon, Inc.	X	X				

ACTIVITIES

	MATERIALS	CONCEPTS					
		1	2	3	4	5	6
1. Make a mobile showing various types of sea animals.	13	X					
2. Start a shell collection. Try to find out the shells' names.	12	X					
3. Make a shadow box of what the ocean floor looks like.	10,12	X					
4. Make a globe. Show the routes of some early explorers.	8		X				
5. Build a model of an early sailing ship.	8		X				
6. Build a model of a submarine or of an oceanographic vessel.	12		X				
7. Collect different types of seaweed. Try to find out the different names.	10	X					
8. Write a letter to the Navy asking for information about a submarine.			X				
9. Find out all you can about Jacques Cousteau. What are some of the problems he and his divers face?	14,15		X				
10. Report on sponges. Look at a real (not man-made) sponge.	10	X					
11. Could a pet goldfish live in the ocean? Why or why not?							
*12. Classroom discussion: Ocean Life.		X					

	MATERIALS	CONCEPTS 1	2	3	4	5	6
*13. Classroom discussion: Adventures in and on the Ocean.			X				
14. Read "Sea Fever" and do the study guide.	18,27		X				
15. Read *Call It Courage* and do the study guide.	6,26		X				
16. Read Chapters 1 and 2 *The Sea Around Us* and do study guide.	10,28	X					
17. Crossword puzzle.	29	X					
18. Word game—Double Trouble.	32	X					
*19. Content Reading Lesson "The Great Wave" and "Outgoing Tide"	35, 37	X					
20. Read a book about ocean explorers.	1, 5, 14, 15		X				
21. View a movie or a filmstrip.	20, 21, 22, 23, 24	X	X				
22. Make a display on beach or boating safety.					X		
23. Put up a bulletin board in the classroom: "Jobs that Depend on the Ocean."	2,7,8,10			X			
24. Make a display about foods from the ocean. Include your favorite recipes.					X	X	
25. Make shell jewelry or artwork.					X	X	
26. Do a report on whaling. Would you like to have been a whaler?	10			X			
27. Write a story: "A Day at the Beach."					X		
28. Make a photo album of your favorite water sport—swimming, sailing, water-skiing, fishing, scuba diving.					X		
29. Demonstrate swimming strokes to the class. Include dolphin and flutter kicks, freestyle, breaststroke, and butterfly arm motions.					X		
30. Bring in a snorkel, mask and flippers, or pictures of an oxygen tank. What is the importance of each to the diver? Demonstrate how each is used.					X		

	MATERIALS	CONCEPTS 1	2	3	4	5	6
31. Look at a Coast Guard chart. Identify shallow and deep water, rocks, sunken obstructions, current and channel markers. Why are these important to the sailor?					X		
32. Write a story about fishing. What types of fish can live in the waters around (your state)? What types have you ever caught? What kind of equipment did you use?					X		
33. Talk to a fisherman who sells his fish. What special equipment does he need? Does he need a fishing license? Where does he catch the most fish?				X			
34. Read a poem. "Where go the Boats?" "Break, Break, Break", "After the Sea Ships", "Fog", "The Whale"	17, 18, 19			X	X		
35. Read and illustrate the nonsense situations in "The Uses of Ocean."	18			X	X		
36. Read *Island of the Blue Dolphins* and do study guide.	4, 25	X	X	X	X		
37. Read a book about fun at the ocean.	3, 5				X		
*38. Structured overview: Fishing—Not Just for Fun!	30			X			
*39. Classroom discussion: Ocean economy	30			X			
*40. Classroom discussion: Fun in the Sun					X		
*41. Content Reading Lesson "Water All Over . . ." and "Ghost of the Lagoon"	36, 38						
42. word game: Alphabet Soup	31	X	X	X	X		
43. Make "Polluting Puppets." Have a show about contaminating oceans.						X	
44. Role playing skit: Convince boaters not to throw their junk in the water.						X	
45. Make a poster about pollution.						X	
46. Demonstrate making salt water into fresh water (desalination).	16					X	X

		MATERIALS	CONCEPTS					
			1	2	3	4	5	6
47.	Role playing skit: It is the year 2020 and you live in Sealab. Discuss food, school, toys, pets, etc. that are way down deep.	34						X
48.	Have a debate. Should fishing/lobster licenses be required?						X	
49.	Look up magazine and newspaper articles about something that has affected ocean and/or river life in your state.						X	
50.	Make a list of ways to save water.	16					X	
51.	Make a newspaper with your group. You live in an underwater city. Include articles on tranportation, entertainment, houses, politics, etc.							X
*52.	Classroom discussion: Misuse of ocean resources						X	
*53.	Classroom discussion: Food and fuel from the ocean							X
*54.	Content Reading Lesson *Sealab 2020*	34					X	X
55.	vocabulary game: *Sealab 2020*	33					X	X
56.	Read a book about people living under the sea.	1, 3, 11, 16						X
*57.	Field trip to local beach.		X	X	X	X	X	

* Activity is required.

Material 18	THREE-LEVEL STUDY GUIDE
Activity 14	

"Sea Fever" by John Masefield

I. Check what the poem is about.

_____ 1. The man wants to go down to the ocean and sail on a big ship.

_____ 2. The man wants to go to sleep and dream about the ocean.

_____ 3. There is a big storm. A ship breaks up and sea gulls are crying.

_____ 4. The man wants to be a gypsy.

II. Check what the author means in his poem.

_____ 1. The man misses being a sailor.

_____ 2. The man thinks a sailor's life is boring.

_____ 3. He is afraid of the ocean.

_____ 4. He loves the ocean.

_____ 5. The man is tired of his life, and longs for the freedom of the sea.

III. Check what the poem can tell us.

_____ 1. You can't teach an old dog new tricks.

_____ 2. We like to relive good experiences from the past.

_____ 3. The best thing to do on a boat is sleep.

_____ 4. Oceans are terrifying.

_____ 5. People need freedom and choice of lifestyles.

Material 25
Activity 36

THREE-LEVEL STUDY GUIDE

Island of the Blue Dolphins

I. Circle the best answer.

1. Karana did not punish Ramo when she reached shore because
   A. She was tired from swimming
   B. He hadn't done anything wrong
   C. He looked so forlorn

2. Karana decided to make the weapon even though the law said not to because
   A. No one would see her
   B. She was so afraid of the dogs
   C. She liked to disobey rules

3. Karana returned to the island after her canoe leaked. The next day she felt
   A. Very happy to be back
   B. Sad that she was back
   C. Fearful of the dogs

4. Karana did not shoot the leader dog for the second time because
   A. She thought he'd bite her
   B. She thought he was already dead
   C. He lay there without moving

5. When Tutok left, Karana still made up words to say to her.
   A. Karana thought Tutok might hear her
   B. Karana was practicing her new language
   C. Karana wished Tutok was still on the island

II. Check the statements that are true.

_____ 1. Karana loved Ramo very much.

_____ 2. The tribe would have been mad at Karana for making the spears.

_____ 3. The island seemed like home for Karana, because she had no other.

_____ 4. Karana felt sorry for the leader dog after she injured him.

_____ 5. Karana didn't miss people, because she had Rontu.

III. Check the statements that *Island* tells about.

_____ 1. Love makes people act unselfishly.

_____ 2. All laws are good laws, and should never be broken.

_____ 3. We should make the best of things that happen to us.

_____ 4. Animals are better friends than people.

_____ 5. People need other people.

Material 26
Activity 15

COMBINATION STUDY GUIDE

Call It Courage

I. After reading the book, look at the words listed below. Do they describe Mafatu before his voyage? After his voyage? Do they describe Tavana Nui before his son's trip? After? If a word doesn't seem to fit anyone, cross it out.

strong	brave	mean
lucky	smart	loving
weak	proud	ashamed
afraid	happy	courageous
understanding		resourceful

Mafatu
before

Tavana Nui
before

after

after

II. Check the statements *Call It Courage* tells about.

_____ 1. The best way to overcome fear is to face what you're afraid of.

_____ 2. Cowardly people should be ashamed.

_____ 3. Courage is something we all have to work at.

_____ 4. People are born either brave or cowardly.

_____ 5. Someone can overcome fear for you.

Material 28
Activity 16

CONCEPT GUIDE

The Sea Around Us (Ch. 1 and 2)

I.   Fill in the blanks after reading chapters 1 and 2.

    1.   _____ and _____ are two animals that can live in the coldest oceans.

    2.   Fish can grow much faster if the water temperature is _____.

    3.   There are more minerals if the water temperature is _____.

    4.   The _____ is the saltiest ocean.

    5.   There are more different kinds of ocean animals if the water temperature is _____.

    6.   There is (much life, very little life) in the middle of the ocean.

    7.   There is (much life, very little life) at the surface of the ocean.

    8.   Tiny fish and plants called _____ are needed for food by larger ocean animals.

    9.   There are many more ocean animals if the water temperature is _____.

    10.   _____ and _____ are types of animals that can live only in Tropic oceans.

II.   Look back at your answers. Under the first column, list anything that wi‹
lead to lots of plants and ocean animals. Under the second column, list thing
that will prevent lots of plants and ocean animals from growing.

Much Life	*Very Little Life*
light—at the surface	darkness—down deep

Material 29
Activity 17

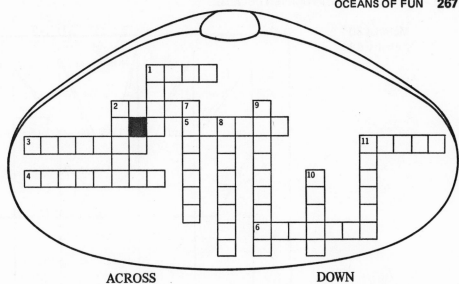

ACROSS

1. a shellfish; to *shut* up
2. periwinkle; s-l-o-w
3. very well "armed"
4. flat, tasty fish; struggle
5. has a "pearly" shell
11. Jaws; a tricky person

DOWN

1. an 8-legged shellfish; a grouch
2. the giant is deadly
7. is caught in a pot
8. a very "bright" fish; You may see it in the sky!
9. has many stingers; Great with peanut butter.
11. small, curved shellfish; a puny person
10. underwater mammal; huge

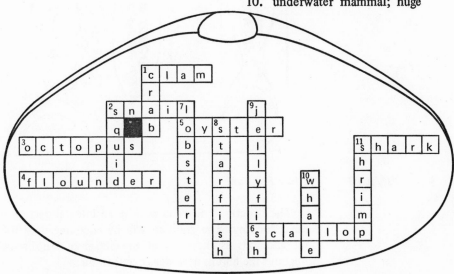

Material 30
Activity 38

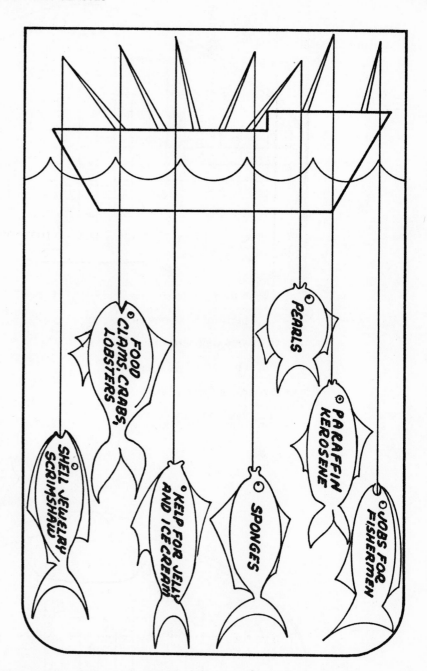

FISHING   *Not Just For Fun!*

The structured overview will be an integral part of our classroom discussion: Ocean Economy. The children will be encouraged to list as many ocean-related goods and jobs as they can at the outset of the discussion, and to add "fish" throughout the unit as new ideas occur to them.

ALPHABET SOUP

This is a game for two or more players.

Materials   Word cards—teacher-made: Atlantic

Pacific

bathyscaphe

oceanography

other long words

Unit resource books

paper and pencils, with a "soup bowl" drawn

To play, child picks one word card out of a hat. All players write the word at the tops of their papers. They must now write an ocean-related word starting with each letter of the base word. Students may use all resource books they need.

Play continues until one player has completed an Alphabet Soup bowl, or when all players are stumped.

All players must then be able to pronounce and explain every word on their papers. For each accurately described meaning (as judged by the other players), one point is scored. High total wins.

Variations   For each different word a player can explain on other children's soup bowls, he gets one additional point.

For each missed word a player can look up, read about, and refresh his memory on, he gets one additional point.

DOUBLE TROUBLE!

All of the underlined words have at least two meanings. One has to do with the ocean. You must decide what the other is, or you're in double trouble.

1. An animal who moves at <u>a snail's pace</u> is a:
   a) rabbit.
   b) turtle.
   c) cougar.

2. Someone who might be called a <u>shrimp</u> is:
   a) Wilt Chamberlain.
   b) Dennis the Menace.
   c) Muhammed Ali.

3. Charlie Brown would call which of his friends a <u>crab</u>?
   a) Snoopy
   b) Lucy
   c) Linus

4. If you were <u>floundering</u> in math, you would:
   a) ask for help.
   b) laugh.
   c) get an A.

Draw a crazy picture for the following Double Trouble situations.

1. Our picnic was a *whale* of a good time.

2. When the principal came in, she *clammed up.*

3. King's Dominion is *oceans* of fun.

4. There's something *fishy* going on around here.

5. Her dress has a *scalloped* edge.

SEALAB 2020

I. Unscramble the following words from *Sealab 2020*. Then match up each word with its meaning.

1. caetvaeu _____   a. injury when a person comes up too fast

2. gbokool _____   b. went to the top

3. vahnis _____   c. to leave

4. rtspineoc _____   d. disappear

5. rfsacdeu _____   e. diary

6. dbsne _____   f. folds

7. dnaritaoi _____   g. person who looks closely at
                                 something

                              h. energy

II. Using the unscrambled words, finish these sentences taken from *Sealab.*

1. The Chief Diver and the Captain were reading the Sealab's
   _____.

2. _____ could kill everyone in Sealab!

3. When he heard about the leak, the _____ looked worried.

4. If Bobby and Sali _____ safely, it would take two days.

5. Because of the leak, the Captain ordered everyone to _____
   Sealab.

6. If Paul and Sali panic and head for the surface, they will get the
   _____.

7. We must find Sealab before the sun will _____.

Index